AF371468

IMAGES & MEMORIES

GEORGIA TECH: 1885-1985

B. Eugene Griessman

Sarah Evelyn Jackson

Annibel Jenkins

Copyright © 1985 The Georgia Tech Foundation

Library of Congress Cataloging-in-Publication Data
Griessman, B. Eugene
  Images & memories.

  Includes index.
  1. Georgia Institute of Technology — History.
I. Jackson, Sarah Evelyn, 1929-   . II. Jenkins,
Annibel. III. Title. IV. Title: Images and memories.
T171.G59G75   1985   607'.11758'231   85-21898
ISBN 0-9615650-0-4

Manufactured in U.S.A.

First printing, 1985

To Paul G. Mayer

Regents' Professor, Civil Engineering
Co-chairman, Georgia Tech Centennial Committee
Staunch Supporter of the Centennial Histories

1923-1985

This photo was taken from the hill upon which the Tech tower now stands. The view is to the east. The marshy area just beyond the Confederate fort is Tanyard Branch, which now flows under Grant Field. On the skyline, immediately right of center is a larger earthwork — a fort armed with heavy guns capable of reaching great ranges. This fort crowned the highest point of Prescott Street just behind Crawford W. Long Hospital.

Acknowledgements

To acknowledge by name each person who has assisted us would require a small book in itself. Such a book would include the names of all the people who found wonderful old photographs and scrapbooks tucked away in attics and storage rooms or told us stories about the way it was in former times. It would also include the people who helped us identify places and dates which, it turns out, is no mean feat when years have passed and memories have gotten rusty. We hope this book itself will be a way of remembering what they have done.

In a way, the photographs tell their own story — the story of Everyman going off to school, overcoming obstacles, finding new friends and, perhaps, a mentor, learning a trade, playing, failing at one thing, succeeding at another, growing up, going off to war, dying if unlucky or extraordinarily brave, coming back to school, graduating, leaving behind old buddies and textbooks in order to make it in the outside world. This book recalls some of those events and faces and places, enlivens them with anecdotes and celebrates some of the moments from Tech's first century.

But not all the moments. Choices had to be made, so we enlisted the editorial committee of the Centennial Pictorial History Project to help make decisions about photographs and historical material: Dr. Helen E. Grenga, Dr. Robert C. McMath, Dr. Paul G. Mayer, Dr. A.D. Van Nostrand and Charles R. Yates. All of us wish the book could have been longer and included more,

because after a while each photograph became a friend with its own history. It made us sad when, due to space limitations, we had to leave out some interesting faces and stories.

The idea of writing this book was proposed by the co-chairmen of Georgia Tech's Centennial Celebration — Regents' Professor of Civil Engineering Paul G. Mayer, and Vice President, Development, Warren Heemann. Their idea for this kind of history of Georgia Tech was supported by President Joseph Mayo Pettit, who subsequently gave continuing encouragement to the endeavor.

J. Erskine Love Jr. and Gay M. Love generously provided financial support for the preparation of the book, as did the Price Gilbert Jr. Charitable Fund, the late William C. Wardlaw and his widow and son, Edna Raine Wardlaw and William C. Wardlaw III. The Georgia Tech Foundation provided additional funding. The Board of Trustees of the Georgia Tech Alumni Association has shown a continuing interest in the project. Rush S. Smith Jr., a member of the Alumni Board and former editor of the *Technique*, has helped see the project through to completion.

John Dunn at the Alumni Publications Office; Charles Harmon, Jill Sewell Rice, Kathy McDowell, and Pam Rountree at the News Bureau; Ray Moore and his staff at the Office of Research Communications; Catherine Inabnit and Laura Zipperer at the Office of Constituency Research; Cecil R. Phillips and all our colleagues at Institute Relations and Development (IR&D) have assisted us in ways too numerous to count. We are particularly grateful to the people who preserve information — when others are throwing it away — and know where to find it, like Anne Bartlow, her assistant Gail Garfinkle and Mary Evelyn Gibert at the Price Gilbert Memorial Library. Moreover, the historians who wrote the companion volume for Tech's centennial have given us invaluable guidance: Dr. James E. Brittain, Dr. Germaine M. Reed, Dr. Ronald H. Bayor, Dr. August W. Giebelhaus, Dr. Lawrence Foster and Dr. Robert C. McMath.

Several students contributed to the project: Warren Drury, who wrote his master's thesis on the architecture of the campus buildings and shared his research with us; Edmund Wall, who worked on the project for two years until his graduation; and Susan Cole, Chris Mundy and Debbie Massara. Kevin Able and Neil Kutchera spent long hours at the word processor patiently putting into print various drafts of the manuscript as the book evolved.

News Bureau photographers were colleagues from the beginning of the project — first Alan David and his assistant Harris Johnson, and later Gary Meek. They photographed and printed, made forays to the Atlanta newspapers, the Atlanta Historical Society and various sites on campus. As this book will attest, they did superb work. Deloye R. Burrell, former staff photographer for the *Technique*, provided anecdotes of the 1960's as well as prints from his files.

Our thanks go to Lee Walburn, Diane Hunter, Andrew Sparks, and Nancy Roquemore at *The Atlanta Journal, The Atlanta Constitution* and *The Atlanta Weekly*; to Franklin Miller Garrett, Elaine Kirkland and Donald Rooney at the Atlanta Historical Society; to the staffs of the Emory University Library and the Georgia Department of Archives and History; and to Dean Emeritus George C. Griffin for notes in his inimitable handwriting, for pictures, for identifications, for stories and for his friendship.

In addition, much appreciation is extended to Jeff Ausband, Creative Director at Hunter Publishing Company, who designed the book and has taken as much pride as we have in its appearance, and to his assistant, Lori T. Lowery, who devoted many hours to the preparation of the book; to Bill Meason, Account Executive at Hunter, who worked with us as it was being written and published; to all the staff of Hunter Publishing Company; and to Kenneth P. Carlson Jr., whose editing tuned the finished product.

Thanks go to our colleagues and members of our families for providing a listening ear, a critical eye, a caution now and then, and never a discouraging word.

Finally, we acknowledge the painstaking research of Ruth C. Hale, scholar and verifier *extraordinaire*. We are grateful.

FOREWORD

By President Joseph Mayo Pettit

It is indeed a rare privilege to write a few words of introduction to a centennial history, especially this one which presents the first one hundred years of the Georgia Institute of Technology. I congratulate the authors, and commend the volume to all readers.

A pictorial history has a special appeal. It conveys in a unique way a feeling for the persons and their times. Words are necessary, of course, and you will find good ones — in the chapter introductions and in the picture captions. But to get the feel of the campus and of student life, only pictures will do. The pictures in this book are marvelous. And what a labor to gather them — from the archives, from alumni and friends!

Of course, while the pictures show the changing fashions of dress and autos, the reader must remember that during 1885-1985 the world was changing too. Tech did not sail through this century on calm waters, but often had to push ahead resolutely through a turbulent sea. Economic crises in the 1890's and 1930's, together with five wars: Spanish-American, World War I, World War II, Korea, and Vietnam, all affected the lives of Tech students and the institution itself.

And the technology to be taught and learned was also changing, almost more rapidly than it could be mastered and brought into the classroom. During the century we progressed from the Wright brothers' flight in 1903 to the Apollo landing on the moon in 1969. The telephone was barely established for local service in 1885 and it would not be until 1915 that the first transcontinental telephone line was completed. The first century of radio coincides approximately with Tech's first century, commencing with Marconi's first successful "wireless" transmissions, and culminating in today's communication satellite, which permits us to talk anywhere in the world. Television came later, with local broadcasting of black and white pictures demonstrated in the late 1930's. And now in the 1980's we have seen beautiful color television pictures relayed from Saturn and Jupiter, millions of miles away. The whole field of electronic computers has come to us during this century — indeed during the latter half — and is still evolving at a rapid pace, with a flow of machines and systems which are ever larger in function and smaller in size and cost.

And so it has been for a century. How little of it could have been foreseen by Tech's founders. Now, here we stand, on the threshold of Tech's *second* century. What will it embrace? How can we be sure that Tech's engineers, scientists, architects and managers will not only follow the changes ahead, but will be among the leaders? First we will continue to seek the best faculty and students. Then we will undergird their endeavors with the necessary resources, built on support from the state of Georgia but increasingly augmented by support from the private sector, as exemplified by the Centennial Campaign, Tech's first major venture into a capital campaign.

As this fine book illustrates so well, we can go a long way in a century. We can face our second century with enthusiasm and keen anticipation.

CONTENTS

Section One

A New Way to a New South:
1885-1905

At noon on October 5, 1888, in a stark brick building on a dirt road called North Avenue on the outskirts of Atlanta, Georgia, a dream about a new way to a New South was taking shape. Inside the building, a crowd watched Nellie Inman, the 18-year-old daughter of Atlanta philanthropist Samuel Inman, take the throttle of a flag-draped 40-horsepower engine. "The steam hissed and spurted," *The Atlanta Constitution* reported, "the eccentrics jumped back and forth, waving the flags as they moved the steam valves, and the big flywheel drove the machinery."

Georgia's School of Technology was open and ready for business. Later that day in the DeGive Opera House in downtown Atlanta, Nathaniel E. Harris, chairman of the commission that had originally recommended establishing a school of technology in Georgia, formally presented the institution to Governor John B. Gordon: "Sir," Harris said, "our work is done and with our hands outstretched in blessing and in prayer, we commit the child to the keeping of that great people into whose favor and affection it must now struggle to make its way."

For Nathaniel Harris, this moment had been long in coming. Six years earlier he had first learned of the concept of a technological school from Major John F. Hanson, a prominent Georgian who later became President of the Central of Georgia Railroad. Hanson, then owner of the *Macon Telegraph and Messenger*, knew that technological schools existed in Europe and convinced Harris that Georgia needed such a school. In that conversation, Harris made his well-known comment: "I would rather be the author of a law establishing such a school than to be Governor of Georgia." Major Hanson replied, "Why don't you become that author?" Harris eventually accepted the challenge and, with Hanson's strong support, successfully ran for a seat in the General Assembly on the issue of a needed school of technology.

After taking office in the General Assembly in 1882, Harris kept his promise and introduced a resolution authorizing the appointment of a committee to study the issue of technological education in Georgia. A committee was formed with Harris as Chairman, and it began visiting some of the few existing technological schools in

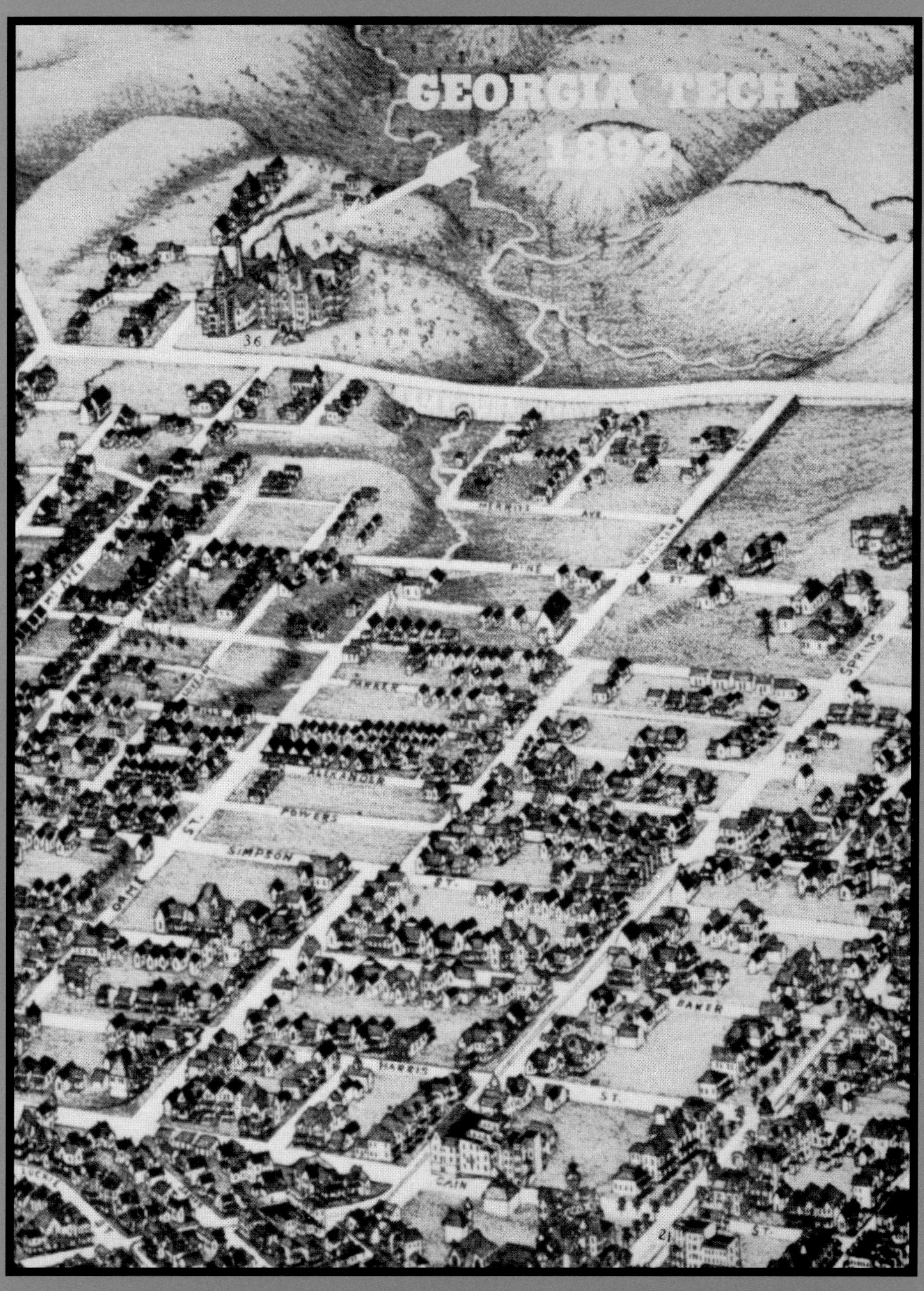

In this 1892 illustrated map, the tall
towers of Tech's shops and academic
buildings dominate Atlanta's northern
landscape.

Tech's first President, Isaac Stiles Hopkins, a scholarly man, yearned for a time when the laborer and the thinker would understand and complement each other. As President of Emory at Oxford from 1884 to 1888, he tried to combine manual training with traditional classical instruction. Discouraged by Emory's lack of support, he enthusiastically accepted the offer to head a new school in Atlanta. In addition to his presidential duties, he taught physics at Tech and served as pastor of the Merritts Avenue Methodist Church from 1890 to 1894.

the country. In particular, the committee visited Cooper Union in New York, Stevens Institute of Technology in New Jersey, the Massachusetts Institute of Technology and the Worcester Free Institute of Industrial Sciences (now Worcester Polytechnic Institute) in Massachusetts. The committee favored Worcester, and the school became Tech's role model, primarily because it manufactured products from its shops to help defray expenses.

The committee's recommendation was not immediately approved by the state Legislature, however. In fact, unexpectedly strong opposition came from several quarters. The problem was that the concept of a technological school was new. This was not a traditional college with Latin, Greek and classical studies. Moreover, some University of Georgia supporters feared that another school in the state would weaken support for the Athens institution. And there was always the nagging problem of money. The state's coffers were almost empty, and most legislators wanted to spend what little money existed on something other than a new school. Therefore, it was July 1885 — three years after Harris took office — before the measure passed the House by a vote of 94 to 62. (Eighty-eight votes in favor were needed for passage.) Later, the bill was approved by the Senate and on October 13, 1885, was signed into law.

Five places vied for the proposed school: Athens, Macon, Penfield (which had lost Mercer University), Milledgeville (the old state capital) and Atlanta. Atlanta's bid of $50,000 (and a promise to give $2,500 annually for 20 years) plus $20,000 from private subscribers and a four-acre site donated by the Peters family decided the contest. In the fall of 1888, the first academic building with its distinctive Tech tower and the shops building with a tower of its own were ready for students. The School's first staff and faculty included five professors and five shop supervisors, directed by its first President, Isaac Stiles Hopkins.

Hopkins, who was the ninth President of Emory College in Oxford, Georgia, before coming to Tech, had a broad educational background. He was schooled in theology, medicine, the natural

Tech's first two buildings suggested a balance between the practical and the academic. When a fire destroyed the Shops Building in 1892, it was rebuilt without a tower, but the emphasis on practical training remained. The buildings were designed by Alexander C. Bruce and Thomas H. Morgan.

Dignitaries from throughout the state joined Atlantans at the DeGive Opera House (left front) at 29 Marietta Street to conclude the opening ceremonies for the Tech. Julius L. DeGive graduated from the School in 1891 and became manager of the opera house founded and owned by his father, Laurent DeGive.

The first official seal of the Georgia School of Technology bears little resemblance to the three that later replaced it. Whether President Hopkins helped design it is unknown, but it embodies his attitudes. Tools and equipment attest to the practical emphasis of the curriculum in the early decades: a telegraph pole, anvil, tongs, a gear and a transit. The motto arching over them, "To Know, To Do, To Be," is no longer on the official seal. A new seal was approved in 1918 but the old one was still used in the 1921 *Catalogue.* Tech's Centennial Campaign commemorates the three-year period from 1885, when the bill that established Tech became law, to 1888 when Tech's doors opened.

In 1882 Nathaniel Edwin Harris, a Macon attorney, said while commenting on the possibility of a technological school in Georgia: "I would rather be the author of a law establishing such a school than to be Governor of Georgia." He became both. As a member of Georgia's General Assembly, his committee's recommendation was signed into law in October 1885. Harris was Governor of Georgia from 1915 to 1917.

sciences, Latin, English literature, "Mental and Moral Sciences," Biblical literature and, most important, industrial education. A workshop located in Hopkins' yard at Oxford had been listed as a "Manual Training Cottage."

Tech's first President came to Atlanta with high hopes and proclaimed soon after he arrived that "No movement in education within the entire history of education has met with such universal recognition and welcome as has this one of technical education of high grade."

One of Tech's first faculty members came from Worcester — Milton P. Higgins, Superintendent of Worcester's shops — as overseer of Tech's four shop foremen. The School's first Professor of Mathematics was Lyman Hall, an 1881 graduate of West Point and native of Americus, Georgia. Other faculty members included William H. Emerson, an 1880 graduate of the U.S. Naval Academy with a Ph.D. from Johns Hopkins, as Professor of Chemistry; John Saylor Coon, an 1877 graduate of Cornell, Professor of Mechanical Engineering and later Superintendent of Shops; and the Reverend Mr. Charles Lane of Macon, Professor of English.

During those early years, each county could send the same number of students to Tech as it had representatives in the state Legislature. Tuition was free for in-state students, but those from

Tech's faculty in the 1890's. From left to right: (front row) John Saylor "Uncle Si" Coon, Professor of Mechanics and Mechanical Drawing; Isaac Hopkins, President from 1888 to 1896; A. Jessop, Superintendent of Shops; the Reverend Mr. Charles Lane, Professor of English; (second row) D.B. Oviatt, Professor of Drawing; Ernest E. West, Adjunct Professor of Physics and coach of the first football team in its three games in 1892; Lyman Hall, Professor of Mathematics; (third row) F.O. Spain, Professor of Mathematics and center on the 1892 team coached by Leonard Wood; William H. Emerson, a Naval Academy graduate with a Ph.D. from Johns Hopkins, Professor of Chemistry and Dean. "Big Doc" Emerson served Tech from 1888 to 1924. The inserts show the first two Presidents — Hopkins, left, and Hall, right.

The first issue of *The Technologian,* the first student publication, appeared in March 1891. It was an eight-page monthly printed by *The Atlanta Constitution* job office, with a subscription price of $1.00.

Contract work was important during the first few years and had to pass inspection by both the shop foreman and the purchaser. Students sold their work until the mid-1890's.

outside the state paid a hefty $150 a year. Not surprisingly, there was only one out-of-state student in the first class: O. B. Stone from Chattanooga, Tennessee. Not until 1893 did more students come from other states.

During the 1870's and 1880's, men such as Benjamin H. Hill and Henry W. Grady toured the state urging its leaders to establish local industries and to educate Georgia's sons and daughters at home. If industrial independence could be achieved, they argued, subservience to the North would forever end.

As stated by Hill and Grady, the creed of the New South had two essential parts: education and freedom from economic bondage. Benjamin Hill told the University of Georgia alumni, "We must have schools of agriculture, of commerce, of manufacturing, of mining, of technology, and, in short, of all polytechnics, and we must have them as sources of power, of respectability, and our sons must be qualified to take the lead and point the way."

Henry W. Grady, in his last public address, spoke of a funeral he had attended in Pickens County, Georgia: "It was a poor 'one gallus' fellow whose breeches struck him under the armpit and hit at the other end about the knee.... They buried him in the midst of a marble quarry; they cut through solid marble to make his grave; and yet a

Detours and torn up streets have been noticeable evidence of Atlanta's progress for more than 100 years. Atlanta's first railway lines, completed in 1889, ran from Edgewood Avenue to what would become Inman Park. Joel Hurt, the moving force behind the project, continued expanding the lines and his electric cars soon replaced the mules on Atlanta's streets. These 1892 lines curve around the artesian well, downtown Atlanta's water supply located at Five Points at the juncture of Peachtree Street and Edgewood Avenue. In the background is the nearly completed Equitable Building (now Trust Company of Georgia).

The charter of the first fraternity on the Tech campus was issued in 1888 to the Beta Iota Chapter of Alpha Tau Omega. Isaac Hopkins, Tech's first President, was an honorary member of the Emory College Chapter of ATO prior to coming to Tech in 1888. The first five members included W.P. "Billy" Walthall, seated right. Editor of *The Technologian,* Walthall is also identified by classmate H.D. Cutter, seated left, as the author of "Ramblin' Wreck."

little tombstone which they put above him, was from Vermont. They buried him in the heart of a pine forest, and yet the pine coffin was imported from Cincinnati. They buried him within touch of an iron mine, and yet, the nails in his coffin and the iron in the shovel that dug his grave were imported from Pittsburgh. They buried him by the side of the best sheep-grazing country on the earth and yet the wool in the coffin bands and the coffin bands themselves were brought from the North. The South did not furnish a thing on earth for that funeral but the corpse and the hole in the ground. There they buried him in a New York coat and Boston pair of shoes and a pair of breeches from Chicago, and a shirt from Cincinnati, leaving him nothing to carry into the next world with him to remind him of the country in which he lived, and for which he fought for four years, but the chill of blood in his veins and the marrow of his bones."

Tech's new President soon discovered that changing Grady's lament into positive action was not easy. The School had started with 129 students in 1888. The *Annual Catalogue* for 1894-95 (spelling was changed in 1971 to the *Annual Catalog*), the last year of Hopkins' administration, indicates that enrollment stood at only 124 students, five fewer than when he arrived. The General Assembly had given steady but conservative support to the School with appropriations that ranged from $18,000 to $22,500 a year. The city of Atlanta kept its end of the bargain, making annual appropriations of $2,500. Other funds came from tuition fees called "contingent expenses" and from gifts. During the early years the School tried to produce items that could be sold commercially, but the project was abandoned because it failed to show a profit and perhaps also because local businessmen opposed it. The practice was gradually eliminated. However, the idea of practical applications continued to provide a rationale for the School's curriculum. The *Annual Announcements* for 1895-96 reported: "The sooner the student can be put into productive industry the better."

The Georgia Tech was first published in 1894. The Commencement Issue served as a kind of yearbook for students, reviewed sporting events and gave a history of each class.

The 1895 Cotton States and International Exposition at Piedmont Park gave Tech students an opportunity to see the latest developments in technology. The first commercial movie theater in the world was one of the Exposition's attractions.

All students were required to take four years of mechanical drawing. Efficiency in the drawing room was considered second only to proficiency in the shop. From free-hand drawing in the apprentice year, students progressed through various drawing problems to the drawing of machine parts and, finally as seniors, to detailed machine design. Instruments cost about $13.00, according to the *Catalogue* for 1899-1900, and classes met each week for 2 1/2 hours. Coats and ties were mandatory for classes but apparently coats could be removed during the extended lab period.

The Georgia School of Technology, or "the Tech" as it was called, was never meant to compete with the University of Georgia in Athens, and its curriculum attested to their differences. Courses in the liberal arts were kept to a bare minimum at Tech, and courses in mathematics and the natural sciences emphasized application rather than theory. Entrance examinations, somewhat like those administered at West Point and Annapolis, were required of all entering students. First-year students devoted two eight-hour days to woodworking and, later in the year, added one day a week of molding and pattern making in the foundry. Second and third-year students spent a day a week and an additional 200 hours each year in the School's four shops: wood shop, foundry, smith shop and machine shop. At the time, just one degree was conferred — a Bachelor of Science in Mechanical Engineering.

The School's first student publication was *The Technologian*, a short-lived newspaper published in the spring of 1891. *The Technologian* was succeeded in February 1894 by *The Georgia Tech,* which lasted 14 years.

Football came to Georgia Tech during the Hopkins administration. At that time the game bore little resemblance to today's closely regulated, well-coached and popularly acclaimed "big-time" sport. Then, it was an improvised affair that was often brutal and sometimes regarded with suspicion and hostility. Georgia Tech's first coach was Ernest E. West, a graduate of the U.S. Naval Academy and Adjunct Professor of Physics at the School. F.O. Spain, Mathematics Professor, assisted him. Tech fielded a team and played three

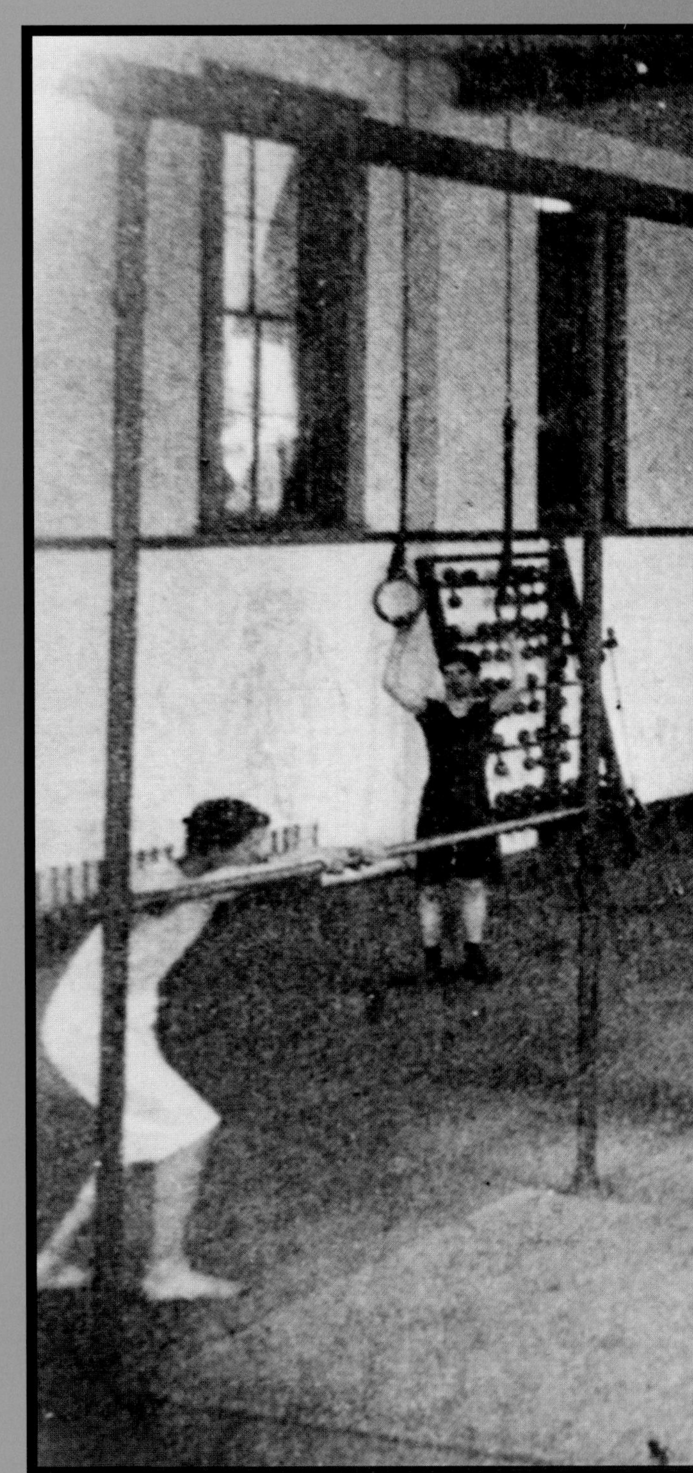

The School insisted on a thorough physical examination for all students, and the instructor in "Physical Culture" then gave them exercises suited to their particular needs and abilities. The Department kept a log which, at set intervals, indicated the increase in each student's measurements during the year. The following statement appears in the *Catalogue* for 1897-98: "Especial attention is paid to track athletics, and students preparing for events in this line of athletic work are subjected to the most rigid training with regard to diet and exercise. While under training, no student is allowed to smoke or indulge in excesses of any kind."

games in 1892. Then, on November 4, 1893, the team played the University of Georgia at Athens for the first time in a game that was historical as well as controversial. The star of that game was Leonard Wood, an Army officer stationed at Fort McPherson, who had enrolled at Tech. Tech won the game 28-6 largely because of Wood's ability and experience. But University of Georgia partisans charged that Wood was a "ringer," a non-student who had matriculated for the purpose of playing football. (Wood apparently formally enrolled at Tech as a sub-apprentice two days before the game, along with one other player, and left Tech the same month. Three other players formally enrolled the day before the game.)

Although Athens fans reportedly threw rocks at the Tech team during the game, all seems to have ended well. "When the game was over," *The Atlanta Constitution* reported, "Captain Butler of the University posed three cheers for the Tech team which was given with a will by the students." Sparing no expense, the Tech team returned to Atlanta after the game in a railroad car that usually hauled coal.

Instructors and middle and senior classes in 1890 include, on the top row: T.S. Grimes, wood shop instructor; Percy C. Brooks; Henry L. Smith; John Toy, machine shop instructor; and George G. Crawford. Middle row: J.B. McCrary; J.P. Goldsmith; J. Hardin Jones; and Julius L. DeGive. Bottom row: William H. Glenn; J.S. Moore; T.S. Setze; W.H.E. Duncan, foreman of machine shop; Oscar Elsas; and Charles M. Pritchett. Smith and Crawford were the first two graduates of Tech. Smith recalls: "George Crawford and I got together before graduation and agreed that this decision was too important to make on an alphabetical basis so out came a coin — it was a 50-cent piece — and I won the toss. It was the greatest honor I ever received, and I received it through chance."

BOARD AND EXPENSES.

Two dormitories and a mess-hall have been built for the students this year (1896). They afford accommodations for thirty students. Mrs. S. E. Capers, a highly accomplished lady of long experience in such work, will take charge of the boarding department. The price of board for students exclusive of washing, fuel, and lights, will be ten dollars per month. Mrs. Capers comes to the school with the highest recommendations for her efficiency in dealing with students, caring for the sick, and exerting a refining and beneficial influence over all who have been associated with her in her work as matron.

The following ladies, in localities of easy access to the school, offer to take students at the prices mentioned:

Mrs. Wood, 128 Plum, $15.
Mrs. Camp, 343 Luckie, $16.
Mrs. Harris, 114 West Baker, $17.50.
Mrs. Hollingsworth, 135 Auburn Ave., $17.
Mrs. Farr, 327 Luckie, $16.
Mrs. Sims, 58 Cherry, $16.
Mrs. Hutcheson, 195 Hunnicutt, $14.50 to $15.
Mrs. Martin, 184 Fowler, $15.
Miss Hodgson, 169 Mills, $15.
Mrs. Morris, 450 Luckie, $15 to $16.
Mrs. Young, 90 Plum, $14.
Mrs. Martin, 41 Gresham, $15.
Mrs. Collins, 177 Alexander, $15.50
Miss Swords, 340 Luckie, $15.
Mrs. McRae, 152 Courtland, $15 to $20.
Miss Wilkinson, 256 Luckie, $15 to $20.
Mrs. Hooten, 6 Cherry, $14 to $15.
Mrs. Winters, 89 Plum, $15.
Mrs. Patterson, 230 West Peachtree, $18.
Mrs. Hamilton, 24 Alexander, $14 to $15.
Mrs. W. L. Saye, 237 Luckie, $16.
Mrs. McDonald, 165 Alexander, $14.
Mrs. Long, 196 Kimball, $12.50 to $15.
Mrs. T. A. Higdon, 430 Luckie, $15.
Mrs. Baker, 226 State, $13.
Mrs. E. Barricklo, 98 West Peachtree, $14 to $18.
Mrs. Saye, 237 Luckie, $15.

With the information given above students may easily come to Atlanta without preliminary correspondence and be located, at least temporarily, a few hours after their arrival.

Washing costs from $1.50 to $2.00 per month. During the winter months coal may be purchased from the school at wholesale prices

Many young men had to seek lodging off campus because the two frame dormitories, better known as the "shacks," accommodated only about 30 students.

In 1892 the first Tech football team was coached by Adjunct Professor of Physics Ernest E. West. *The Technologian* reports: "Great interest is being manifested in foot-ball and we are playing the game to win." The football in those days was rounder than it is today and resembled a rugby ball. Padding and protection equipment were virtually unknown. A newspaper clipping from a later time identifies the members. Top row: Stafford Nash, manager; [W.C.] Jordan; Phil Ogletree; George Forrest; E.A. Greene; [A.W.] Hall; and Trezevant Holmes. Second row: "a boy named Dugger [D.E. Duggan] from Hawkinsville, Georgia; W.O. Conner of Cave Springs; William Dennis of Talbotton, with the football..., and two boys named [J.T.] Elder and Daniels [G.G. Daniel], first names not remembered. Bottom row: Ernest B. Merry of Augusta; William W. Hunter, Captain, of Washington, Georgia; Eddy R. Whitney of Augusta, and Edward A. Werner of Atlanta....Frank O. Spain, mathematics instructor (not in picture), also took an active part."

Baseball was the most popular game on campus. Accounts differ, but 1890 seems to have been the year when Tech played its first intercollegiate baseball game — against Georgia. In 1948, H.D. Cutter, class of 1892, recalled that game: "Nearly the whole school went....A classmate of mine [A.D. "Duke" Black of Rome] pitched and we brought home the bacon, and I know that 'Ramblin' Wreck' was sung by our boys at the time, and I am sure that Billy Walthall, of Palmetto, Georgia, another classmate, was the author." Dean George C. Griffin's records for 1892 show that Tech lost that year to its arch-rival 8-3.

In 1895, Dr. Hopkins resigned from his post at Tech to return to the full-time Christian ministry and efforts to find a successor began. The Trustees' search led them back to the Tech campus to Lyman Hall, the iron-willed West Point graduate who was already Head of the Department of Mathematics. On January 3, 1896, the Trustees named him Chairman of the faculty, raised his salary $50 a month and stipulated that he be "clothed with the authority of president" while completing the unexpired term of Dr. Hopkins. Then, on June 24,

This photograph was taken just before Tech's 1893 football team defeated Georgia 28-6 in the first meeting between the two schools. Coach Leonard Wood, No. 15, an Army lieutenant and member of the sub-apprentice class, scored the first touchdown for the record book. Others in the picture include — back row: Ed Werner, Nourse or Charles Warren Hill, George Forrest, Frank O. Spain (Professor of Mathematics), M. W. McRae, J. Frank Ogletree Jr., Trezevant Holmes, Guley V. Heidt. Front row: Ed Whitney, Ed Hunter (captain), John Kimball, Park Howell, Haskell, Thomas W. Raoul and Wood. Ferd Kaufman and W.G. Mealor served as managers. (Two players — No. 10 and No. 12 — have noseguards hanging around their necks.) Authorities differ on identification.

The machine and wood shops stood just west of the Academic Building. Here, hundreds of Tech students learned the rudiments of working with wood, forges, smith equipment and machines. The building fell to the wrecking ball in 1968.

Tech's dress code from 7 a.m. until 1 p.m. required a coat and tie. After lunch, students donned bib overalls and an oilcloth apron or smock to work in the wood shop with "Uncle Heinie" Henika, in the foundry with "Mr. Billy" Van Houten, in the smith shop with Horace A. Thompson and in the machine shop with J.A. Bailey.

after six hours of closed-door debate, they officially named him President of the Georgia School of
Technology. Hall was 36 years old.

Tech's second, and youngest, President was
born in Americus in 1859, the son of John Hall, a
prominent merchant. He attended public schools
in Americus and for three years was a student at
Mercer University prior to his appointment to
West Point, where he graduated in 1881. Before
coming to Tech as its first Mathematics Professor,
Hall served on the faculty of the Georgia Military
Academy at Kirkwood, the South Carolina
Military Academy and the Moreland Park Military
Academy near Atlanta.

The 1906 *Annual Catalogue* included this photograph of freshman
wood shop students standing on the steps of the Shops Building. At
the top left stands young Uncle Heinie sporting his famous beard.
Shop memories were often fond. The historian of the 1908 senior
class wrote in the first edition of *The Blue Print* (changed to *The
Blueprint* in 1963): "The machine shop was the one haven where we
sought rest. Who of us does not remember with pleasure the
afternoons we spent riding leisurely back and forth on the machine
planers, almost lulled to forgetfulness by the narcotic effect of its
gliding motion?"

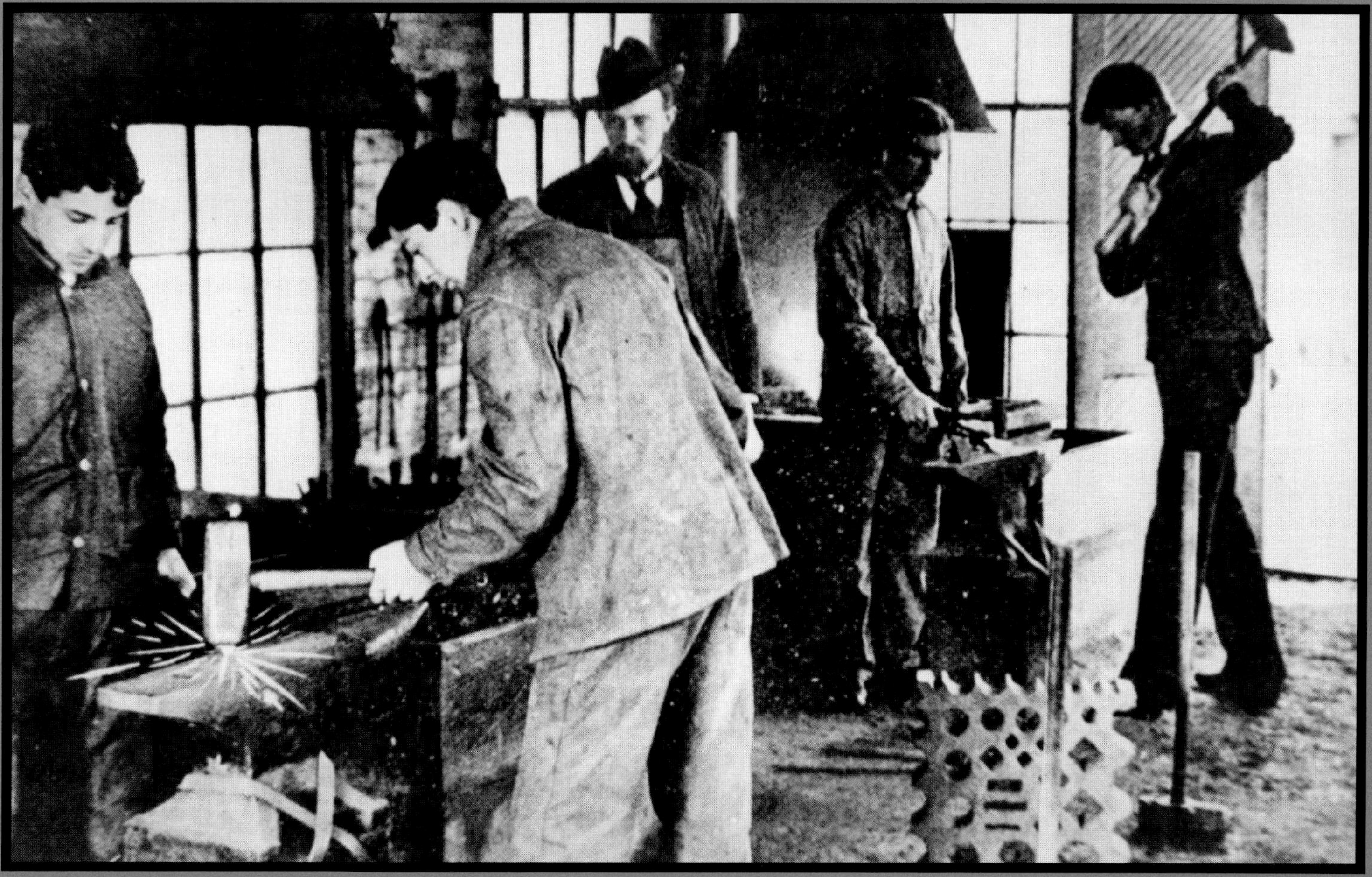

The anvil became a symbol for the School. It was the focal point of
the first seal and was prominently displayed on the cover of the 1896
Commencement Issue of *The Georgia Tech.*

According to Tech's 1898-99 *Catalogue*,
students working in the foundry received
instruction in "green and dry-sand
moulding, core-making, mixtures of iron,
brass-founding, and the mixtures of the
various useful bronzes, aluminum-casting,
and the aluminum bronzes."

All students were required to take four different shops: wood shop, foundry, smith shop and machine shop. The apprentice year was devoted to woodwork, especially the careful use of tools. As soon as a student could do pattern work, he was sent to the foundry to put his skills into practice. During his last three years, he divided his time in the shops doing pattern making, foundry, smith shop and machine shop. Equipment in the machine shop included lathes, planers, grinding tools, a milling machine, a shaper and small tools. At the Cotton States and International Exposition, the shop received a silver medal for its entry — an iron planer.

Hall was a highly regarded mathematician as well as administrator. He wrote three textbooks and was once offered considerably more money than Tech paid him to accept a similar position at the University of Tennessee.

Hall was unbending, strict, disciplined, reserved and aloof. M.L. Brittain, who knew him personally, wrote that Hall was "intimate with no one." Locally, he became prominent as Commanding Officer of a popular volunteer military organization known as the Grady Cadets.

When Hall was named to complete the unexpired term of Hopkins, the School had many needs. There were just two buildings, no dormitories and a severely restricted curriculum (the *Annual Catalogue* for 1895-96 called Tech a "school of mechanical engineering"). Its library

Lyman Hall, second row center (standing and wearing a "straw boater"), became President in 1896. By 1899 the student body had more than doubled, the faculty was larger and there were three new departments: Civil Engineering, Electrical Engineering and the Textile School. Seated second from the left is the man who would succeed Hall in 1905, English Professor Kenneth G. Matheson.

The first degree in chemistry — Engineering Chemistry, offered in 1901 — required quantitative analysis. By 1906, students worked in the newly completed 60-student laboratory in the Lyman Hall Laboratory of Chemistry. Professor William H. Emerson, a member of the first faculty, stands in the rear.

By 1905 seniors in Mechanical, Civil and Textile Engineering, as well as those in Engineering Chemistry, were required to take courses in dynamo electric machinery.

consisted of a shelf of books in Professor Matheson's classroom. "To put it bluntly," Robert B. Wallace Jr. later wrote, "in its early days Tech was a trade school."

Hall immediately began transforming the trade school into a college, and the muddy hill on North Avenue into a campus. Two frame dormitories, dubbed the "shacks," accommodated a few boarding students until the completion of Knowles Dormitory, which also housed the dining hall. Another dormitory and gymnasium soon followed, then the Aaron French Textile School and the Electrical Engineering Building. These

On June 28, 1896, *The Atlanta Constitution* gave this warm reception to Lyman Hall, the new President of Tech.

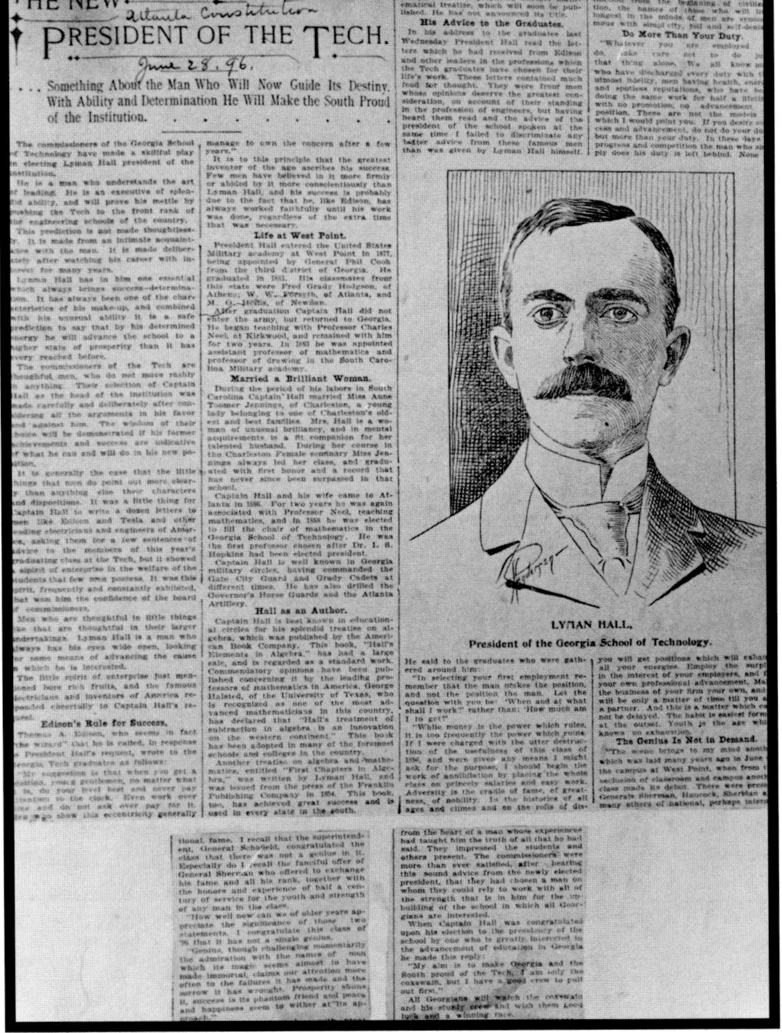

THE NEW *Atlanta Constitution*
PRESIDENT OF THE TECH.
June 28, 96

Something About the Man Who Will Now Guide Its Destiny. With Ability and Determination He Will Make the South Proud of the Institution.

The commissioners of the Georgia School of Technology have made a skillful play in electing Lyman Hall president of the institution.

He is a man who understands the art of leading. He is an executive of splendid ability, and will prove his mettle by pushing the Tech to the front rank of the engineering schools of the country.

This prediction is not made thoughtlessly. It is made from an intimate acquaintance with the man. It is made deliberately after watching his career with interest for many years.

Lyman Hall has in him one essential which always brings success—determination. It has always been one of the characteristics of his make-up, and combined with his unusual ability it is a safe prediction to say that by his determined energy he will advance the school to a higher state of prosperity than it has ever reached before.

The commissioners of the Tech are thoughtful men, who do not move rashly in anything. Their selection of Captain Hall as the head of the institution was made carefully and deliberately after considering all the arguments in his favor and against him. The wisdom of their choice will be demonstrated if his former achievements and success are indicative of what he can and will do in his new position.

It is generally the case that the little things that men do point out more clearly than anything else their characters and dispositions. It was a little thing for Captain Hall to write a dozen letters to men like Edison and Tesla and other leading electricians and engineers of America, asking them for a few sentences of advice to the members of this year's graduating class at the Tech, but it showed a spirit of enterprise in the welfare of the students that few men possess. It was this spirit, frequently and constantly exhibited, that won him the confidence of the board of commissioners.

Men who are thoughtful in little things are those that are thoughtful in their larger undertakings. Lyman Hall is a man who always has his eyes wide open, looking for some means of advancing the cause in which he is interested.

The little spirit of enterprise just mentioned bore rich fruits, and the famous electricians and inventors of America responded cheerfully to Captain Hall's request.

Edison's Rule for Success.

Thomas A. Edison, who seems in fact the "wizard" that he is called, in response to President Hall's request, wrote to the Georgia Tech graduates as follows:

"My suggestion is that when you get a position, even a position, no matter what it is, do your level best and never pay attention to the clock. Have work every time and do not ask ever pay nor time. [...] show this eccentricity generally manage to own the concern after a few years."

It is to this principle that the greatest inventor of the age ascribes his success. Few men have believed in it more firmly or abided by it more conscientiously than Lyman Hall, and his success is probably due to the fact that he, like Edison, has always worked faithfully until his work was done, regardless of the extra time that was necessary.

Life at West Point.

President Hall entered the United States Military academy at West Point in 1877, being appointed by General Phil Cook from the third district of Georgia. He graduated in 1881. His classmates from this state were Fred Grady Hodgson, of Athens; W. W. Erwyth, of Atlanta, and M. G. Joffit, of Newnan.

After graduation Captain Hall did not enter the army, but returned to Georgia. He began teaching with Professor Charles Neel, at Kirkwood, and remained with him for two years. In 1882 he was appointed assistant professor of mathematics and professor of drawing in the South Carolina Military academy.

Married a Brilliant Woman.

During the period of his labors in South Carolina Captain Hall married Miss Anne Toomer Jennings, of Charleston, a young lady belonging to one of Charleston's oldest and best families. Mrs. Hall is a woman of unusual brilliancy, and in mental acquirements is a fit companion for her talented husband. During her course in the Charleston Female seminary Miss Jennings always led her class, and graduated with first honor and a record that has never since been surpassed in that school.

Captain Hall and his wife came to Atlanta in 1886. For two years he was again associated with Professor Neel, teaching mathematics, and in 1888 he was elected to fill the chair of mathematics in the Georgia School of Technology. He was the first professor chosen after Dr. I. S. Hopkins had been elected president.

Captain Hall is well known in Georgia military circles, having commanded the Gate City Guard and Grady Cadets at different times. He has also drilled the Governor's Horse Guards and the Atlanta Artillery.

Hall as an Author.

Captain Hall is best known in educational circles for his splendid treatise on algebra, which was published by the American Book Company. This book, "Hall's Elements in Algebra," has had a large sale, and is regarded as a standard work. Commendatory opinions have been published concerning it by the leading professors of mathematics in America. George Halsted, of the University of Texas, who is recognized as one of the most advanced mathematicians in this country, has declared that "Hall's treatment of subtraction in algebra is an innovation on the western continent." This book has been adopted in many of the foremost schools and colleges in the country.

Another treatise, on algebra and mathematics, entitled "First Chapters in Algebra," was written by Lyman Hall, and was issued from the press of the Franklin Publishing Company in 1894. This book, too, has achieved great success and is used in every state in the south.

Captain Hall is preparing another mathematical treatise, which will soon be published. He has received from Edison and other leaders in the profession, which the Tech graduates have chosen for their life's work. These letters contained much food for thought. They were from men whose opinions deserve the greatest consideration, on account of their standing in the profession of engineers, but having heard them read and the advice of the president of the school spoken at the same time I failed to discriminate any better advice from these famous men than was given by Lyman Hall himself.

His Advice to the Graduates.

In his address to the graduates last Wednesday President Hall read the letters which he had received from Edison and other leaders in the profession, which the Tech graduates have chosen for their life's work. These letters contained much food for thought. They were from men whose opinions deserve the greatest consideration, on account of their standing in the profession of engineers, but having heard them read and the advice of the president of the school spoken at the same time I failed to discriminate any better advice from these famous men than was given by Lyman Hall himself.

Do More Than Your Duty.

"Whatever you are employed do, take care not to do just that thing alone. We all know men who have discharged every duty with the utmost fidelity, men having health, energy and spotless reputations, who have been doing the same work for half a lifetime with no promotion, no advancement, no position. There are not the men which I would point you. If you desire success and advancement, do not do your duty, but more than your duty. In these days progress and competition the man who simply does his duty is left behind. None

LYMAN HALL,
President of the Georgia School of Technology.

He said to the graduates who were gathered around him:

"In selecting your first employment remember that the man makes the position, and not the position the man. Let the question with you be: 'When and at what shall I work?' rather than: 'How much am I to get?'

"While money is the power which rules, it is too frequently the power which pains. If I were charged with the utter destruction of the usefulness of this class of 1896, and were given my means I might ask for the purpose, I should begin the work of annihilation by placing the whole class on princely salaries and easy work. Adversity is the cradle of fame; of greatness, of nobility. In the histories of all ages and climes and on the rolls of distinction from the beginning of civilization, the names of those who will be longest in the minds of men are renoun more with simplicity, toil and self-denial.

You will get positions which will exhaust all your energies. Employ the surplus in the interest of your employers, and for your own professional advancement. Make the business of your firm your own, and will be only a matter of time till you are a partner. And this is a matter which can not be delayed. The habit is easiest formed at the outset. Youth is the age when known no exhaustion.

The Genius Is Not in Demand.

"The scene brings to my mind another which was laid many years ago in June—the campus at West Point, when from seclusion of classroom and campus another class made its debut. There were great Generals Sherman, Hancock, Sheridan and many others of national, perhaps international, fame. I recall that the superintendent, General Schofield, congratulated the class that there was not a genius in it. Especially do I recall the fanciful offer of General Sherman who offered to exchange his fame and all his rank, together with the honors and experience of half a century of service for the youth and strength of any man in the class.

"How well now can we of older years appreciate the significance of those two statements. I congratulate this class of '96 that it has not a single genius.

"Genius, though challenging momentarily the admiration with the meteor of men which its magic seems almost to have made immortal, claims our attention more often to the failures it has made and the sorrow it has wrought. Prosperity shines it, success is its phantom friend and peace and happiness seem to wither at its approach.

from the heart of a man whose experience had taught him the truth of all that he had said. They impressed the students and others present. The commissioners were more than ever satisfied, after hearing this sound advice from the newly elected president, that they had chosen a man to whom they could rely to work with all of the strength that is in him for the upbuilding of the school in which all Georgians are interested.

When Captain Hall was congratulated upon his election to the presidency of the school by one who is greatly interested in the advancement of education in Georgia he made this reply:

"My aim is to make Georgia and the South proud of the Tech. I am only the coxswain, but I have a good crew to pull out first."

All Georgians will watch the coxswain and his sturdy crew and wish them good luck and a winning race.

In 1897 the Apprentice Class gathered in front of the Academic Building with Professor Matheson for their first official picture. Sitting under the tree is Julian P. Benjamin (third from right). In 1901 the seniors of this class defied the administration, refusing to return to campus from Christmas holidays on December 31. When they did return on January 2, President Hall called them in one by one, told them they were guilty of "insubordination," and ordered them out of the dormitories for six weeks. They were compelled to return to classes for six weeks in the fall in order to graduate. This photograph was taken following their special graduation exercises which were held in November 1901.

The Insubordinate Seniors held reunions every five years and posed on the west side of the Academic Building for group photographs. In 1961 Julian P. Benjamin returned to sit in his spot for a final picture.

new buildings also signified a steady curriculum expansion with more majors for more students. A start was made at a library when a room in the Academic Building was stacked with appropriate books.

Hall was unequaled at fund raising and he worked at it even on vacations. While at a North Carolina resort, he met Aaron French, a prominent Pennsylvania millionaire, and persuaded him to support the struggling institution. French subsequently contributed thousands of dollars for scholarships and for the School's textile program.

The Textile Department was, in Hall's opinion, one of his best dreams come true. Two years after

From the beginning, mathematics was heavily emphasized. Three of the names on the blackboard in this section in descriptive geometry are the names of students in the class of 1897, Mechanical Engineering: E.F. Huff from Bibb County, R.M. Crumley from Fulton County and Rex Van Den Corput from DeKalb County. (Positive identification is unavailable for Mr. West, the young man explaining his problem.)

Tech's 1901 baseball team was managed by Roy Merry and had a successful season. The team saved the Athletic Association from bankruptcy by raising $1,800 in two days — selling seats for games during those days for 25 and 50 cents. One of its pitchers, Weldon Henley, later gained fame with the Philadelphia Athletics. James Wayne Moore, the team's center fielder, is at the far right with a bandaged hand. Other members included Robert Lee Hicks, Murphy, Neal, J.J. McCathern, Jacob Henry Paulsen, McKibben, Eugene C. Patterson, Waddill, Joseph A. Brinson, Lindley McClure and Morrison.

his inauguration, he called its establishment "the most important step in education ever taken in Georgia." He declared that "When the first brick is layed [sic] in the textile department of the Georgia School of Technology, the South declares war against New England; a war not of secession but of aggression, a war against slavery, and we are the slaves who shall be free."

Hall had the distinction of being in office when John Heisman, the famous football coach, came to Tech. During the pre-Heisman years, Tech had had just one winning season and had suffered a number of defeats by Heisman-coached teams (Auburn and Clemson). By 1903 Tech had decided to change that record. Frank Turner, an 1899 graduate and instructor at Tech, proposed a

A young man sits with the nurse on the steps of the Isolation House built to confine Tech men with contagious diseases.

solution: hire Heisman. He collected money from faculty and students, helped convince the reluctant Hall that Tech needed a full-time coach, then helped persuade Heisman to leave Clemson and come to Tech, where there was not even a playing field. When Tech's offer rose to $2,250 a year plus 30 percent of the gate, Heisman accepted.

Al Loeb, one of Heisman's star players, recalls Heisman's strict rules: "No fried foods and no pork, but hearty meals of meat and potatoes, vegetables, and sweet milk; no alcohol and no smoking, except after a victory when a bottle of beer and a cigar were sometimes permitted; cold showers only, except after a game, when players could luxuriate in warm water; and no sex."

Heisman coached elsewhere — at Oberlin, Buchtel (University of Akron), Auburn, Clemson, Pennsylvania, Washington and Jefferson, and Rice, but his greatest days were at Tech. Each year when the Heisman Memorial Trophy is awarded to the nation's most outstanding football player, Tech fans are reminded of their first full-time coach and his long list of outstanding players, teams and memorable afternoons.

Tech has had a grand tradition of beloved teachers, such as John Saylor Coon — "Uncle Si" — who came to Tech the year after it opened. He had misgivings about teaching at Tech because he considered himself too unorthodox to please most Georgians. Eventually, however, he not only pleased most Georgians but became part of Tech lore. He headed the Mechanical Engineering Department from 1889 until he retired in 1923. There were others: William Perry, who became Head of the English Department and was best known for his "Hour of Charm," as his literature classes were called; and J.B. Crenshaw — "Little Doc" — the feisty Head of the Modern Language Department.

In the early days, state-supported schools like Tech were often called "godless" by clergymen. Hall, in fact, had a running battle with churchmen over the alleged use of wine at social events attended by Tech students and faculty. In reality, most of the Tech community were anything but godless, and many students and faculty were active in local churches and the Y.M.C.A..

Middlers and juniors battle it out in 1904.

Lyman Hall, a native of Americus, Georgia, and a graduate of the United States Military Academy at West Point, came to Tech in 1888 at the age of 29 as its first Professor of Mathematics. Selected President in 1896, he remained at Tech until his death in 1905. Hall was known as a strict disciplinarian and his emphasis on precision, thoroughness and careful attention to detail remain as distinguishing characteristics of the Tech student. He began the shift away from shop training and toward more diversified engineering. After his death, the chemistry building — completed in 1906, and for which he had raised the funds — was named for him. The inscription on the cornerstone reflects his philosophy: "In the first place I would put accuracy (Geikie)."

When Tech first opened, students found lodging and board in the surrounding area because no dormitory or dining hall was available on campus. One of Hall's actions was to erect at a cost of $4,000 two frame buildings to house students (dormitories on the left in the above picture). Students called these buildings the "shacks." Then Hall approached the Legislature for money to build a suitable dormitory. Clarence Knowles of Fulton County took a leading part in getting the appropriation and, in recognition of his help, the Institute named the new dormitory, built in 1897, Knowles.

This was the Victorian Era, and life at Tech mirrored its norms. Students were expected to behave as gentlemen; duty was all-important and discipline an essential part of character. Daily chapel attendance was required, and in the dorms an inflexible schedule began at 6:30 a.m. and ended with room inspection at 10:30 p.m. The President himself inspected dormitory rooms on Saturdays. Strict rules were made and enforced by administrators and "inspectors" — student assistants. During the Hall regime, the following regulations were posted throughout the School:

Students found with playing cards in their possession will be required to leave the Dormitory.

Students must not leave the school property without permission, except to visit the ball-ground or walk on North Avenue, between Plum and West Peachtree Streets, during the day hours.

Students who desire to go bicycle riding must get leave of absence from the professor in charge.

In 1904, Field Day was held on the front campus laid out with running tracks, jumping and pole vaulting paths, circles for shot, hammer, etc.

Students must deposit their firearms with the
  professor in charge.
Students may not hire any one to attend to
  room, but must take alternate weeks in
  performance of this duty.
The rising-bell will ring in the hall at 6:30
  A.M., daily, except Sunday.
The time at the dormitory will be regulated by
  the clock in the Academic building.

Prior to the opening of Tech's first dormitory in
1896, students from other towns boarded with
local families whose names and rates appeared in
the *Annual Catalogue.* But by 1899, parents were
advised to *require* their sons to board in the dormitories for several reasons: cost, convenience and
discipline. "The regulations," the *Catalogue*
advised, "protect them from the evil influences of
a great city."

Even with Tech's restrictions, students had
time for many activities. Atlanta was certainly no
sleepy college town and never had been. Its
population was almost 90,000; its national and international expositions drew crowds as large as
300,000; its industries were growing, and important cultural and political events were taking
place. Other colleges were attracting students into
the area — Agnes Scott, Morris Brown, Spelman,
Atlanta University and Emory; and a syrup
developed in 1886 as a remedy for headaches,
called "Coca-Cola," had already begun to create
new jobs and fortunes in the capital city.

If Atlanta's attractions lacked appeal — and
Hall seems to have hoped they would — there
were ample opportunities for extracurricular
activities on campus. Fraternities (Alpha Tau
Omega was the first), literary societies such as Phi
Eta Sigma, and publications such as *The Georgia
Tech* provided faculty and students with outlets for
literary and other approved social expression.

The physical training of all students was important to the school administrators. Apprentice
students were required to take "physical culture,"
and all other students were encouraged to participate in these classes or at least in some physical
activity. The 1897-98 *Announcements* refers to
"the gymnasium, a baseball-ground, tennis-court,
football-ground and running-track."

44

Aaron French of Pittsburgh became a faithful friend of Tech, providing donations for the Textile School building, machinery and a self-perpetuating scholarship in textiles. In 1900, French helped keep the doors open for the sub-apprentice class by his contribution of $3,500.

Hall wanted to open the textile courses to women and felt women's skills would be particularly suited to the work of design, weaving, drawing and chemistry. "Co-education," Hall stated in a letter to Mrs. Robert Parks, "is not only feasible, but productive of much good in stimulating ambitious students to higher efforts and exemplary conduct." Hall did not live to see this idea implemented.

The A. French Textile School began instruction in 1899. Lyman Hall waxed eloquent in a letter to Clark Howell, Editor of *The Atlanta Constitution:* "When the first brick is layed [sic] in the textile department of the Georgia School of Technology, the South declares war against New England; a war not of secession but of aggression, a war against slavery, and we are the slaves who shall be free."

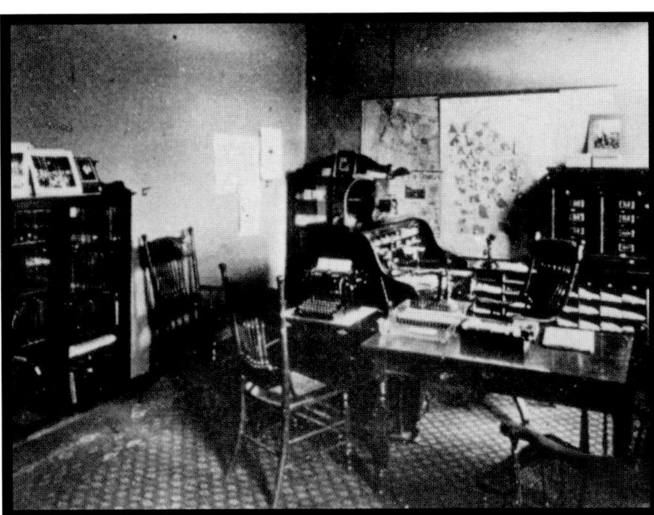

Isaac Hopkins and Lyman Hall used this office in the Academic Building during their presidencies.

The Professor in Charge had general oversight of student rules and regulations.

Crowds of spectators pass alongside the picket fence built in 1897 and move across the quadrangle to the Tech Flats for an afternoon of football. A 1910 issue of *The Yellow Jacket* notes that the 1897 fence as well as all barbed wire fences on campus were to be replaced by a privet hedge to beautify the campus. "We ought, all of us," the article continues, "to be old enough not to need barbed wire fences to keep us off the grass."

Both Swann Dormitory and the Electrical Engineering Building were added to the campus in 1901. James Swann of New York offered the School $20,000 if it raised an additional $15,000. Named for Swann's wife, Janie Austell Swann, the building has served several occupants through the years. George Griffin tells of the time he and C.D. "Dummy" LeBey found a loose mule on campus, took it to Swann and tied it to the door of Professor A.H. Armstrong's room. Swann's rooms today are the offices and classrooms for Continuing Education and the Department of Modern Languages. The Electrical Building was given the name of Professor and Dean of Electrical Engineering D.P. Savant. It currently houses the Cooperative Division, the Graduate Division and other offices.

For in-state students the cost of attending Tech was low. There was an annual $20 fee for "contingent expenses" and an additional $5 fee deposited with the Treasurer upon enrollment to cover possible damages to college buildings or furniture. Students not in dorms or in improvised quarters, like "Middlers Mansion," could board with "good families" who charged $12.50 to $20 a month with "special arrangements for fuel and light, plus a charge for washing costs."

Local boys walked to school and packed their lunches because there were no restaurants or cafeterias nearby. (Drug stores sold just drugs and cosmetics.) According to first graduate Henry L. Smith, Jacobs' was the only place in Atlanta that sold Coca-Cola and "even [Mr. Jacobs] would not have thought of selling hamburgers, hot dogs, or even milk across the counter."

Middlers Mansion gave free rein to the creativity of its builders, middlers S.L. Snowden of Macon and W.M. Fambrough of Boston, Georgia. The little shack served both as a class project and as living quarters. Edward C. Peters, owner of the rough wooded hollow north of campus, permitted the building to be erected and the School gave the students credit for their after-hours project. The roof sloped in only one direction and a gutter emptied rain water into a whiskey barrel, from which the water flowed by gravity through filtering charcoal into a wash basin in the house. The wallpaper consisted of drawings — "from the free-hand sketches of by-gone unsophisticated 'preps' to the machine designs of the wiley [sic] Senior." The bunks five feet off the floor predate the modern skyracks; draperies hanging from them made large "cupboards." Other furnishings included a coal-burning stove, a table, stuffed chairs, rugs and typical college wall decorations; and an assortment of groceries and toiletries filled a box nailed to the wall. According to a January 1902 *Georgia Tech* article, "A Tech Snuggery," a telephone system put Fambrough and Snowden in direct communication with R.H. "Pudd'n" Lowndes and B.F. "Fatty" Markert. The two students remained undisturbed by room inspections and curfews.

John W. Heisman came to Tech in 1904. During 16 football seasons he recorded 102 victories, 29 losses and 7 ties; and in 14 baseball seasons, 161 victories and 97 losses. Robert B. Wallace Jr. credits Frank Turner, an 1899 graduate and drawing instructor at Tech, with being the moving force behind the push to get Heisman. An 1892 graduate of Pennsylvania, Heisman continued to wear his sweater with a large "P" on the front. The Heisman Memorial Trophy is named for the famous Tech coach.

This agreement entered into this the twenty-fifth day of November, 1904, between J. W. Heisman and the Athletic Association of the Georgia School of Technology and stipulates as follows:

1. J. W. Heisman agrees to coach both Varsity, Foot Ball and Base Ball teams of the Georgia School of Technology.

2. The Athletic Association of the Georgia School of Technology agrees to pay J. W. Heisman for the above services the sum of Twenty-two Hundred and Fifty dollars and thirty per cent of the gate receipts annually.

Net gate receipts to mean Tech's gross share of all gate receipts, less park rent, less $2,250.00, (coache's salary), less $500.00 for foot ball and base ball supplies, less reasonable advertising expenses. This sum of $2,250.00 to be paid in twelve equal installments, one at the end of each calendar month.

This contract extends over a period of three years, becoming void on December 31, 1907.

Athletic Association of the Georgia School of Technolo

Per. _Frank C. Turner Grd. Mgr._

J. W. Heisman.

Frank C. Turner

Witness

President Lyman Hall sent John W. Heisman this contract, allowing him 13 days to make a decision.

When James Walter Estes lined up to register as a sub-apprentice in 1900, he was told no money was left for new students. Bitterly disappointed, he took a train to Locust Grove, Georgia, to enroll in a school there. Upon arrival, he found a message from his father informing him that Aaron French had donated money toward Tech's scholarship fund and the School was once again accepting students. Estes graduated in 1904 in Electrical Engineering and, at the time of his death at age 102 in 1985, he was Tech's oldest living alumnus. This photograph shows Estes (left) and Frank Davenport leaving General Electric's Schenectady, New York, plant where the two worked for 25 cents an hour shortly after graduating from Tech.

Hall's brief tenure as President was highly successful. The year he took office, Tech graduated 10 men. And by 1905, Hall's last year, there were 29 graduates and the School's enrollment was more than 500 students. The campus, no longer a muddy hill, now consisted of nine buildings.

Hall labored incessantly on behalf of Georgia Tech. Exhausted from his efforts at fund raising and by his administrative responsibilities, he entered the Jackson Health Resort in Danville, N.Y., and died there on August 16, 1905. Three months later, the cornerstone was laid for the building named in his honor, the Lyman Hall Laboratory of Chemistry. The 1905-06 *Annual Announcements* states: "During his nine years' incumbency of office, President Hall was chiefly instrumental in building the school from an insignificant and struggling existence to a proud position of equality with the other great engineering institutions of the country."

J.B. Crenshaw joined the faculty in 1904 as Professor of Modern Languages. A Randolph-Macon graduate, he earned his Ph.D. at Johns Hopkins and did further graduate work at the University of Berlin. Known affectionately as "Little Doc," he served for years on the athletic board, as Faculty Chairman of athletics and coach of the first lacrosse team. He personally sponsored a yearly prize in both Spanish and French.

On top of the Empire Building, then Atlanta's highest, E.A.J. Seddon and W.M. Fambrough use Tech-made equipment under the direction of Professor Arthur H. Ford and Professor Floyd C. Furlow. From Tech's Academic Building two miles away, Professor J.B. Edwards sent this long distance wireless message: "Tech sends greeting to Empire." Tech constructed both sending and receiving equipment. Floyd Furlow, class of 1897, achieved distinction as Tech's first graduate to become a faculty member. He later became President of the Otis Elevator Company.

A Bag of Wind

WHAT THE WINDS FLUTTER

WHITE AND OLD GOLD

WHAT THE WINDS WHISPER

Ve—vi—ve—vo—ve—vi—vo—vum!
Johnny get a rat trap bigger than a cat trap!
Bum—bum!
Hannibal—cannibal—sis—boom—bah!
Tech of Georgia—rah—rah—rah!
Tech—e—ty—reck—reck—reck!
Tech—e—ty—reck—reck—reck!
Boom—rah! Boom—rah!
Georgia Tech!
Bow—wow—hi—yi!
Hot—cold—wet—dry!
Get—there—E—li!
Tech!

WHAT CAUSES WHITLOCK TO BLUSH

(Sung only on the bleachers)

I wish I had a barrel of rum and of sugar three thousand pound,
A college bell to put it in, and a clapper to stir it round.
Like all good honest fellows, I take my whiskey clear:
I'm a rambling wreck
From Georgia Tech,
And the ——— of an engineer.

Oh, if I had a daughter, sir, I'd dress her in white and gold,
And take her on the campus to cheer the brave and bold;
But if I had a son, sir, I tell you what he'd do—
He'd yell like ——— for the Georgia Tech, like his daddy used to do.

I'm a ——— of a, ——— of a, ——— of a, ——— of a, ——— of an engineer;
I'm a ——— of a, ——— of a, ——— of a, ——— of a, ——— of an engineer;
Like all good honest fellows, I take my whiskey clear;
I'm a rambling wreck
From Georgia Tech,
And the ——— of an engineer.

(Owing to the melting of the type, it has been impossible to print the parts of the above song represented by blank spaces.)

The "Ramblin' Wreck," possibly the best-known fight song in the world, was sung as early as 1890 in Athens at the first intercollegiate baseball game Tech played. H.D. Cutter, who graduated in 1892, wrote in *The Atlanta Journal* in 1948: "Nearly the whole school went to Athens....This must have been in 1890. A classmate of mine pitched and we brought home the bacon, and I know that 'Ramblin' Wreck' was sung by our boys at the time, and I am sure that Billy Walthall of Palmetto, Georgia, another classmate, was the author...." Tech, incidentally, won the game.

Tech's band in 1908 played the piece to the tune of an old drinking song, "The Son of a Gambolier." When Mike A. Greenblatt organized the first official band in 1910, he made the first arrangement. The next band director, Frank Roman, had the words and music printed under his name sometime before 1924. Wally Butts, long-time coach at the University of Georgia, was quoted as saying, "I would give half a year's salary if I had a battle hymn like that."

The yell, too, was also an early student creation. F.E. Whitney, class of 1892, wrote in the November 1925 *Alumnus* his recollections of the first time for Techety Reck and the wearing of the white and gold: "In the fall of 1891...Tech did not know the first rudiments of football. The students were invited to attend an Auburn and University of Georgia game and root for Auburn. A committee of the senior class composed of A.R. Colcord, Arthur Solomon, Whitney and others selected the colors and suggested several yells, with Techity Rex [sic] the runaway choice. The approximately 200 students who attended their first college football game cheered the Auburn Tigers to victory, an event long since forgotten by both teams."

This winter scene reveals the bank sloping down to the Flats. At the south end of Knowles is one of the two wooden bridges crossing the deep gully that cut through the campus in the early days. The two "shacks" on the right still have their front porches.

Lyman Hall's sudden death at age 45 set off a heated contest for his vacant post. There were letters and petitions in support of various candidates, mainly by supporters of Dr. H.S. Bradley, a prominent Georgia clergyman. But after two stormy sessions, the Board of Trustees chose Kenneth Gordon Matheson, a member of Tech's English Department since 1896. The Trustees temporized for a few months, calling Matheson "chairman of the faculty," but in 1906 named him President. He was 42 years old and, though not an engineer, was a military man like his predecessor.

Born in Cheraw, South Carolina, Matheson graduated from The Citadel in 1885 and received an M.A. degree from Stanford University in 1897. A year later, he married Belle Seddon Fleet of Culver, Indiana, and served briefly as Commandant of Cadets at the Georgia Military College before coming to Tech.

Matheson is remembered as a quiet, diplomatic man, distinguished in appearance and action, but demanding if the occasion called for it. He was patient and persistent, but in the end was beset by political battles, setbacks and nagging money problems that eventually broke his health.

From the beginning it rankled Matheson to hear the institution he headed referred to as a trade school, and he immediately started improving its academic program. First he tidied up Tech's nomenclature of sub-apprentice, apprentice, junior, middle and senior, changing it to apprentice, freshman, sophomore, junior and senior. Then he turned to his career-long obsession, the library.

Tech's library, as it was generously and perhaps facetiously called in the early days, consisted of a few random books on shelves in Matheson's office. According to one probably exaggerated story, then-Professor Matheson told his students that to pass his courses they had to donate books to the library. Lyman Hall eventually moved the books to a room in the Academic Building and soon thereafter was mentioning the library in Tech advertisements as one of the school's strengths. In 1901 the collection had about 2,000 volumes, many of them duplicates and cast-offs from other college libraries.

Kenneth Gordon Matheson married Belle
Seddon Fleet on December 27, 1898, a
year after he came to Tech as Professor
of English. Students gave Matheson the
sobriquet "KG" — short for "King
George."

Lyman Hall had asked Andrew Carnegie for funds to construct a library building, knowing the philanthropist was interested in libraries. Carnegie had already donated $100,000 for the public library in Atlanta, and in 1899 had written: "I have especial interest in doing something for the South, a portion of the country to which I have always been attached and in whose problems I am deeply interested."

Consequently, only a few months after Hall's death on March 12, 1906, Carnegie donated $20,000 to Tech with the stipulation that the School appropriate $2,000 a year to support the library. The Legislature appropriated $5,000 and

The Rockefeller Y.M.C.A. building, built in 1912 on the corner of North Avenue and Fowler, became the focal point for student activities. "Its splendid home offers a wholesome atmosphere and adequate amusement, making it unnecessary for a boy to go to the city to spend his idle hours," states the 1921 *Bulletin.* The large house next door served as the President's home from its completion in 1904 until a new home was built in 1949. The small frame buildings next to the "Y" were replaced by the Roosevelt House and Techwood Homes.

Young William Leckie Mattox was the mascot of the baseball team in 1907-08. He became a Navy flier in World War I and later worked with the Navy ROTC at Tech. A tank destroyer battalion commander in World War II, Mattox was killed on Okinawa in 1945. At the time of the picture R.W. "Bob" Mattox, his father, was completing his senior year in Special Textiles at the age of 36. According to the 1908 *Blue Print*, Bob prepared for Tech at Cornell, and at Tech he was President of the Athletic Association and "Head Promoter of everything." Bob Mattox's grandson, Leckie Jr., attended Tech, as did his great-grandson, William Leckie III, who graduated in Civil Engineering in June 1982.

construction began.

The library was only one of several building projects that transformed the Tech campus during Matheson's presidency. The Lyman Hall Laboratory of Chemistry, which commemorates the man whose efforts gave it birth, opened in 1906. A handsome new Y.M.C.A. building was constructed in 1912 when another benefactor of the School, John D. Rockefeller, matched two-for-one each dollar raised by the School for constructing the $75,000 building. The "Y" housed student activities and provided dormitory space as well.

In 1910, Matheson received word of the largest bequest Tech had yet received: two-thirds of the estate of Julius L. Brown, a prominent Atlanta lawyer and business executive, oldest son of Georgia Civil War Governor Joseph E. Brown and

Coach Heisman's 1906 team posted a record of 23 wins and three losses. Heisman is seated with "Woo," his pet poodle.

On October 20, 1905, President
Theodore Roosevelt spoke at Tech on the
importance of technological education.
"America can be the first nation only by
the kind of training and effort which is
developed and is symbolized in
institutions of this kind," Roosevelt
declared. "Every triumph of engineering
skill credited to an American is credited
to America....It is incumbent upon you to
do well, not only for your individual
sakes, but for the sake of that collective
American citizenship which dominates the
American nation." Roosevelt's mother,
Martha Bulloch, was reared in
Roswell, Georgia, at Bulloch Hall.

brother of Georgia Governor Joseph M. Brown. His estate included property in Georgia and more than 4,000 acres in Texas, as well as books and furnishings. Brown, who made the bequest without the knowledge of Tech's administrators, stated in his will, "I believe that the Georgia School of Technology is worth more to the State of Georgia than all the rest of her colleges combined." Although the bequest was designated in part "to found and maintain a professorship in the department of electricity and chemistry to be known as the Julius L. Brown Professorship," the income at the time apparently was not sufficient to fulfill this stipulation. Since 1910, however, the gift has generated millions of dollars — $248,000 in 1981-82 alone. The Institute sold most of the Texas land in 1983 for $1.7 million.

There were other new buildings on the Tech campus: a power station that contained $100,000 worth of equipment donated by manufacturers; the Mechanical Engineering Building, later named for John Saylor Coon; the Military Building built in 1917; the Automobile Building in

On November 21, 1906, the cornerstone was laid for the new Andrew Carnegie Library. The library was built to accommodate a few hundred Tech students. By 1924 the number of volumes had increased from a few shelves full to approximately 16,000, but the number of students had reached 2,820, causing severe overcrowding.

The Georgia Tech served as newspaper, literary magazine and yearbook in the early days of the School. The issue for November 16, 1906, carried this list of 11 commandments for the sub-apprentice class issued by the class of 1909, the "shining, celestial stars of sober Sophomores."

THE GEORGIA TECH   3

BEWARE! YE SUBS!

SKIDOO, ye sulky, subordinate, suckling, slouchy, subby subs; ye sneaky, snobbish, squealing, stupid soppers of sorghum syrup; and swaggering, skunky scurts.

UGLY, umbrageous, unsophisticated urchins; ye unmuzzled usurpers of onions; uppity, uncivilized, unbearable, underclass upstarts!

BEGONE! brainless, bedecked buttermilks; blasted brats, and biped, boot-blacks, wearers of box-toed brogans! Beware of boogher bears' bad breath!

SALAAM to the shining, celestial stars of sober SOPHOMORES; smokers of strong segars; supreme society swells; sumptuous sages of superior sovereignity; and studious scholars of select science.

BEHOLD THE 11 COMMANDMENTS FOR THE CLASS OF '11.

1. We, the all-wise SOPHOMORES, do hereby adopt LOUD GREEN and NOISY PINK as colors for the insignificant Subs.

2. No Sub shall wear any class hat or cap unless it be of these colors and bear the inscription S-U-B!

3. All Subs must wear their colors to all intercollegiate contests.

4. To the loyal Subs who would gain the favor of the mighty and brilliant SOPHOMORES, we recommend the wearing of the green skiddoo hats with pink bands.

5. No smoking of pipes unless carved with the insignia S-U-B! Also, the owner must possess a written permit signed by the PRESIDENT of the SOPHOMORE CLASS or the GOVERNOR OF GEORGIA.

6. No cigarette smoking to be allowed under any circumstances unless the vile weed be tied with a GREEN and PINK ribbon.

7. All Subs must subscribe to the college paper immediately. Failure to do this will bring upon his head the wrath of the mighty SOPHOMORES.

8. All Subs must recognize the authority of the SOPHOMORE CLASS and all other upper classmen at all times.

9. Subs must never wear celluloid collars.

10. For a Sub to wear a mustache or let his whiskers grow to any undue length, shall be considered the heighth of rebellion and shall be punished accordingly.

11. Subs must always give up seats on street cars to the LADIES AND SOPHOMORES.

Signed, Sealed and Delivered in Secret Council of Tech '09.

Endorsed by Class '08.

October 23, 1906.

The above is a copy of the "order" given to the Subs, by the Sophs, on November 3d. It was our intention to write an editorial concerning this, but the whole thing has been so ably discussed in the editorial page of the Atlanta Georgian that we feel that we could not do better than reproduce a part of this editorial:—

"But seriously, or humorously as you will, this is a good live thing in the Sophs. of the Tech to do. It is a good, bold burst of college spirit that brings the Tech up in the ranks of the republic's great schools. The cane-rushes at Harvard and the tugs of war at Yale and Princeton —the class wars at Cornell and Michigan and Oberlin and Wisconsin are a part of the great big life of these great big schools.

Godspeed to the manly boys in their mimic battles which are fitting them for the big real battle of the world.

Only this: The limit of good humor and self control must never be overstepped. This is not real but mimic war. This is good humor on trial as well as strength. This is merely a battle of brotherly brawn and strength, and any man of any class who, forgetting the spirit of the college, would strike with temper or use a weapon, reflects upon his own manhood and foreshadows a dangerous and unpopular career upon the larger field of strife.

The class battles are, like football contests, meant to be fought to the last amiable limit of strength and skill, but finished in friendship, with the best men and the next best always shaking hands upon the field."

—Atlanta Georgian, Nov. 5, 1906.

"Have we played Sewanee yet."
"No, not yet."

1918; and Grant Field. Grant Field was made possible by gifts from Tech Trustee John W. Grant and named in memory of his deceased son Hugh Inman Grant. Assistance in completing Grant Field came from the Legislature, with its appropriation of funds for campus expansion; from Fulton County, with a contribution of convict labor to grade the field and put in the drainage system to convert the "rough and wet tract into an unexcelled athletic field"; and from Tech students, who contributed their labor to build the 5,600-seat concrete west stands.

Meanwhile, Matheson fulfilled his promise to freshman Ernest D. Ivey to establish a Department of Architecture if Ivey found 15 students to enroll in it. Ivey found 20 and, in 1908, one of Tech's most important programs was begun. One of its early graduates was Philip Trammell Shutze, who designed some of Atlanta's most famous landmarks, including the Inman residence (the Swan House) and the Academy of Medicine. Shutze taught at Tech for one year after his graduation.

The Joseph B. Whitehead Memorial Hospital, named in honor of a Coca-Cola executive whose widow donated $5,000 to its construction, opened in 1911. That event was described in the first issue of the Technique: "The halls and wards were decorated in the school colors, four young ladies presided over the punch bowls, and the Tech orchestra provided music." Today this building houses the offices of various student deans, the Student Counseling and Career Planning Center, and FASET (Familiarization and Adaptation to the Surrounding Environment at Tech.)

The 1907-08 track team appeared in the
first *Blue Print* with a page of Tech
records:

    100-yard dash 10 2/5 sec.
    1-mile run 5 min. 10 4/5 sec.
    Pole vault 10 ft. 2 in.
    16-lb. shot put 33 ft. 10 1/2 in.
    16-lb. hammer throw 89 ft. 9 in.

Members included L.E. Goodier Jr.
(captain), C.E. Jones, D.I. MacIntyre,
L.W. "Chip" Robert Jr., L.R. Munroe,
J.E. Davenport, C.W. Pittard, L.A.
Emerson (manager) and E.W. Smith
(assistant manager).

The series with Clemson began in 1898.
However, Tech's first victory over the
Tigers did not come until 1905, 17-10,
with L.W. "Chip" Robert Jr. starring and
winning his first football "T." At the end
of the 1984 season, the record between
the old rivals stood at 35 Tech victories,
12 defeats and two ties.

William A. Alexander stands in front of the Lyman Hall Laboratory of Chemistry. Students in the background are lined up to go into the dining hall. He entered Tech in 1908, played under Heisman and remained to coach. When young Alexander arrived on campus, William Van Houten recalled he was a "true country boy, right down to his yellow socks." In addition to coaching, Alexander taught mathematics in a makeshift classroom located in the basement storage area of the Academic Building.

The whistle is one of Tech's earliest symbols. Blown for classes and after football victories, it soon became a focal point for student ingenuity. When Georgia students tried to steal it, Tech students guarded it with their lives. Tech students also stole it occasionally, assuming no whistle, no class. But these popular pranks lost their appeal when the faculty imposed a 10-cent tax on each student every time the whistle was stolen.

Land was purchased in all directions. Several lots acquired in 1906 to the west and four acres to the east were just the beginning. Seven more acres were added by 1913, in addition to another lot given by the Peters Land Company. In 1917 Tech purchased Newton Hall at 36 E. North Avenue from Washington Seminary to use as a freshman dormitory. Mathematics Professor D.M. Smith served as dormitory counselor. One student commented in the October 2, 1917, *Technique* about Newton Hall's only disadvantage: "A fellow works up too big an appetite walking down to meals only to be disappointed upon arrival."

Tech's Evening School was also begun during the Matheson administration. It opened in the 1907-08 academic year with 135 students and offered vocational training and academic courses below the level of college work. Companies throughout the city paid tuition for their employees to take the Evening School's practical courses.

Later, regular courses in business were added to the curriculum and the unit became the School of

Three students test boilers at the Atlanta
Water Works and three others indicate an
engine at the Georgia Railway and
Electric Company. This kind of practical
experience became a significant part of
the educational process at Tech,
especially after the Co-op Plan began in
1912.

Commerce. During World War I, women were admitted to the School of Commerce and, in 1919, Mrs. Annie Teitlebaum Wise became Tech's first woman graduate. She also became the first woman to teach at Tech when she held a position in the Evening School.

Not until 1920 did the General Assembly formally ratify a provision making it legal for women to attend the School of Commerce: "Be it enacted by the Assembly of the State of Georgia...it shall be lawful to admit women to the School of Commerce of the Georgia School of Technology at the branch thereof *which is not located on the campus,* and will confer degrees upon them under the regulations to be adopted by the local Board of Trustees." [Italics added by editor.] By 1923, enrollment in the School of Commerce

Noon break meant lunch, running errands and changing into shop clothes.

The Department of Physics had grown to six staff members by 1921, with six different courses. The lecture room had "running water, gas, and electricity from dynamo and storage battery" as well as "a good stereopticon" and "a projecting lantern." The equipment in electricity, according to the *Announcements,* was "especially good, all new galvanometers, bridges and resistances being of high grade." In 1923 the Department moved to the D.M. Smith Building.

exceeded that of any other division of the Institute, with 343 full-time students and 452 Evening School students. (The Electrical Engineering Department was second in size with 234 students.)

The Cooperative Plan began during the Matheson era, in 1912, six years after the first such program was inaugurated at the University of Cincinnati. Tech's program started with 12 mechanical engineering and electrical engineering students who alternated on a weekly basis between school and jobs at the Central of Georgia Railroad. The co-op time periods were gradually lengthened until they reached three-month segments in 1929. Money for school seems to have been the primary motivation for students during the early years, but companies and students alike realized the value of the cooperative time as a learning experience.

Meanwhile, the fame of the School was spreading. International students were enrolling, too. The 1909 *Blue Print* lists Ramiro Antonio Fernandez from Cuba, Howard Yoemans Round from England and Philip Bernard Wolfe from Ireland.

Some students came as day students, many of them walking several miles or perhaps taking a streetcar to Peachtree Street and North Avenue. George W. Woodruff remembers riding an Indian motorcycle over bumpy cobblestone streets from his home at 708 Edgewood Avenue in Inman Park to the Tech campus. In those days dormitory rooms cost $5 a month and a bed in the "shacks" even less. The shacks — four-room buildings behind the Lyman Hall Laboratory of Chemistry —

The entire first floor of the rear wing of the Lyman Hall Laboratory of Chemistry was devoted to freshman chemistry and could accommodate about 500 students.

Civil Engineering was introduced in 1896 shortly after Lyman Hall became President. A great deal of attention was paid to sanitary engineering, and the facilities included laboratories for bacterial analysis and the study of purification methods. Here, four seniors make surveys for a water and sewage system for Kirkwood, Georgia.

After a sumptuous "marsupial," (*i.e.*, possum) banquet given by the Chamber of Commerce, President-elect William H. Taft spoke at Tech on January 16, 1909, emphasizing character and integrity: "I don't think I can inculcate a better lesson in dealing with you gentlemen who are to exercise great influence in all the public works of this country than to ask you to be honest with yourselves....You are engaged in testifying what the fact is from an expert standpoint, and therefore you have no right to be influenced by anything but the exact facts."

Anak is unique to Georgia Tech. Founded in 1908 by four seniors, Charles Sweet, George McCarty, C.H. Vaughn and Lewis Goodier, the society served as the Institute's student government until the Student Association was organized in the 1912-13 academic year.

Tech's Evening School opened for business in the 1907-08 academic year with 135 students and offered vocational training and courses below the college level. The unit later became the School of Commerce.

provided a stark atmosphere but were still home for the eight to twelve students who occupied them for at least one year. According to James Herty Lucas, if a Knowles Dormitory boy jumped on a shack boy, the entire shack would empty in his support. Shack residents stored vivid memories for a lifetime — gathering firewood on the campus to feed the pot-bellied stoves and studying in the quiet of the shacks by kerosene lamps. Lucas, incidentally, earned an ME degree in 1915, an MSCE in 1921, and taught from 1920 to 1961 in the School of Civil Engineering.

"Fixins" for a lunch could be bought at Comer's

William Van Houten worked at Tech from age 16 in 1888 until his death in 1944. Generation after generation passed through the required courses in foundry and grew to love "Mr. Billy." Three of his four sons and four of his grandsons, including William Van Houten III, graduated from the Institute. John Bourke Van Houten Jr. is the only student trainer in the Tech Football Hall of Fame. Two of Van Houten's daughters, Madge and Isabelle, still live in the house he built on the Tech campus (on 5th Street) in 1927. In addition to being a great favorite of Tech presidents, he was a friend of Atlanta mayors and other officials. He was always free on Monday to attend City Council meetings to plead Tech causes.

"Mr. Billy" Van Houten devised a memorable system for students who needed to work off demerits. They were required to move a large pile of pig iron from one spot to another 40 feet away. He assigned other students to laying sidewalks on campus. Contract work was done in the foundry, including all the castings and window weights for the old Loew's Grand Theater in Atlanta.

STUDENTS LAYING CEMENT WALK ON THE CAMPUS

Textile Department students were "able to carry out the entire process from the bale to the finished fabric." Students designed patterns to weave on the Jacquard loom.

Grocery just across Hemphill Avenue. Meals served "down-below" in the basement of Knowles were remembered as filling but plain: meat, potatoes, turnip greens, cornbread, pitchers of iced tea, coffee and sweet milk (no buttermilk for the country boys). Biscuits, baked only on Monday, were reportedly "hard as the desks" by the end of the week.

"Uncle Gus" Allen, who cooked meals for the dormitory students, also ran a small commissary adjacent to Grant Field. His commissary business thrived on the students' sometimes desperate attempts to supplement their diets. On one occasion, students actually stalked out of the mess hall *en masse.* When President Matheson heard about the mini-rebellion, he chided the errant students: "Gentlemen, this will not do. Uncle Gus is in tears." Subsequent protests seem to have been more subtle.

Ernest Daniel Ivey, second from left in
this 1910 photograph of Tech's Artist
Society, was instrumental in the
successful drive to establish the
Department of Architecture in 1907. The
club's motto was "Art for the model's
sake, Architecture for the money's sake."

The Architectural Society appeared in the
1911 *Blue Print*. Classmates of Philip T.
Shutze recognized his creative talents and
had him illustrate the yearbook with
drawings such as those bordering the
picture. Seated, left to right: P.H. Clarke,
F.H. Ogletree, J.T. Clarke, unidentified,
Shutze; second row: three unidentified,
H.D. Stubbs, unidentified, I.M. Auld, W.
Pope Barney, D.A. Finlayson, J.C.
Dennis; back row: three unidentified,
P.A. Burroughs, M.H. Levy. Other
members that year included J.E. Crane,
T.R. Benning, G.H. Bond, W. Levin,
W.A. Markley, H.S. McCrary, W.L.
Oliphant and A.B. Swain.

Gene Turner, Y.M.C.A. secretary (back row, center), coached the 1908 basketball team. The School had no practice facilities until 1912, when $500 was spent to renovate the foundry. When Turner left Tech to go to China as a missionary, Tech alumni raised $1,000 and continued to support him each year.

Intercollegiate athletics came of age at Tech during Matheson's tenure as President. John Heisman, who had come to Tech during Lyman Hall's administration, enjoyed his greatest success under Matheson. This complex czar of the gridiron — part actor, part scholar, part businessman — had an uncanny ability to inspire confidence and dogged will among his players.

During his 16 years at Tech, Heisman football teams never had a losing season. The record stands at 102 victories, 29 losses and 7 ties. His team's 222-0 win over Cumberland University in 1916 is in the *Guinness Book of World Records* and his 1917 team won the national championship, the first Southern team to accomplish this feat. In 1918, Tech's skein of 33 unbeaten games came to an end in Pittsburgh. During those 33 contests, Tech outscored its opponents 1,599 to 99.

What is not widely known is that Heisman coached baseball as well — for 14 years — with only two losing seasons. He won 161 games and lost 97. Heisman also tried coaching basketball, but with less success. In 1909-10 his team had a woeful 1-5 record; in 1913-14, two wins and six losses; and in 1914-15, six wins and two losses.

For as long as Tech students remember, the familiar four words have been sung, chanted and flashed in the card section at ballgames. However, when they appeared on one of the "shacks" in 1914, President Matheson announced the game would not be played as long as the words remained in view of the Georgia fans. "Mr. Billy" Van Houten supplied asphalt and brushes for a dozen students who covered up the offensive expression. The game then proceeded.
Later, when Matheson objected to a chant at a football game, the students came up with a new one:

    Tutti frutti
    Punch and Judy
    Tech will always
    Do her duty
Matheson said no more about Tech chants and yells.

Both the baseball diamond and the football field were located on the Tech Flats in 1911. The scoreboard erected for baseball suggests the ambivalent feelings toward the faculty.

Ernest Kennon Thomason stands beside Albert Lorch Loeb. The press called Loeb the "Yiddisher Vildcat." Heisman called the scrappy little center a "physical misfortune" because of his size. However, Heisman selected his "snapper" as the receiver for one of the first forward passes in Southern football, having him snap the ball from his position on the end of the line and then go out for the pass. Thomason, who wore a brace to protect his bruised back, played end on defense and fullback on offense on the 1911, 1912 and 1913 Heisman-coached teams. Both Loeb and Thomason attended Tech games during the 1984 season.

Team Leaving
No

The Athletic Association hired a "tallyho" to transport the team to
the streetcar line to go to Ponce de Leon Park for the Vanderbilt
game November 12, 1910.

When John Heisman left Tech in 1919 to return to the University of Pennsylvania, his alma mater, he was succeeded by William A. Alexander, who created new records of his own. Few could have forecast success at the time of Alexander's elevation, except perhaps the football team, which threatened to mutiny if he were not named Heisman's replacement. Many Tech alumni and fans wanted a big-name coach when Heisman departed, but strong support from players and students tipped the scales in Alexander's favor. He responded by coaching the team to a brilliant record his first season, suffering just one loss — a 3-10 squeaker to Pitt.

Coach Alexander scheduled intersectional contests with football powers that helped firmly establish Tech on the national football map. "They will beat us nine times out of ten, but in losing we will learn a lot of football," said Alexander, defending a strategy unpopular in some quarters. "We will gain a lot of prestige nationally." And that Tech did. Alexander's lifetime record is 134 won, 95 lost and 15 tied — including a sensational 1929 Rose Bowl win over California.

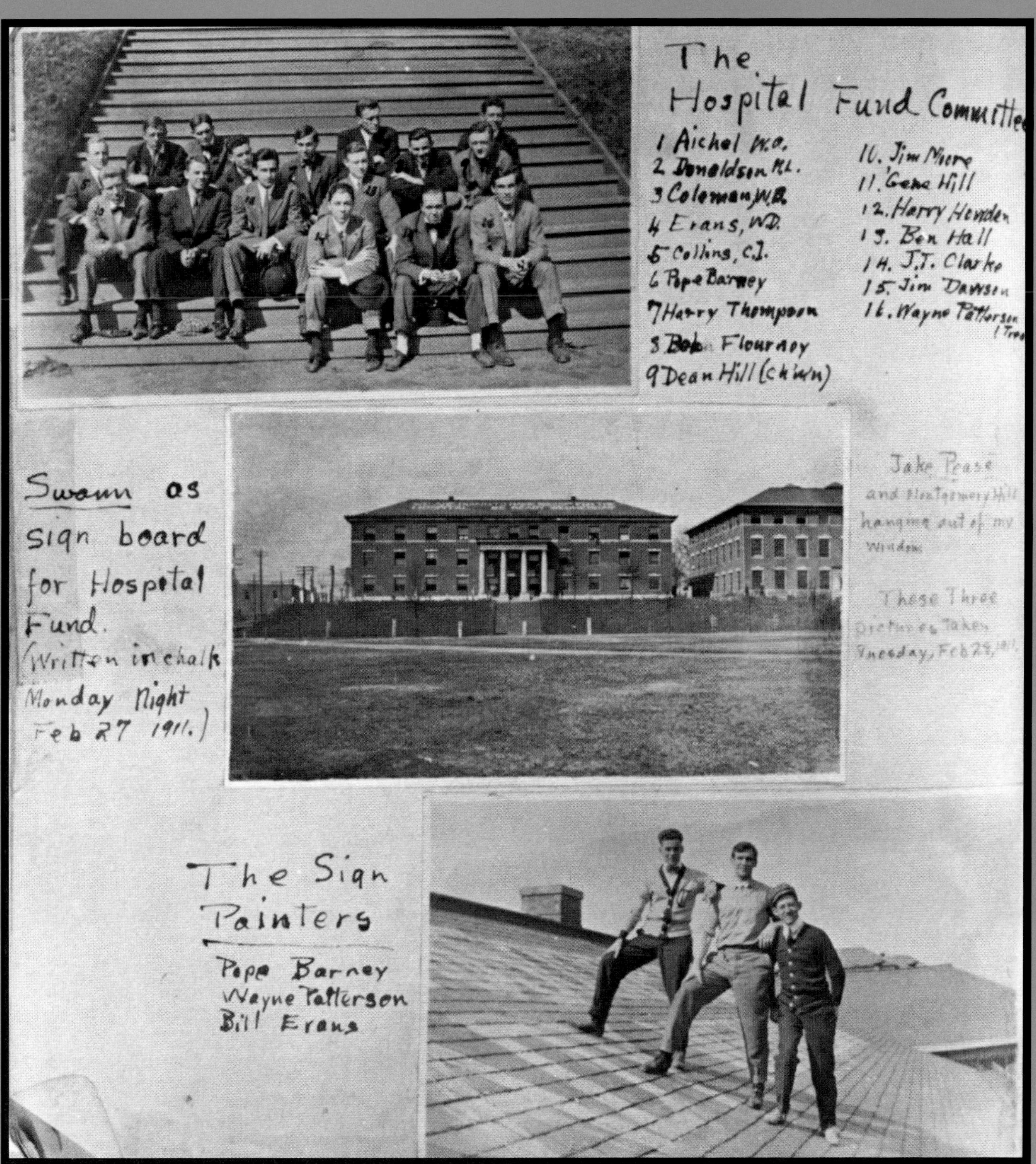

The sight of the half-completed hospital motivated a group of students to organize a committee to help finish the job. These pictures and captions tell the story of their efforts.

H. Wayne Patterson took photographs of
the campus, the people and various events
during his college years when he was
captain of the football team, captain of
the track team, dormitory inspector,
editor of *The Blue Print,* a member of the
Mandolin Club, exchange editor of *The
Yellow Jacket* and an SAE.

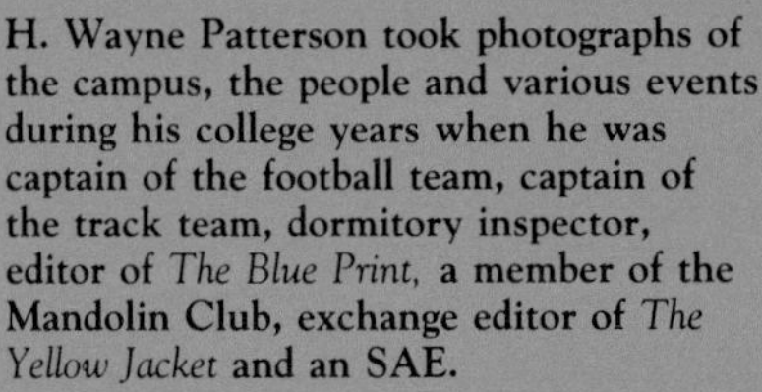

The chapel used as the drawing room.

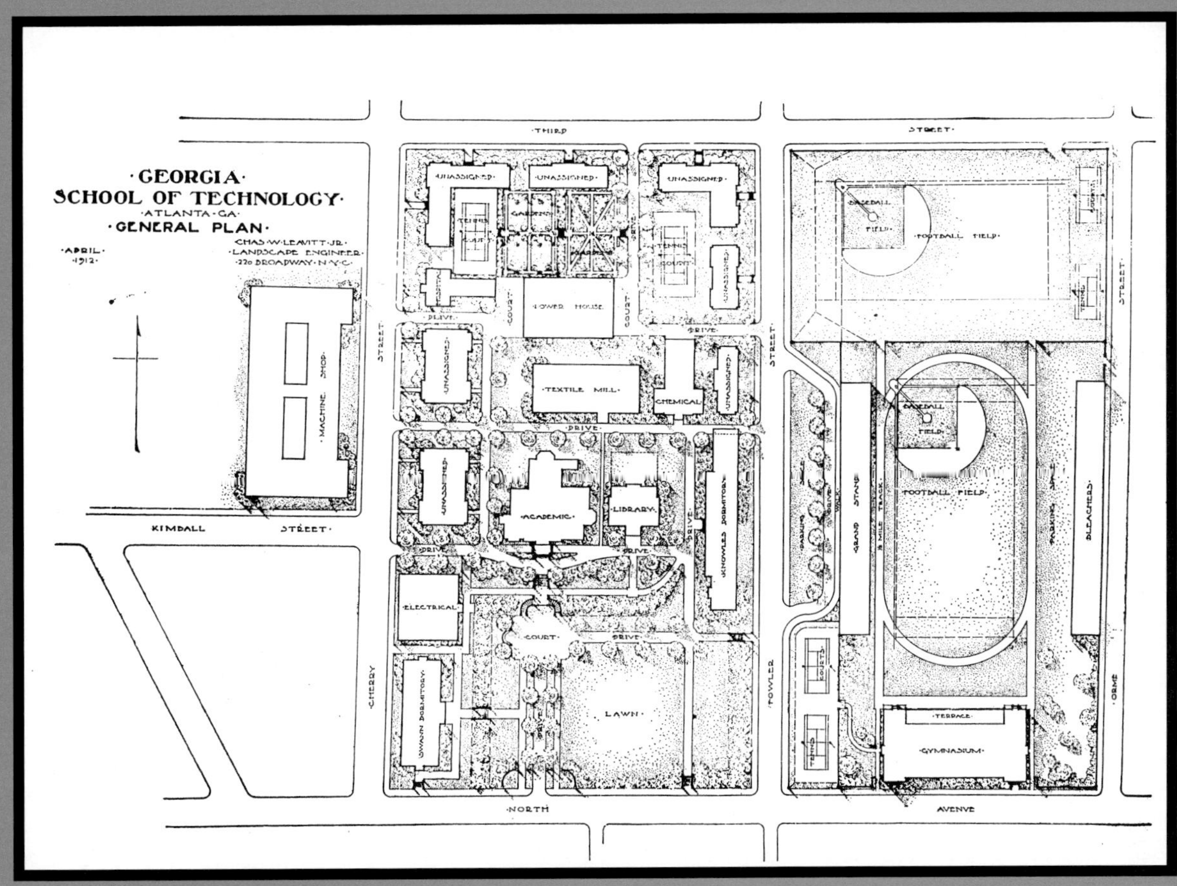

The Blue Print documents the steady increase in student organizations and activities during Matheson's tenure. Twenty-two fraternities vied for student members. There is a picture of the band, organized in 1908, plus one photo each for organizations formed by students from various towns in Georgia and other states — the Americus Boys, the Elberton Club, the Macon Club, the "Geechee" Club of Savannah, the Mississippians and the Florida Alligators. In 1918, pictures show the Sub Club — the "remains of the 1913 Sub Class," as well as the boys of the Rockefeller Apartments, Newton Hall and "That !*!*!*!*?*?* Dormitory."

Lowell S. Terrell, who made this violin at age 16, was urged by his friends to attend Tech because he was "technically minded." His father owned farmland, a gin, several mills and a country store located near today's Hartsfield International Airport. He followed his friends' advice and attended Tech, walking three miles to the car line in Hapeville, riding an hour to school and returning in the evening after dark. After graduating, he worked 44 years for the Western Union Telegraph Company. (The millstone in the floor is from one of his father's mills.)

In an uncharacteristic pose in 1912, Coach Heisman holds his prize catch of the day in a photo snapped by William E. Palen. The football team was in Florida to play the University of Florida in Jacksonville.

Student publications mirrored the interests of the times. *The Yellow Jacket,* started in 1908 as a serious publication in which articles written by students and faculty discussed scientific and engineering topics as well as school affairs, gradually became a monthly collection of jokes, lampoons and tall tales.

On Friday, November 17, 1911, the *Technique,* "The South's Livest [sic] College Weekly," began operation. It was started by Gene Turner, then Secretary of the Y.M.C.A. and later a missionary in China. The editors filled all four pages with articles about student life and the upcoming games, but the advertisements also suggest other

The grassy "Flats" served as a playing field from September 1905 — when Tech defeated Dahlonega (North Georgia College) 54-0 in the first football game played there — until 1913, when blasting began for building the concrete west stands.

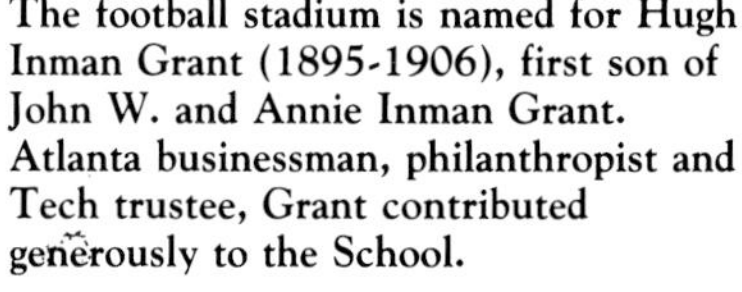
The football stadium is named for Hugh Inman Grant (1895-1906), first son of John W. and Annie Inman Grant. Atlanta businessman, philanthropist and Tech trustee, Grant contributed generously to the School.

86

William E. Palen climbed the wobbly iron rungs and straddled the top of the smokestack to take these photographs. Behind the wooden east stands is the quarry, where students stashed moonshine whiskey. To the right is the fashionable North Avenue district with the silhouette of the Georgian Terrace in the background.

Folklore about the 222-0 Tech rout of Cumberland University in 1916 includes this tale: "J.C. 'Canty' Alexander, a senior lineman from Decatur, had never had his hands on the football. It was his last game. Teammates ran the ball down to the one-yard line, lined up, slapped the ball in Canty's stomach, and carried him in for a touchdown. The crowd roared approval." That season a 7-7 tie with Washington and Lee prevented the team from having a perfect season.

entertainment and diversions. On Saturday evening after a game, the Atlanta Theater offered "The Speediest of all Comedies," *The Girl in the Taxi*; the following week Ty Cobb was to be featured in *The College Widow*, which undoubtedly attracted baseball fans on campus. Prices ranged from $.25 to $1.50.

The fourth issue carried the following advertisement for Tech: "A Technical Institute of the highest rank, whose graduates occupy prominent and lucrative positions in engineering and

In 1911 the Flats and Tech's neighbors
looked like this.

Students, faculty and friends gather for a production by the Ben Greet Players of Shakespeare's *As You Like It* in the spring of 1915. The stage stands in front of the Lyman Hall Laboratory of Chemistry. One of the "shacks" is visible on the right.

All is ready in the basement of Knowles for the arrival of students. After waiting in line outside, they marched in, stood behind their chairs while a selected student said the blessing and then were served by the dining room waiters.

commercial life. Located in the most progressive city in the South, with the abounding opportunities offered its graduates in the South's present remarkable development. Advanced courses in Mechanical, Electrical, Textile and Civil Engineering, Engineering Chemistry, Chemistry, and Architecture. Extensive and new equipment of Shop, Mill, Laboratories, etc. New Hospital and splendid new Y.M.C.A. and Shop buildings. Cost reasonable. Each county in Georgia entitled to 15 free scholarships. The demand for the school's graduates is greater than the supply."

In 1916 Noye H. Nesbit borrowed a cap and gown and diploma to have his picture made in anticipation of graduating the following year. However, after Congress declared war in April 1917, course work at Tech was accelerated with members of the senior class reporting for duty on May 13 at Fort McPherson. They returned for graduation in uniform.

For the Commencement speaker in 1917 the administration appropriately selected a military leader to speak to the graduates, more than half of whom had already been in the service for several weeks. General Leonard Wood, Tech football coach and player during the 1893 season and later Governor-General of Cuba, gave the soldier-graduates their diplomas. Others on the front row include Governor John M. Slaton, who commuted Leo Frank's death sentence, Nat E. Harris, President Kenneth G. Matheson, Chancellor David C. Barrow and Dr. M.L. Brittain, who was then State Superintendent of Schools.

Later editions of the *Technique* told of students contributing to help needy students in Italy; new societies on campus — the Society of Mechanical Engineers, the Society of Electrical Engineers and the Emerson Chemical Society; a plea for payment of subscription fees; jokes and cartoons; a Glee Club concert directed by Billy Arno, who reportedly was "as good at getting work out of boys as another Mr. Billy" (Billy Van Houten of the foundry); praise and appreciation to Agnes Scott College for its support at the Tech-Georgia game; and a report on the Southern Educational Conference in Houston in the fall of 1911, where "Tech came in for high praise, being named the best school of its kind in the South."

Tech was one of the institutions across the country chosen for the Student Army Training Corps (SATC) program. Tech's SATC program included 700 Army personnel, 175 Navy personnel and 100 Marines. Students were instructed in "auto mechanics, truck driving, machine shop, electric wiring, radio telegraph, blacksmithing, carpentry and surveying" in the four-year course which was compressed to 24 consecutive months.

Training detachments assigned to Tech in 1917-18 transformed the curriculum and the campus. Max Herzog remembers: "We assembled at regular intervals on the athletic field, formed into squads, companies and battalions and drilled....The campus took on quite a warlike look, especially after a detachment of machine gunners was assigned to Tech and began daily practice in a sort of sunken area next to the then-unused new power plant."

The U.S. Army Training Detachment was at Tech from June to December 1918, providing military and vocational instruction for 1,164 students.

Campus life was enriched by a growing number of organizations like the Cotillion Club, which sponsored formal dances twice a year at town clubs. Skull and Key, a sophomore group reputed to be "a little bad," could not match the reputation of the Bulldog Club, started in 1909, as the "bad boy club." However, the bad boys were not very bad by today's standards. "Fraternity meetings were very solemn," George W. Woodruff, a KA, recalls. "There was mighty little hell raisin' in those days...I don't remember ever getting drunk." One student remembers that for his initiation he was sent to a young lady's home

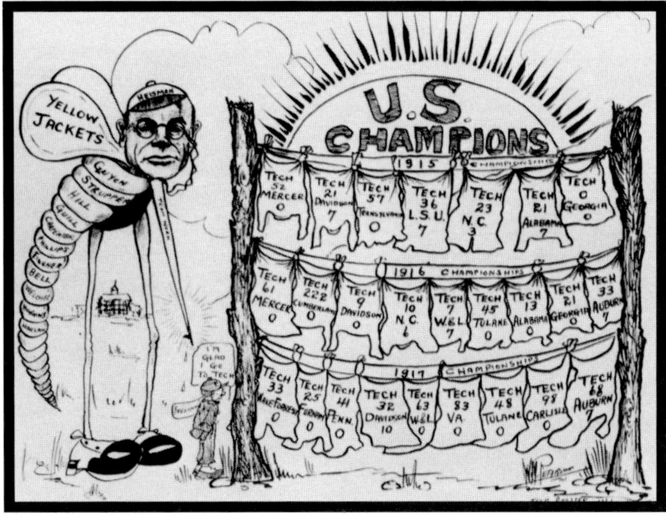

Drawn by Moore Pearson, "Tech Booster," this cartoon appeared in the *Technique* on December 4, 1917.

Acclaimed by *The New York Sun* as "the greatest eleven in the country," Coach John Heisman's 1917 Golden Tornado squad scored 491 points to the 17 points of its nine opponents. All-Americas on the team included Carpenter, Fincher, Guyon and Strupper. Bill Fincher often intimidated his opponents by rising after a vicious tackle, holding his artificial right eye in his hand. Front row, from left to right: John Vandergrift, J.H. "Ham" Dowling, Everett "Strup" Strupper, Albert B. Hill, Marshall Guill, Willard Simpson, Alton Colcord and John Rogers; second row: Robert Bell, Buzz Shaver, Clark Mathis, Walker "Big Six" Carpenter (captain), Charlie Johnson, Dan Whelchel and William Thweatt; third row: Bill Fincher, Joe Guyon, Babe Higgins, Coach John W. Heisman, G.M. "Pup" Phillips, Wally Smith, J.W. "Judy" Harlan and Ray Ulrich.

for Sunday dinner. He was forbidden to talk to anyone at the table and, at the end of the meal, did as he was instructed, tossing two nickels on the table and saying, "Most terrible dinner I've ever eaten." Groups included Koseme for juniors; Phi Kappa Phi; and Anak, a 12-man senior group organized in 1908. Koseme and Anak are unique to Tech.

World War I brought major changes to Tech. Military drill began by order of the faculty in April 1917, and students were in uniform in the fall. The War Department sent military officers to run the newly formed Department of Military Science. During the last year-and-a-half of the war, Tech had a variety of programs, including a ground

John Saylor Coon, Head of Mechanical Engineering, enjoyed football and often watched practice. At game time and during practice he would seek his favorite seat — the top of the stands.

The four-floor building for the Department of Mechanical Engineering, completed in 1912 and later named for John Saylor Coon, housed offices, a museum, a library, 700 lockers, classrooms, a drawing room and, on the top floor, office space and two large drawing rooms for the Department of Architecture. Later, wood shops and machine shops were added to the building's north side. The 1921 *Bulletin* notes: "All work done in the shops is from our own design from beginning to end."

Wilfred E. Gross, far right, and three wily classmates staged this picture to send to their parents. The clock on the table shows 2:00 a.m. and their harried expressions suggest "pulling another all-nighter."

In 1919 Mrs. Annie Teitlebaum Wise, a native of Budapest, Hungary, became the first woman to graduate from Tech. She received a Bachelor of Commercial Studies degree. The following year Wise was appointed for one year as an instructor in Commercial Studies in the Evening School — Tech's first woman instructor. She entered Tech in 1917, though the Georgia General Assembly did not legalize such enrollment until 1920. By 1932, 25 women had received degrees in Commerce from Tech.

A.R. "Buck" Flowers is one of seven Tech players in the National Football Hall of Fame.

The Chicago Tribune used the caption "Gridiron Ginger" for this famous 1921 picture of Captain J.W. "Judy" Harlan running interference for 1922 Captain David Irenus "Red" Barron in the Rutgers game. Tech won 48-0. In 1921 Barron set a season rushing record of 1,495 yards in nine games and Tech repeated its 1920 Southern Conference championship with an 8-1 season. Photographers snapped the two Tech "greats" before Tech's one loss of the season to Penn State on New York's Polo Grounds.

Twenty-five-year-old Arthur Murray
made history on March 27, 1920, with
the first dance to radio music. The
dancers gathered on the roof of the
Capital City Club outfitted with
earphones to hear music being played by
the band on the Tech campus. The
system worked, but there was some
controversy. Back-up musicians Leon
Levy, drums, and Abel Winburn, piano,
protested vigorously when Murray refused
to pay them because they did not play.

Arthur Murray discovered a successful
way to pay his bills while at Tech. He is
pictured here with an early class.

Only electrical engineering students could enroll in the Signal Corps unit of the ROTC. The government provided each student with $36 a year for uniforms and students attended a six-week summer camp at Camp Vail, New Jersey. By 1921 the government had provided Tech with $450,000 worth of equipment for ROTC instruction in all units.

school for air cadets, training programs for Air Corps supply officers and Navy personnel, and finally the ROTC. Courses with military applications appeared in the curriculum, an accelerated degree program was inaugurated and graduates began to take their diplomas in uniform. Pup tents of the Student Army Training Corps (SATC) dotted the green in front of the Academic Building during the war. Forty-three percent (556) of Tech's graduates served in the war and many gave their lives. President Matheson was himself mobilized and spent six months in France with the American Expeditionary Force doing welfare work for the Y.M.C.A. In 1918, when victory finally came, Tech units marched in Atlanta's colorful victory parade.

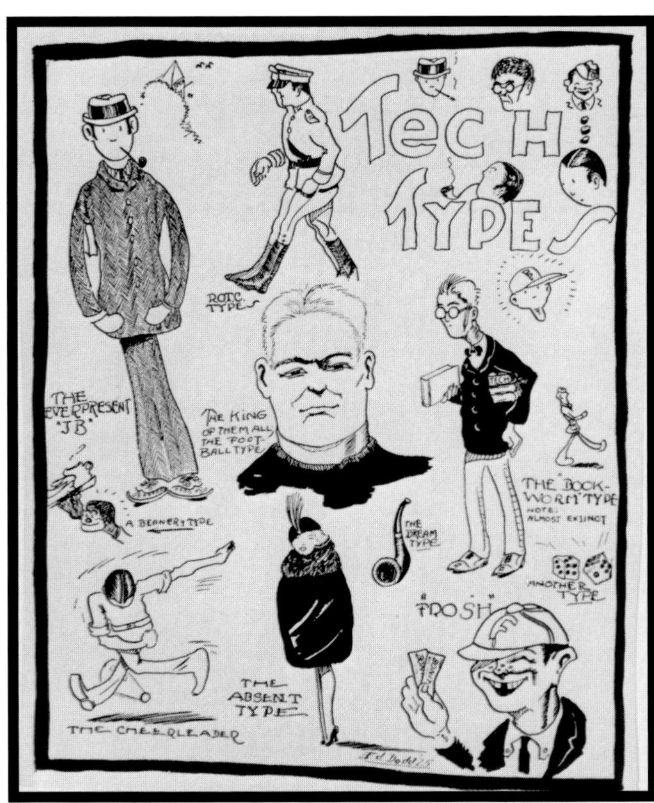

Edward Benton Dodd portrayed Tech types in 1922. Dodd later created the syndicated comic strip "Mark Trail."

Participating in local parades is an old Tech tradition. Pictured here are two notable entries from the early 1900's.

One of Tech's best-remembered faculty members came to the Institute during Matheson's administration — D.M. Smith, a mathematician and graduate of Vanderbilt and Chicago. Smith taught at Tech from 1913 until 1954. Andrew Alexander "Andy" Mahoff recalls never taking a book to class because Smith explained theories and problems better than the text. A lover of football, Smith helped Coach Alexander establish a tutoring program for athletes that has been envied by many coaches and still functions admirably today.

In 1910 William Henry Emerson, who had come to Tech in 1888 as Head of the Chemistry Department, became Dean of the School, a position that today is roughly equivalent to Vice President, Academic Affairs. For 36 years, Emerson served the Institute with distinction; his contributions to Tech are memorialized by the building named in his honor.

Shortly after World War I, Matheson became involved in a bitter intercampus dispute with President Andrew Soule of the State College of Agriculture (a powerful unit of the University of Georgia at Athens) over the appropriation of funds from the Smith-Howard Act. Under the Act, funds would have been available to develop engineering research programs at state-supported colleges and universities, but the bill never passed. Even though little engineering research was taking place at the University, Soule claimed that the prospective funds should go to Athens. However, a Tech campaign to gain access to those funds was successful and, in 1919, the General Assembly passed legislation establishing the Engineering Experiment Station at Georgia Tech. Unfortunately for Tech, what the General Assembly gave with one hand it took away with the other, for it did not appropriate any money for the project. Tech received no funds for this purpose until 1934, when the state appropriated $15,000.

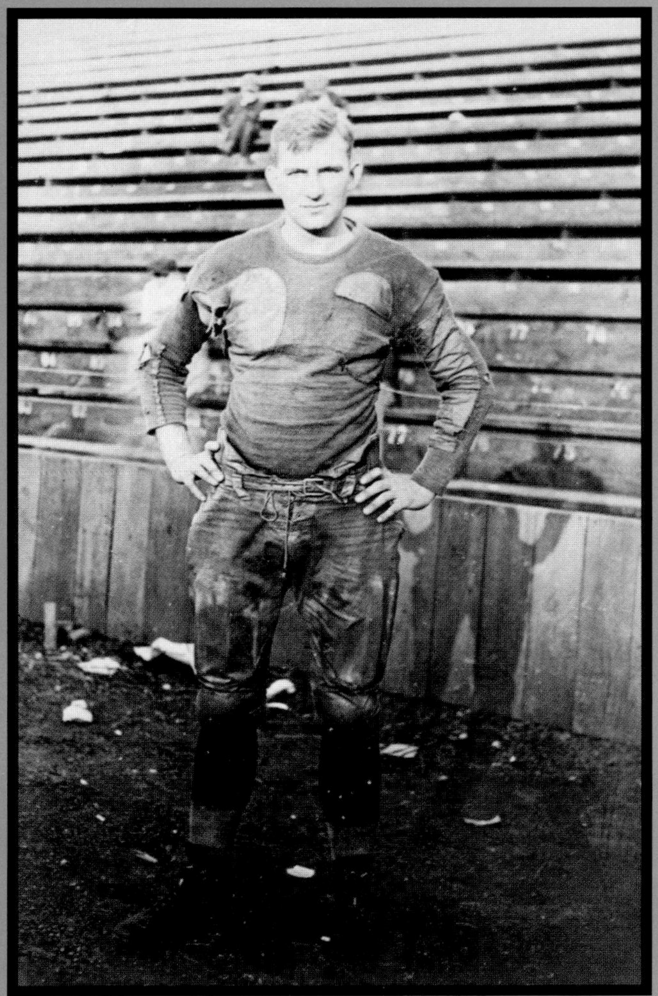 

Oscar G. Davis, Albert H. Staton and John Staton epitomized Tech as students and later as alumni. Oscar Davis and Al Staton starred under Heisman and Alexander, and John Staton under Alexander. As juniors and seniors, Davis and Al Staton tied for top academic honors in their class of more than 200. John Staton was one of 12 sophomores on the Honor Roll in 1922. That year *The Atlanta Georgian* spoke highly of the three: "The people of Atlanta are proud of them, not only as athletes but as gentlemen and scholars." In 1923 Al Staton became the first paid Secretary of the Alumni Association and started the *Alumnus* magazine. In 1966 Al and John Staton received Tech's highest honor, the Alumni Distinguished Service Award. In 1970 Oscar Davis was the recipient.

There also was bad blood between Athens and Atlanta over athletics. In fact things got so bad that, following the Tech-Georgia game of 1919, all athletic contests between the two campuses were suspended for five years.

Matheson's difficulties with the General Assembly were not over either. In 1919 Tech received almost the full amount it requested; but in 1920, as a result of conflict between the two houses of the Legislature, Tech received about half the money it sought. The situation was desperate. The Board of Trustees issued notes, the General Education Board made an emergency grant of $40,000, the Rotary Club of Atlanta loaned $29,500, and the Atlanta City Council made a generous $19,000 grant in addition to its yearly appropriation of $25,000. In 1921 the familiar story continued. Only half the requested appropriation was granted and once again Tech faced a large deficit.

All these frustrations took a physical toll on the 57-year-old Matheson, who quietly told friends he wanted to avoid the fate that had befallen Lyman Hall. As he remembered too well, Hall had literally exhausted himself raising funds for the School. It came as no surprise that in 1921 Matheson resigned to accept the presidency of Drexel Institute.

Margaret Mitchell in 1922 interviews Tech students for a magazine article. According to one of her contemporaries, "Peggy Mitchell interviewed all sorts of people about every subject in the human interest field."

Frank C. "Hop" Owens played on the 1919 championship tennis team. His student activities reveal his broad interests and the esteem of fellow students: track, cross country and swimming teams; Koseme; Chi Phi Fraternity; President of the Marionettes; and editor of the *Technique* and *The Blue Print.* In 1978 he was named to the Georgia Athletic Hall of Fame. His close association with the Institute continued until his death in 1984.

Following a practice of the times in which convicts worked on public projects, the city of Atlanta contributed convict labor to grade the land and put in a drainage system in the area that would become Grant Field. As many as 300 convicts, some in a chain gang, worked on the field at one time, singing while armed guards stood watch. The west bank was soon ready for building to begin. In an earlier time a creek had run through the bottom and, later, sewer lines had been laid there. Drainage from Spring Street to North Avenue made the land a veritable marsh, with artesian wells that sprang up all over the field after a heavy rain. When the field was finished, a seven-foot manhole was put in center field. Upperclassmen used it for their own purposes, hanging in it disobedient freshmen by their heels until they agreed to follow the rat (*i.e.*, freshman) rules. This photograph shows students about 1905 in the required coats and ties watching the progress on the west bank. In the background are the Academic Building with the TECH barely visible, the rear of Knowles Dormitory, the Lyman Hall Laboratory of Chemistry and the "shacks."

The west stands of Grant Field serve as a backdrop for 34 members of the first freshman football team and Coach George C. Griffin (in coat and tie). Fred Moore sits in the middle of the front row, the captain of the team that finished 6-1-1, losing their one game to the varsity from Erskine College.

When Matheson departed, the School had 2,579 students, more than twice the maximum number of students forecast when Tech first opened its doors. The annual budget had increased from $62,522 to $350,000; the level of instruction was more rigorous and unquestionably college-level; discipline was still strict; the curriculum had expanded; a graduate program was being planned; and, especially important for Matheson, Tech now had a library worthy of the name.

The students dedicated the 1922 *Blue Print* to their scholarly President. The *Technique* called Matheson an "unstammering Demosthenes, who can use the candied words, the honeyed sentence and the sugar-coated rhetoric when occasion demands, but who can with equal facility make a logical, forceful speech, convincing in the extreme; a man, whose tongue never tires of telling outsiders what a glorious institution Tech is; whose purse, heart, sympathies and influence are always at the command of one who wishes to better Tech; lastly, one but for whose labors Tech would be an insignificant work-shop, alike unknown to Georgians and Americans."

In 1921 the band, under the direction of Frank Roman, accompanied 100 Georgians on a week-long train tour through Georgia to raise $5 million for the Greater Georgia Tech Campaign.

Calendar of the 1922 Commencement

JUNE 8TH—JUNE 13TH

THURSDAY FROM EARLY MORN . . . . House party guests hove in

THURSDAY AFTERNOON . . . . Exams finished. A shave, shine, and a hair-cut
(Frantic celebration meanwhile)

THURSDAY EVENING . . . . Junior Prom at Brookhaven

FRIDAY, VERY A.M. . . . . A race to town, and—"sweet dreams, ladies!"

FRIDAY, SLIGHTLY P.M. . . . . Festivities at house parties

FRIDAY EVENING . . . . Senior Hop at Brookhaven

SATURDAY, EXTREMELY A.M. . . . . Repeat of Friday, very A.M.

SATURDAY AFTERNOON . . . . Bridge parties at the fraternity houses

SATURDAY EVENING . . . . . Senior Farewell Banquet. Sophomore American at Brookhaven

SUNDAY MORNING . . . . Baccalaureate sermon by Dr. C. J. Harrell

SUNDAY AFTERNOON AND EVENING . . . . Dates
(I didn't fall, she tripped me)

MONDAY MORNING . . . . Commencement Exercises on the Campus

MONDAY AFTERNOON . . . . Prepared to throw the Last One

MONDAY EVENING . . . . Pan-Hellenic Costume Dance at Brookhaven

MONDAY AT MIDNIGHT . . . . Midnight Luncheon at Brookhaven
(Signals off—then, "On with the dance")

TUESDAY MORNING AT SEVEN . . . . It just simply couldn't last forever

TUESDAY NOON . . . . "All's well that ends well."

The 1922 Commencement Calendar describes a full five days of
activities, from the arrival of houseparty guests on Thursday to the final
departures on Tuesday. Dances at the Brookhaven Country Club
sponsored by the three upper classes occupied the evenings, with bridge
parties and banquets filling other hours. A gala Pan-Hellenic costume
dance with a buffet supper at midnight and breakfast at dawn rounded off
the festivities and ended a Tech era.

Marion Luther Brittain began his 22-year tenure as President of Georgia Tech on August 1, 1922. Born the son of a Baptist minister in Wilkes County, Georgia, in 1865, Brittain earned a degree and a Phi Beta Kappa key at Emory College at Oxford, Georgia, and did graduate work at the University of Chicago. His academic background was in foreign languages and he headed the Department of Languages at Boys High in Atlanta in the 1890's. Brittain was not a military man, like Hall and Matheson. But he came to the job well seasoned in political battles, having served as Georgia's Superintendent of Education for 12 years.

Brittain was a popular choice. The 1923 *Blue Print* called him the "foremost educator of Georgia and the South, a man who has perpetuated himself in the memory of thousands who admire him as a gentleman of the highest type of the old South." His manners and many of his ideas were shaped by the traditions of the Old South, but his years at Emory studying under Isaac Hopkins gave him a clear view of the future. Hopkins' emphasis on practical shop work and his desire to use education as a tool to improve conditions in society profoundly impressed the young Brittain.

When Dr. Brittain, his wife Lettie McDonald and their daughter, Ida, moved into the old President's home on North Avenue, the twenties were roaring. Georgia women were voting, building was booming, F. Scott Fitzgerald's "new world" was emerging and campus drinking sprees and jazz music were the rage. Veterans returning from the trenches of Europe had brought back new ideas along with their wounds and medals. Two Atlanta radio stations took to the air waves in 1922 — *The Atlanta Journal* station, WSB, and *The Atlanta Constitution* station, subsequently named WGST. The $6 million Biltmore Hotel opened its doors and immediately became a proud new Atlanta landmark. Lindbergh made his first nonstop flight across the Atlantic in 1927 and, when he spoke at Grant Field shortly thereafter, 20,000 people came to see him and hear his appeal for intercity air travel. Two years later, Fuller E. Callaway Jr. flew with Eddie Rickenbacker from Atlanta to New York aboard one of Eastern's first passenger flights. By that time Atlanta's Candler

Marion Luther Brittain served as
President from 1922 to 1944. Born in
Wilkes County, Georgia, he studied at
Emory College in Oxford, Georgia, under
Isaac Hopkins, Tech's first President.

In 1928, Brittain spent
three months on a
Mediterranean tour with
colleagues, bringing home
several marble statuaries
and paintings as well as the
Marathon Stone.

Tom Pitts's Cigar Shop was a favorite spot for Tech students. Students would go next door to "Greasy" Witts and buy a weinie "all the way" for a nickel and, for a second nickel, buy chocolate milk with scoops of ice cream and whipped cream on top. Although too small to have tables and chairs, Pitts's shop was *the* meeting place in Atlanta. Fraternities frequently required pledges to dust the globes of the five-branched street lights at Five Points.

Field was scheduling 16 flights a day, behind only New York and Chicago in traffic frequency. This was the decade when sound was added to motion pictures and Atlanta was first linked to Paris by long-distance telephone lines.

Brittain immediately launched a successful program to get Tech accredited by the Southern Association of Colleges and Secondary Schools. His knowledge of legislative procedures and his friendship with government leaders no doubt contributed to his success in this and other undertakings. Although state funding remained small, private contributions increased, new buildings were constructed and the campus began to assume an English collegiate appearance, due mainly to the influence of two Professors of Architecture whom Brittain brought to Tech from Harvard — J.L. Skinner and Harold Bush-Brown. Throughout the decade, there was new construction underway: the Physics Building, which also housed the Department of Architecture; the Emerson addition to the Lyman Hall Laboratory of Chemistry; the Nathaniel F. Harris and the Julius L. Brown dormitories; Brittain Dining Hall; and the baseball stands.

Tech awarded its first advanced degree in 1924 and granted three professional degrees and three Master of Science degrees the following spring.

In 1922 Tech hired Al Staton as the first paid Secretary of the Alumni Association, an organization that had had a checkered existence since its beginnings in 1896 when H.L. Smith first got some alumni together for a meeting. A charter had been granted in 1908 due to the efforts of W.H. Glenn, J.W. Little, J.B. McCrary and W.P. Walthall; various clubs had assisted in the first Greater Georgia Tech Campaign in the summer of 1914; and a reorganization had occurred in 1919. In March 1923, the Association published the first issue of the *Georgia Tech Alumnus,* edited by Al Staton. That year, after Staton departed for Brazil to serve as a missionary, R.J. "Jack" Thiesen became its editor, remaining until 1951.

Early issues of the *Alumnus* tell of a thriving School of Commerce. Instruction included courses in "financial, accounting, managing and advertising problems of business, and journalism." Journalism assignments included working

In 1928 Edward Barton Hamm won the
Southern Conference championship in the
100-yard and 220-yard dashes, with times
of 9.8 and 21.2 seconds respectively, and
in the broad jump, with a distance of 25′
6 3/4″. As Georgia's first Olympic Gold
Medalist, he set an Olympic record of 25′
4 3/4″ in Amsterdam in 1928. Hamm
stayed on at Tech to coach. His
roommate was the new young backfield
coach from Tennessee, Bobby Dodd. In
1930, Hamm served as first President of
ODK. Each year, jumpers vie for the
coveted Hamm Best Performance Trophy
at the Georgia Olympics.

In April 1925, Frank Mayo, outfitted in an Army ROTC uniform, explained the formula of sodium aluminate to his inorganic chemistry class. "When I graduated from Tech, I was offered $18 a week," Mayo recalls, "but I didn't think that was enough money, so I decided to work for myself. If I'd been offered $20, I'd probably have taken the job." The formula on the blackboard proved prophetic. Mayo Chemical Company has manufactured large quantities of sodium aluminate.

During World War I, the War Department made Tech a U.S. Army School of Military Aeronautics — one of eight across the country. More than 1,200 men completed the program and hundreds more attended a school for Supply Officers for Aviation Squadrons, which was discontinued in 1918. In 1921, the War Department established an Air Service Unit of the ROTC. In 1922, Muggsy Smith took his camera to camp at Maxwell Field in Montgomery, Alabama, and covered the summer activities.

evenings as reporters for *The Atlanta Constitution.* Other *Alumnus* articles announced the formation of new alumni clubs in Washington and Chattanooga, described the successful season of the Glee Club and the Marionettes, and appealed for help in securing larger legislative appropriations.

In 1926 a recently hired Tech librarian, Frances Newman, created a sensation when she published *The Hard-Boiled Virgin,* a novel subsequently banned in Boston. Newman remained at Tech only two months after the novel appeared, eventually resigning to pursue her writing career.

By this time the in-state tuition had risen to $118 a year plus $209 for a year's room and board in the dormitories. There was a little "pork and bean place" on what would later be called Uncle Heinie Way, where students could buy a bowl of soup for a nickel. Room and board in the fraternities cost about $25 a month. Fuller E. Callaway Jr. recalls his father asking him to estimate his first semester expenses. According to his tally, they came to $260 — including shoe shines and haircuts. In 1929 one of the co-op students, J.H. Dugger, started with the Central of Georgia Railroad for $.32 per hour with a 2 1/2-cent an hour raise each six months for five years. Hamp Daughtry, a graduate in Textile Engineering, took the best offer he received — $14 for a 66-hour week.

Meanwhile, Brittain established the "Robbery," a restaurant and bookstore in the Academic Building, "to counteract enticing

Cake races were not unique to Tech, but Tech men welcomed the craze. One year Tech faculty and friends baked 160 cakes.

temptations of three or four shops on Cherry Street." Venable Patrick remembers one of those shops where World War I veterans and adventurous younger students could purchase booze, thereby maintaining the myth that engineers had to be robust in body as well as in mind. According to Ernest Kontz, the rock quarry behind the Chi Phi House on North Avenue was an excellent hiding place for bottles containing spiritous liquids. Daughtry "stashed his 'pop skull and coke syrup' in the bushes outside Jan Garber's Dance Hall — a favorite spot on North Avenue and Peachtree where you could dance all evening for seventy-five cents."

The effects of the war lingered for many years. Students took the mandatory ROTC class and wore "Hirschies" — khaki uniforms left from the war years — to save on clothing costs. But there was one minor drawback: students had to provide

Today, dormitories and Brittain Dining Hall stand on the bare fields shown in this photograph. The Arthur B. Edge Jr. Intercollegiate Athletic Center has replaced the gym on the corner of Techwood and Third. The area in the top left was purchased in 1929 with profits from the famous game in California and is now Rose Bowl Field.

"The Tech team," said Lyle Wilson, "is always identifiable. The players wear ties, coats, and hats, and behave themselves as 'young gentlemen.' " Waiting with the team on the Brookwood Station platform to go to New York for the 1925 Penn State game are, center, President Brittain and, left with cane, Dr. Crawford, a physician who frequently traveled with the team. On the far right, front row, is Mercer McCall "Mack" Tharpe, later a Tech football coach. Tech won 16-7.

Fuller E. Callaway Jr., center, accompanied his parents (right) on many of their trips. Equipped with a photographic memory and a penchant for hard work, the elder Callaway left school after the first grade and eventually became a textile magnate. His son Fuller carried on the family business and the tradition of making generous gifts to religious and civic causes. Callaway contributions to Tech include the Fuller E. Callaway Apartments for Married Students, the President's home, the Fuller E. Callaway III Student Athletic Complex, the Arthur B. Edge Jr. Intercollegiate Athletic Center and four Callaway professorships. He continues active involvement in Institute affairs, especially through his role as a Trustee of the Georgia Tech Foundation and the Georgia Tech Research Corporation.

Frances Newman's first reference to her new position, written on blue notepaper with the Tech Library heading and Miss Hammond's name as librarian, says: "Here I am — and charmed with my new job. The youths seem amiable and amenable, and so far they have done nothing worse than steal a Decameron and a page or two out of our best new architectural magazine, which I hope may satisfy them temporarily. Still, I doubt if I'm here for long." To her niece she wrote, "I am very much pleased with the library so far and I really think libraries are about the nicest places in the world."

In February of 1925 she traveled to New York to be honored with a special prize for her story. "Rachel and Her Children," but returned to the campus ill and discouraged about her job. She wrote to her sister, "Tech takes it out of me terribly — some people may be able to write at night after a day's work, but my mind and my body are both too feeble for that. I am sorry I took it, and June will be my limit, *deo volenue* ... I would like to retire in some mountain fastness in June and get the Virgin done,..." (She had already written about a third of her novel, subsequently named *The Hard Boiled Virgin,* and wanted the time and privacy to finish it.) In the summer she resided in a cottage on the McDowell estate in New Hampshire, where she finished the manuscript, and in the fall, when she came back to Atlanta, asked President Brittain for a leave of absence to see it through the press. She never again was officially the librarian at Tech.

When *The Hard Boiled Virgin* was published in 1925, she became an instant celebrity. A student in the class of 1927 remembers much discussion of the publication. Not that the students actually read it, but the stir over its publication raised certain questions of propriety. The rumor that President Brittain dismissed Newman because of the book is not true. However, Kate Faraday, the book's heroine, was a disguised Frances Newman, and Newman's use of details of setting and social life in Atlanta offended a great many people. One critic remarking on the uproar the book caused said, "The Southern Aristocracy — or that portion of it which knew Miss Newman and therefore read the book — was outraged." Miss Newman died in 1928.

their own shoes. By 1923 the Corps had 22 personnel stationed at Tech with 1,400 students, 400 of whom were in the advanced course for juniors and seniors. (Upperclassmen in the Corps received a $12 monthly salary.) The War Department rated Tech a "distinguished college" in 1921, 1922 and 1923. Students were assigned to one of six battalions based on their respective majors: Coast Artillery, Signal Corps, Ordnance, Infantry, Air Service and Motor Transport.

The Navy ROTC started in 1926 thanks to the efforts of many people, especially George C. Griffin. Harvard, Yale, Northwestern, the University of California and the University of Washington were the only other schools selected to have the program. For several consecutive years, the Tech Naval unit won the efficiency trophy as the outstanding unit in the country despite the disadvantage of being the only group without a large body of water nearby. Venable

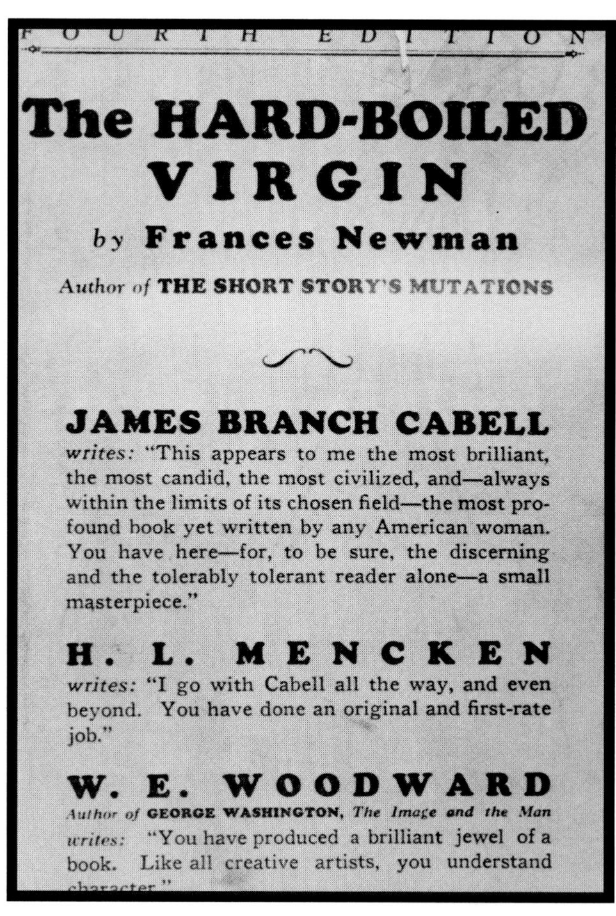

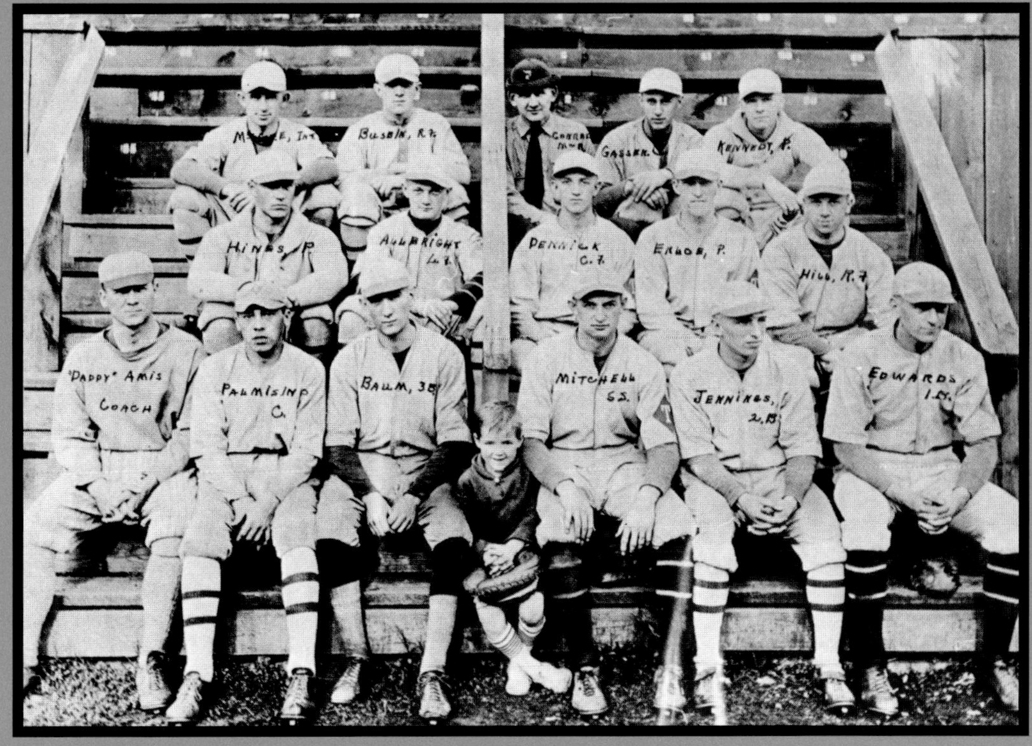

The early 1920's were the heydays of Tech baseball. The 1920 team under Coach Joe Bean won the Southern Intercollegiate Athletic Association championship, and three teams under Kid Clay were Southern Conference champions (1922, 1923, 1926). Even the scrubs were impressive. In 1921, the scrub team finished the season 10-3. Third baseman Johnny Baum was called "one of the most dependable hitters in college baseball."

The Ordnance and Signal Corps units of the Army ROTC spent summer camp at Fort Benning in 1927. The pontoon bridge across the Chattahoochee was built by the Signal Corps and the Corps of Engineers in 32 minutes 5 seconds.

Tech's old radio station may have been the nation's first amateur (school) station. According to Emory Rumble, it began operating at the end of World War I when the government lifted restrictions on amateur operations. Students placed the station's equipment in the power plant, almost in the roof trusses. In 1920 Arthur Murray utilized this equipment when he held his famous dance by radio on the roof of the Capital City Club.

In 1925 Tech's football team, coached by Alexander and still called the Golden Tornado, won impressive victories over Vanderbilt 7-0 and Penn State 16-7.

Patrick remembers the exploits of the "Piedmont Park Navy," including one story in which NROTC cadets transferred three Navy whale boats from the swimming area to an anchorage in the lake, wearing only their skivvies.

The first 200 cadets took courses in "seamanship, navigation, ordnance and gunnery, and naval engineering." By 1935 the Naval Armory occupied the corner of Techwood and Third. A full-size destroyer bridge provided hands-on training. From the USS *Georgia* came the ship's bell, the eagle masthead and the scrollwork. The last was melted to cast the doors to the Armory, designed by 1928 architecture graduate Julian Harris.

There was a great deal of interest in the new field of radio at Tech. Experimental work in wireless broadcasting under the aegis of the Signal Corps had been underway since World War I. Floyd C. Furlow, a Tech graduate, is credited with building the first wireless apparatus in the South. In 1920, two years before the nation's first commercial station in Pittsburgh began regular operations, Signal Corps equipment was used for an unusual radio event concocted by a Tech student, Arthur Murray. Murray arranged for the Tech band, led by Tech's Bandmaster Frank Roman, to play on campus. Two musicians went to the Club to provide live music as well. The band's music was transmitted to dancers wearing headsets who awaited the downbeat on the roof of the Capital City Club over a mile away. The experiment succeeded. The first tune was "Ramblin' Wreck" and the world's first radio dance went into the record books on March 27, 1920. [See page 95.]

Arthur Murray went on to become a world-famous dancing entrepreneur, but other dramatic and lucrative radio ventures lay in store for Georgia Tech. In 1923, Clark Howell, owner and editor of *The Atlanta Constitution*, donated radio equipment originally used by the newspaper to Tech. The station operated as WGM, then as WBBF, but in 1925 the call letters were changed to WGST (Georgia School of Technology). At first the Electrical Engineering Department ran the station, broadcasting about two hours a week, using campus talent and, predictably, making no

Shirttail parades marked Tech football victories for many years. Students in the early 1900's only pulled out their shirttails; but by the 1920's outlandish costumes attracted Atlantans to watch the fun of snarled traffic and disrupted movie houses as students descended on the heart of the city. This photograph was taken after the 15-13 victory over Penn State in 1924.

Before the Ramblin' Wreck parades began, initiates of the Civil Crew entertained the crowds and paraded around Grant Field during the half of the football game. The Civil Crew, founded in 1909, was the junior-senior honorary of Civil Engineering.

Charles A. Lindbergh flew his nonstop trans-Atlantic flight from New York to Paris in May 1927. "Plucky, lucky Lindy," the "Eagle of the U.S.A.," the country sang, and thousands of Atlantans gathered at Grant Field in November 1927 to hear him speak.

money. Then, in 1930, the Southern Broadcasting Company started managing the station and, with Tech remaining its owner, profits increased dramatically.

As possibilities and profits grew, so did efforts by individuals, corporations and state groups to buy the station. President Brittain's daughter, Mrs. Fred Patterson, recalls her father's constant struggles to retain it. As a protective measure, he listed it in the *Catalogue* as a "trust-fund endowment." Once, in response to an anonymous phone caller who told Brittain the Senate was preparing to vote on Governor E.D. Rivers' plan to take the station from Tech and give it to the state, Brittain immediately went to the Senate Chamber. He asked to be heard and stated that the laws did not permit the Governor nor the General Assembly to take away the School's endowment. After hearing Brittain speak, the Governor apologized for not understanding the circumstances and asked Supreme Court Judge W.H. Duckworth to assist Brittain in protecting the asset.

WGST affiliated with two different broadcasting companies during its 50 years at Tech: Columbia Broadcasting System and American Broadcasting Company. In 1974, the 51st anniversary of "the most valuable gift," the station was sold, increasing Tech's endowment by $5 million. During its years of operation, profits from the station also enabled Tech to acquire 90 acres of land.

When Clark Howell made his gift of the radio equipment, he wrote prophetically that a radio station at Tech would be "of great value in its use for instruction purposes for many young men who may later put their knowledge to practical business advantage, for we are but at the threshold of the development of the radio for commercial purposes."

Through the years many Tech students helped make Howell's prediction come true, but none more dramatically than Hazard Reeves. After graduating in 1928, Reeves set off for New York City because, in his words, "I saw all these lights around and I thought, 'Well, where there are a lot of lights, there must be some activity and opportunity.' " He got a job with a phonograph company doing research for $25 a week. Although he knew

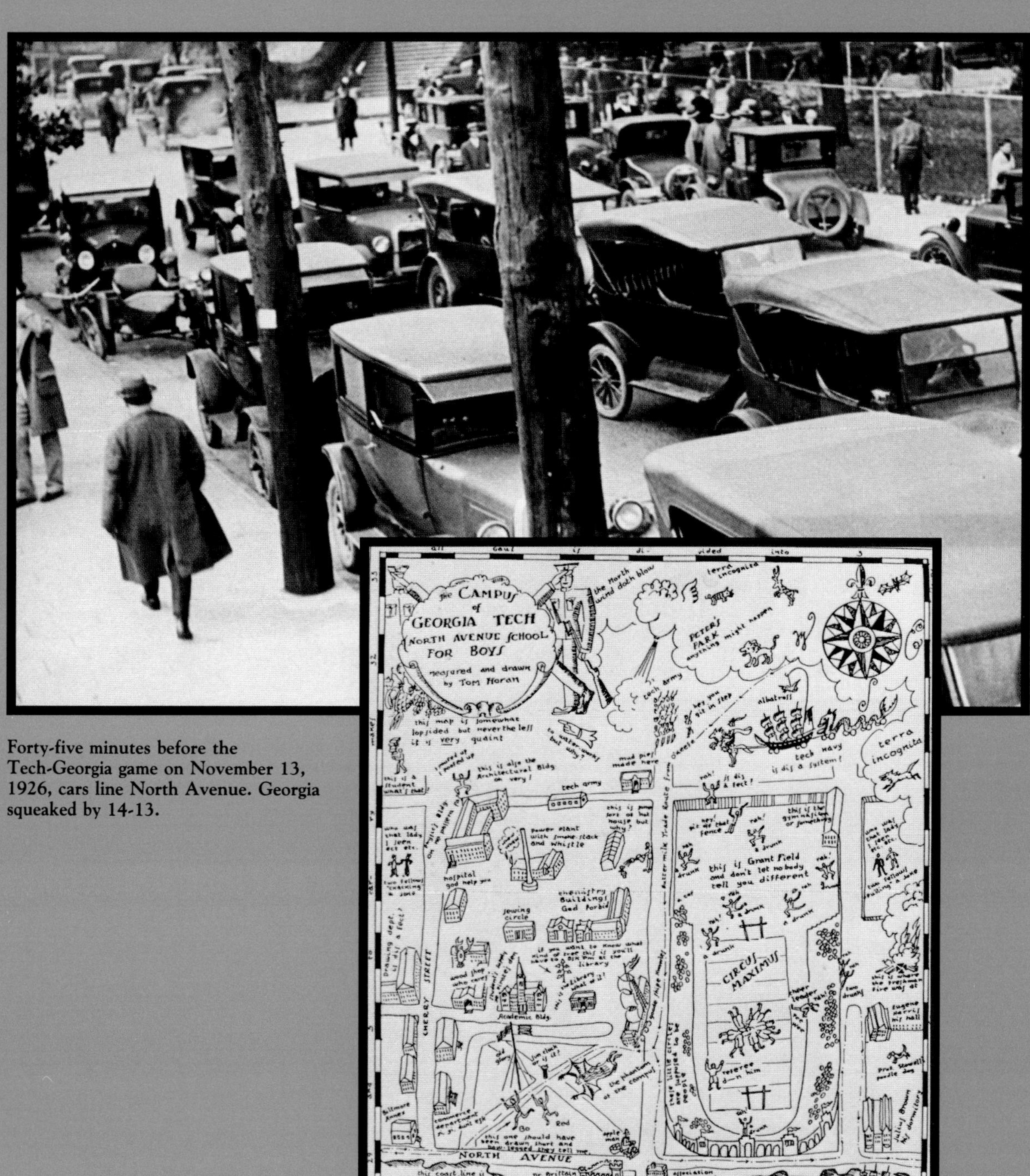

Forty-five minutes before the
Tech-Georgia game on November 13,
1926, cars line North Avenue. Georgia
squeaked by 14-13.

Student Tom Horan prepared this 1926 map of the campus. Clockwise
from upper right: (a) Tech's Navy in Piedmont Park. (b) Students outwit
the guards by presenting tickets to enter at one gate, leaving the field
with rain checks through another gate, selling their tickets and then
piling over the fence. (c) The *Technique* for February 19, 1926, carried a
front-page story of two unidentified architecture students, apparently
"Bo" and "Red," accosted at midnight on Cherry Street by the
"Phantom," a young barefoot woman with streaming hair who spoke wild
words and screamed like a wildcat. (d) Students living in the privately
owned house at North Avenue and Cherry nailed up a sign with the
name "Biltmore Annex." (e) "Uncle Heinie" had a lobster and a picture
of a mangled hand in his wood shop. His first lecture on safety began:
"Gentlemen, a lobster is better than you. He can grow another claw, but
you can't grow another hand." (f) The hothouse belonged to "Uncle
Heinie," hence the drawing of him with a watering can. (g) Horan
summed up student jokes about Ceramic Engineering with the words
"mud pies."

nothing about electrical recording, he learned fast and eventually became involved in quartz crystal manufacturing, radio stations, television stations, cable systems, stereo sound, radar control equipment and eventually Cinerama. The company he formed won three Oscars for Cinerama.

In 1930 Tech received word of what Brittain later called the School's "greatest honor" — the Guggenheim Award. Only six other institutions received the award — Massachusetts Institute of Technology, New York University, Michigan University, California Institute of Technology, the University of Washington and Stanford University — but it came only after intense lobbying by Brittain. Chancellor Kirkland of Vanderbilt

The Class of 1928 on a three-day Senior Trip at the Cliff House in Tallulah Falls.

Few people recall the pink-paper *Razzberry* humor newspaper of April 7 and April 17, 1927. Headlines alleging debauchery in the ranks of administrators and students led to its demise.

Brittain Hall, designed by Tech Professor Harold Bush-Brown, was built in the English collegiate style popular during the 1920's (and preferred by President Brittain). Above the entrance are 18 yellow jackets, wings spread in flight. Two shields at the crest of the arch depict the eagles of the Army and the Navy. In the floor under the tower is the colored ceramic tile seal of the School designed by the Ceramics Department. Along the colonnade on the corbels of the columns are heads of famous men of science designed and carved by architect Julian Harris: Aristotle, Archimedes, Darwin, da Vinci, della Robbia, Edison, Lavoisier, Michelangelo, Newton and Eli Whitney. Harris, who now is Professor Emeritus in the College of Architecture, also won the student competition for the design of the stained glass window, the first three panels of which were given as a memorial by his class.

wrote to offer his congratulations, saying: "I would have secured that award for Vanderbilt if you and D.M. Smith, your fine head of mathematics, had not filled that department at Georgia Tech with those excellent Ph.D. instructors from Harvard." With $300,000 of virtually unrestricted funds in hand, Brittain started building the Department of Aeronautics. Montgomery Knight came to Tech from Langley Field to head the program, which through the years has produced a remarkable number of leaders in the field.

One of its influential graduates, Andy Mahoff, almost failed to be admitted to the new and already prestigious aeronautical program. Hugh H. Caldwell, Tech's Registrar, turned down Mahoff's application in 1938, but the determined applicant journeyed to Atlanta from California and appeared in the Registrar's office at the beginning of summer term. Caldwell admitted Mahoff conditionally and Mahoff completed the term with a 4.0 GPA. Mahoff taught mechanical drawing that fall and later taught Caldwell's son. After graduating, Mahoff took a position at Douglas Aircraft, where his partiality for Tech men became legendary. A new Douglas employee from a Midwestern school once admitted he felt like a foreigner after Mahoff finished introducing him to a room filled with his co-workers — all Tech graduates.

ALMA MATER

HERE IS A COPY OF THE NEW ALMA MATER SONG AND WE ARE GOING TO SING IT DURING THE FIRST HALF. PRESERVE THIS COPY FOR USE AT THE OTHER GAMES OF THE YEAR. WHEN SINGING IT COVER YOUR HEART WITH YOUR HAT.

ALMA MATER

I

Oh Sons of Tech arise, behold!
For the banner as it reigns supreme,
For from on high the White and Gold,
Waves in its triumphant gleam!
The spirit of the cheering throng
Resounds with joy revealing
A brotherhood in praise and song,
In the memory of the days gone by.
Oh Scion of the Southland,
In our hearts you shall forever fly.

II

We cherish thoughts so dear for thee,
Oh Alma Mater in our prayer,
We plead for you in Victory,
And then in Victory we share!
But when the battle seems in vain
Our Spirit never falters,
We're ever one in joy or pain,
And our union is a lasting bond.
Oh may we be united,
'Til the Victory of Life is won.

At the Notre Dame game on October 28, 1922, cheerleaders distributed copies of the new alma mater, with music by Frank Roman and lyrics by Iver Granath.

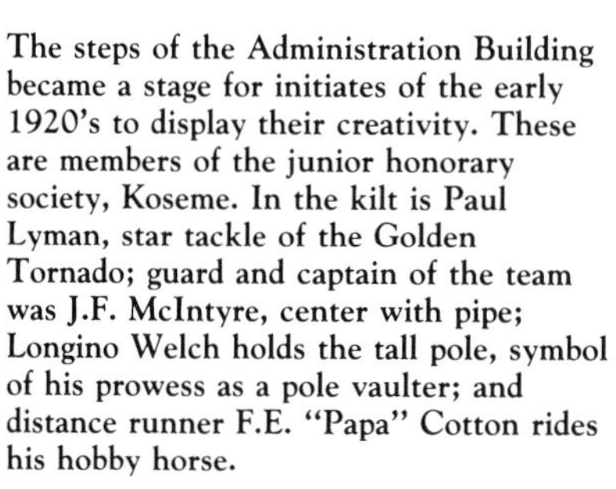

The steps of the Administration Building became a stage for initiates of the early 1920's to display their creativity. These are members of the junior honorary society, Koseme. In the kilt is Paul Lyman, star tackle of the Golden Tornado; guard and captain of the team was J.F. McIntyre, center with pipe; Longino Welch holds the tall pole, symbol of his prowess as a pole vaulter; and distance runner F.E. "Papa" Cotton rides his hobby horse.

President Brittain brought the rectangular marble Marathon Stone from the battlefield in Marathon, Greece. The inscribed words, "Marathon" in Greek and "Victory" in English, suggest Brittain's own ideals as well as those he sought to instill in the "young gentlemen" in his charge. The stone disappeared from Grant Field during construction of the west stands, but in 1983 Mrs. Fred Patterson (Ida Brittain) commissioned a duplicate to be made in Greece and installed on the new George C. Griffin Track adjacent to Rose Bowl Field.

131

The U.S. Amateur Trophy is held by
Thomas B. Paine. Bobby Jones, right, and
Watts Gunn were finalists in the 1925
championship match, with Jones the
winner.

Three Georgia Tech alumni have played
on U.S. teams that compete biennially against
British teams for the famed Walker Cup:
Bobby Jones, Watts Gunn and Charlie Yates.
Jones and Gunn played on the 1926 and
1928 teams. Jones retired from golf in 1930
after his stunning reception but posed for
this photograph taken in 1936, when Yates
was a Walker Cup team member. Yates
competed on the 1938 team, was team
captain in 1953, and was honorary captain in
1985. Yates also was 1934 National
Intercollegiate Golf Champion and 1938
British Amateur Champion.

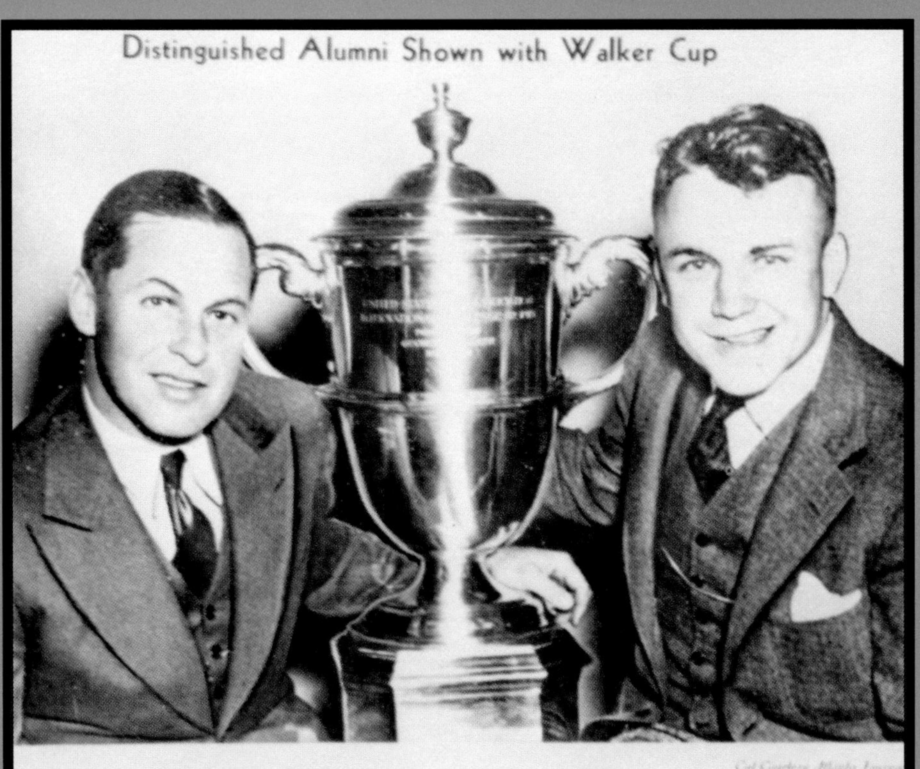

Bob Jones and Charlie Yates shown with the Walker Cup, British-American amateur golfing team emblem, which was recently displayed at the Atlanta Athletic Club. Another A. A. C. member who once played in the international matches is Watts Gunn, now residing in New York. All three are distinguished alumni of Georgia Tech.

The peak of Tech alumnus Robert Tyre "Bobby" Jones's career occurred in 1930 when he won the "Grand Slam" of golf. The Grand Slam comprised the United States Open, the United States Amateur, the British Open and the British Amateur. A ticker tape parade awaited him in New York, and Atlantans thronged the streets around the railway terminal to give him a tremendous hometown welcome.

"You can easily exist in Atlanta by eating only at Jones testimonial dinners," Will Rogers commented. "If all Jones banquet speakers were laid end to end, it would make a fairway with a 288 par. So find a spot on Stone Mountain for Bobby....And just think, ten years ago, all Atlanta had was Coca-Cola."

START
EARLY

40th ANNUAL
TOURNAMENT
OF ROSES

PASADENA
NEW YEAR'S DAY

FLORAL PARADE
10:30 A. M.

FOOTBALL
Georgia Tech vs. University of California
Rose Bowl Stadium—2:15 p.m.

TO OUR PATRONS
We urgently request that you plan to
TRAVEL EARLY

Ample Service will be provided on this date to handle the
large crowds, but to insure the prompt and efficient
handling of the traffic we need the co-operation of the
traveling public. Our advice is—

USE THE EARLY TRAINS
THROUGH SERVICE TO PASADENA

will be operated from some of the principal points on the
system. See Special Notices covering.

START EARLY

Pacific Electric Railway

Permit No. 4504   10M—12-18-28

In the 1928 season the Golden Tornado
made a clean sweep, ending the season
9-0 and receiving a bid to the Rose Bowl.
Dana H. Johnson reminisced, "Georgia
Tech's football team of 1928 inspired
such frantic enthusiasm on the part of us
as underclassmen that we felt like this
was the 'only' thing in life. When we
yelled during those games, it was much
like games where gladiators did their
thing with real swords and shields.
Thumbs down."

On December 21, 1928, four
motor-lorries and a pilot car lined up
outside the Biltmore Hotel, and some 80
Tech supporters piled aboard for the
10-day trip to Pasadena. Randy Whitfield
wheedled a bus ticket from *The Atlanta
Journal* by wiring daily accounts of the
odyssey to the paper.

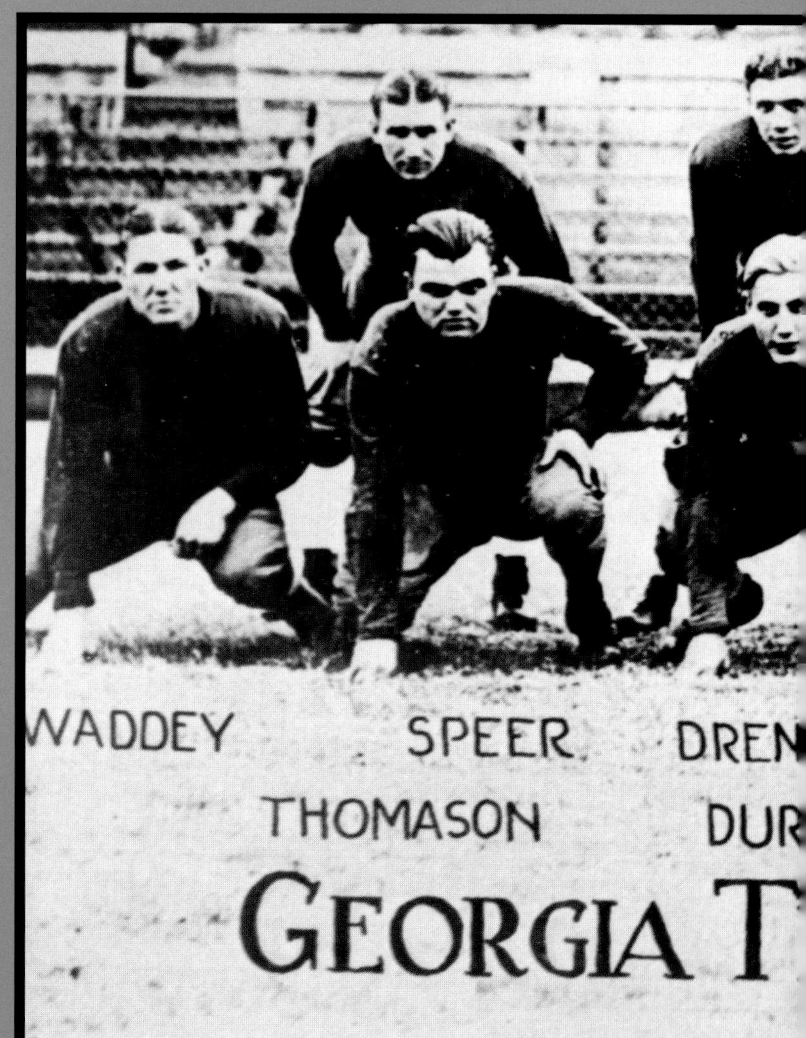

GEORGIA TECH DELEGATION
TECH-CALIFORNIA GAME PASADENA

PUND   WESTBROOK   MAREE   JONES
LUMPKIN   MIZELL   RANDOLPH
H'S GOLDEN TORNADO
1928

Athletics provided much excitement during the 1920's. There was also more diversity in that Coach Alexander emphasized various sports, not just football and baseball. Professor Crenshaw formed a lacrosse team and Jules Gray served as its manager — the official "washer of uniforms." According to rumors, the odds for getting a good grade in Crenshaw's course improved dramatically if a student tried out for the team. Members of the track team traveled regularly to the National Intercollegiate meets. In 1928 Edward Barton Hamm jumped 25′ 4 3/4″ to become Georgia's first Olympic Gold Medalist. On the golf links, Watts Gunn won Tech's first NCAA individual championship in 1927. And of course, there was the "Emperor of Golf " himself, Tech's renowned Robert Tyre "Bobby" Jones. He began his career at age nine, when he won the Junior Championship at the Atlanta Athletic Club. He became known as the "boy wonder" five years later when he competed in the United States Amateur. In 1930 he won the British Amateur, the U.S. Open, the British Open and the U.S. Amateur — the "Grand Slam" of golf. That same year he also was a member of the U.S. team that won the Walker Cup. A ticker tape parade in New York preceded his rousing welcome in Atlanta, where Mayor Isaac N. Ragsdale presented him with a gold key to the city.

Few Tech students experienced such glory, but in keeping with Tech tradition, most of them worked hard and played hard as attested by the many clubs and honor societies. Each discipline had its own group, including the national military fraternity, Scabbard and Blade. The Matheson Literary Society encouraged debating and public speaking, and Anak continued to be a powerful group on campus.

High jinks were also part of the Tech tradition. Venable Patrick's diary tells of a heated sophomore-freshman battle during Thanksgiving week of 1924, when the green and white freshman flag flew for four days from the central flagpole. The sophomores, unable to climb the cosmoline-covered pole and unable to shoot down the flag, finally called in the fire department to remove the hated symbol. In September 1925, students "borrowed" a wagon from the Consumer Ice Plant

Local Color

GEORGIAN
SDAY, JANUARY 2, 1929
ay, Tech Scores
S. TITLE; SCORE 8-7
PEACH FOOTBALL EXTRA

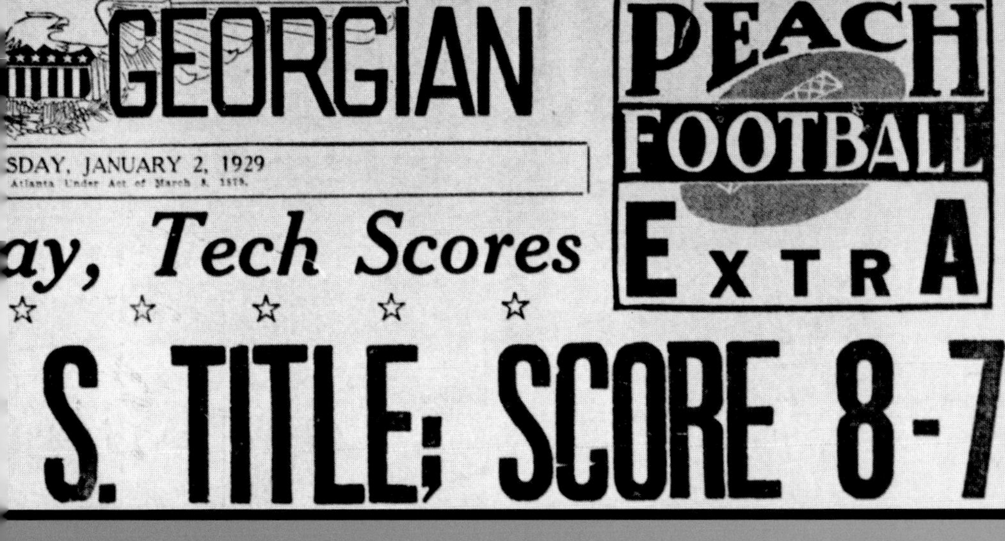

In the 1929 Rose Bowl, Tech defeated California 8-7. The game continues to attract attention because of the famous wrong-way run by Roy Riegels of California. Riegels contends that no one would ever have known his name had it not been for his fatal run after Tech's Jack "Stumpy" Thomason fumbled the ball. A mad pursuit followed, with Riegels' teammate Bennie Lom and Tech player Frank Waddey tackling him on the California one-yard line. According to Randy Whitfield, the stadium was "quiet as a tomb" during the run. When the radio announcer realized what had happened, he spoke just one sentence: "My God, he's run the wrong way!" Many listeners later expressed sharp disapproval of his choice of words. On the first play after the run, California's punt was blocked by Tech's Vance Maree for a safety. From left to right in this photo of Riegels' famous run are Raleigh Drennon of Tech; Lom; Waddey; and Bob Durant, Tech quarterback (behind Riegels' left hand). At the far right with his left hand bandaged is Joe Westbrook of Tech.

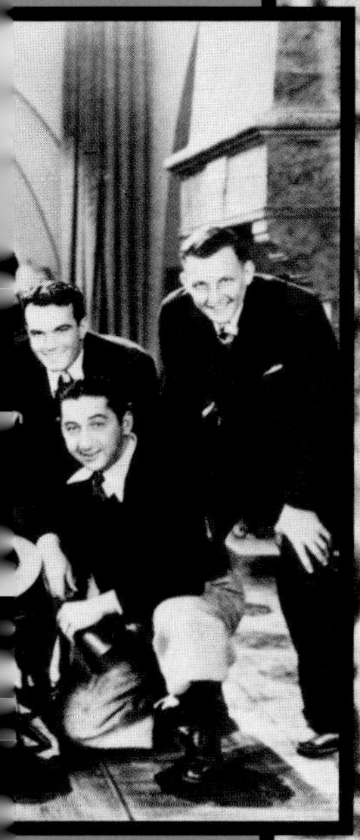

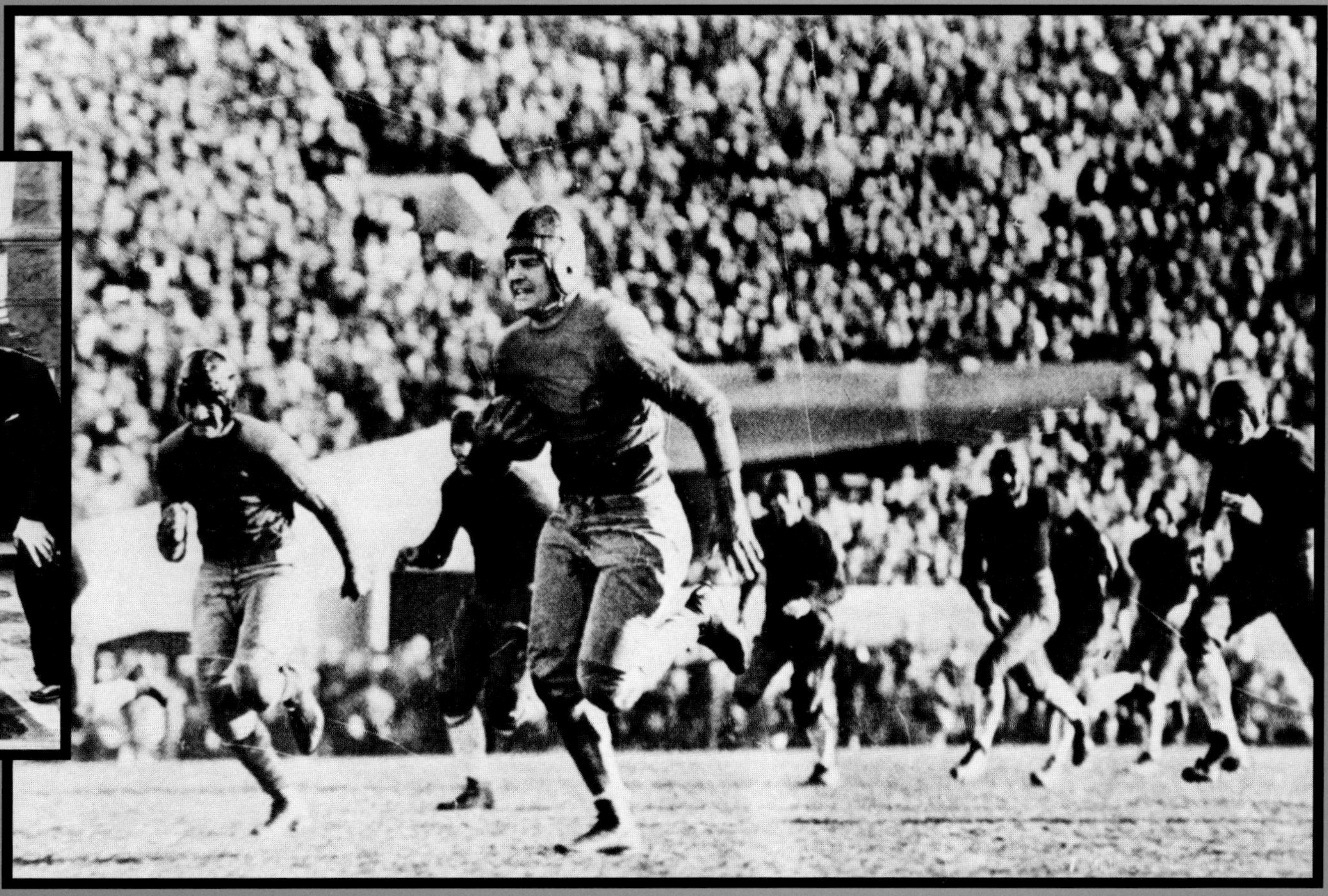

and put it on top of Knowles Dormitory for the east stands football spectators to enjoy. Not until after Thanksgiving Day did the administration succeed in removing it.

One stifling May night in 1926, the Knowles freshmen boarded up the shower room to a depth of four feet, plugged the drains, then relaxed all evening in their homemade swimming pool. According to Joe Westbrook, the culprits remained at large despite "Uncle Gus" Allen's fury over his ruined provisions in the adjacent storeroom.

This same decade produced the most famous legend of them all — George P. Burdell. According to the most faithful accounts, Ed Smith received two application forms by mistake when he entered in 1927. He filled in his own name and personal data on the first form and, on the second, gave the first name and initial of a relative, then the name of his cat for a surname. The hoax quickly spread through the ranks of freshmen who made George P. a respectable class member by writing papers and taking examinations in his name. Smith reminisces:

"As a naval officer in World War II and later at graduate school, I ran into George P. many times. In New York, Chicago, Philadelphia, Memphis, Birmingham, Los Angeles and all over the world, I heard of his showing up.

"I saw him honored with a B.S. degree in 1930 and I am pleased that he now has his masters.

"I am glad to learn that George P. is still very much alive. It is gratifying to know that George P. Burdell, along with the Ramblin' Wreck, became the spirit of Georgia Tech, for, as the ancient Horace is supposed to have said to Caesar Augustus: 'It is pleasant and proper to be foolish once in a while.' "

Omicron Delta Kappa was formed in 1930, the year *The Blue Print* won its first "superior" award in national competition and the Yellow Jacket Club was formed to combat allegedly low morale on campus. The economic boom of the 1920's continued into the early 1930's but there were signs of weakness. The state still depended heavily on agriculture and, in 1933, the average Georgia farm cash wage was very low. Tech's record-breaking enrollment of 3,717 in 1929-30 dropped to 2,126

George P. Burdell entered the world in 1927, the full-grown creation of freshman Ed Smith from Augusta. Inadvertently given two registration blanks, Smith had a brainstorm: Why not register his relative who was the headmaster of his prep school? "George P." was as far as he dared go; "Burdell," the name of his cat, served as surname. The hoax was on. Classmates of Smith joined the fun, writing papers and taking quizzes for the elusive George P. Professor Robert E. Sheppard excused both George and Ed from his class, explaining, "Those two students know more history than I do." Degrees and honors followed — a B.S. in 1930, an M.S., claims of a Regents' Professorship and the Deanship of Humanities and Fine Arts.

Everywhere Tech students go, George is one of the crowd. "As a Naval officer in World War II and later at graduate school I ran into George P. many times," Smith writes. "In New York, Chicago, Philadelphia, Memphis, Birmingham, Los Angeles, and all over the world, I heard of his showing up." He flew missions with the 8th Air Force; he enrolled one quarter for 3,000 hours at Tech.

William D. Monroe Sr. wrote Dean Dull about a tale that Professor Glenn Rainey shared with his class. Rainey accompanied the Tech chorus to the Atlanta Federal Penitentiary for a performance. All the students signed a roster when they entered and checked out as they departed. At the conclusion of the routine check, Rainey noticed some agitation among the guards. When he finally learned the cause — George P. Burdell was missing — he had to use his best argumentative skills. "The authorities were not amused," said Rainey.

The National Social Directory for 1977 lists Burdell in Augusta, Georgia, with a second residence in West Palm Beach. The listing noted his membership in the Society of the Cincinnati, the Piedmont Driving Club, Sigma Chi, the American Legion, Augusta Georgia Tech Alumni Society and Nine O'Clocks. "He is a past member of the Board of Regents and has a son, George P. — Georgia Tech '77."

Society editors unfamiliar with his name publish accounts of the parties he hosts for recent debutantes; and in 1971 his engagement to an Agnes Scott College astronomy major slipped by even the shrewd eye of long-time society editor Yolande Gwin. *The Journal for Computer-Based Instruction* lists several references to his publications, including *Patterns in Neolithic Basketweaving* and *Design of C.B.E. Lessons,* the latter published in Atlanta at the North Avenue Trade School.

He is the bane of insurance salesmen and magazine subscription offices. Burdell's mail and complaints about this delinquent student arrive ultimately at Dean Jim Dull's office. Dull patiently explains that registration forms, insurance policies and magazine subscriptions must simply be cancelled if they bear that name. George P. has recently entered a new field. Fascinated by various telephone services, he has placed orders with them all for installation. In 1975, 48 years after his entrance on the Tech campus, the Co-op Club held its first annual birthday celebration for the most famous Tech man of them all.

Ed Smith, writing about the omnipresence of his creation since that fateful September day in 1927, notes: "I am glad to learn that George P. is still very much alive. It is gratifying to know that George P. Burdell, along with the Ramblin' Wreck, became the spirit of Georgia Tech, for, as the ancient Horace is supposed to have said to Caesar Augustus: 'It is pleasant and proper to be foolish once in a while.' "

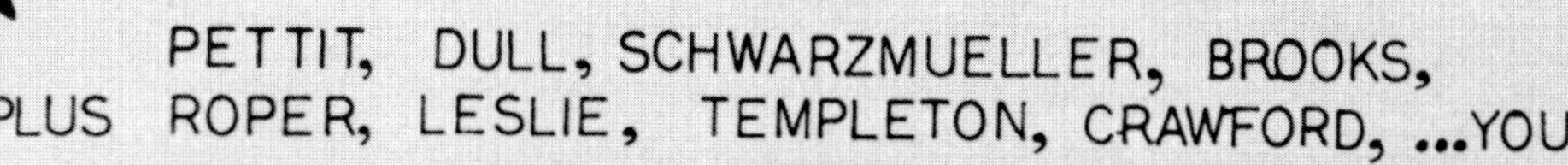

"The Piedmont Park Navy" consisted of whale boats given by the Sixth Naval District for training Navy ROTC cadets.

in 1933. Many Tech men faced a "no-job" market when they graduated, and those fortunate enough to find jobs often had to take pay cuts.

One architecture student, Julian Jett, recalls not getting any offer from architectural firms when he graduated, so he took a position with a contractor for $125 a month in 1928. His pay increased to $150 in 1929-30, then dropped to $120 in 1931, $85 in 1932 and finally, no job. Jett eventually found employment as an architect with a government agency and later with several private firms, but he remembers the 1930's as difficult years.

Nevertheless, Tech men did better than most. When the 1928 class published its update 50 years later, the author recalled those troubled years: "Tech failed to inform us that we were economically disadvantaged during that worst depression; so, not knowing any better, we went out and proved that we weren't."

Two important Tech institutions were formed in 1932, the Tech Placement System and the Georgia Tech Alumni Foundation. The former was begun to help Tech alumni survive those troubled years; the latter, the School itself. Under the leadership of George C. Griffin, the Placement System's founder, a student-compiled publication called the *Senior Personnel History* was sent to potential employers across the country. It was one of several successful projects designed to bring scarce jobs and alumni together.

The Georgia Tech Alumni Foundation began with total annual donations of just $462.37, and by the end of the decade its assets were still less than $3,000. But it was a beginning, and in later years the Foundation would become a major source of enrichment for the School.

In 1932 two visitors who would help direct the course of the world in the forties came to Atlanta — Winston Churchill and Franklin Delano Roosevelt. Churchill, accompanied by his daughter Diana, spoke to a gathering at Grant Field as a result of efforts by Professor R.P. "Rip" Black of Civil Engineering. The Prohibition Era was in full swing and, in acknowledging its norms, the heavy drinking Churchill apologized for the bottle of wine on the lunch table, saying that he was simply obeying "his physician's orders." After

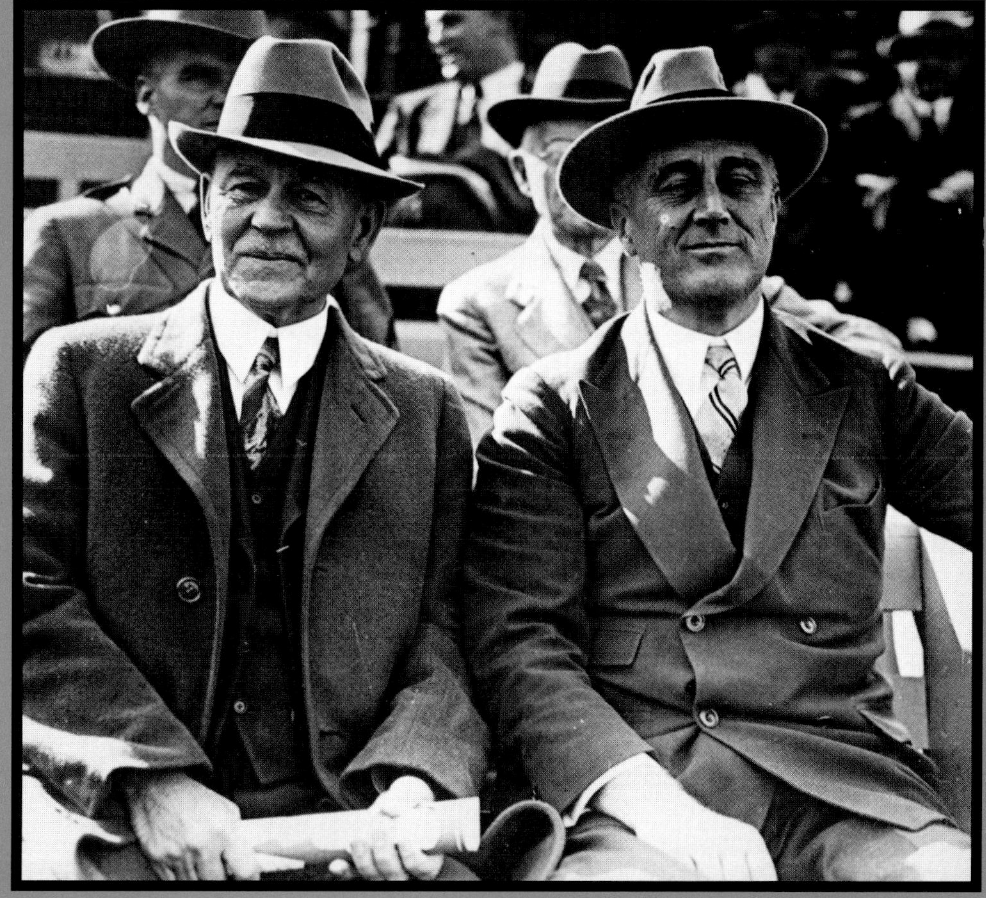

President Franklin D. Roosevelt attended several football games with President Brittain. On November 29, 1935, he signed a "message of greeting" to the students and then spoke to more than 50,000 who filled the stands and playing field of Grant Field for the formal dedication of the Techwood Homes Project, the first low-income housing project in the nation.

In 1932 Winston Churchill visited Atlanta with his daughter Diana (shown here with President Brittain). Speaking from a flower-covered platform on Grant Field, he urged the continued brotherhood of England and the United States: "It is my earnest desire that the two greatest English-speaking nations will always remain united by their common language together with those ties of blood and history that have always made us brothers across the sea."

watching the ROTC drill, he stated: "It is my earnest desire that the two great English-speaking nations will always remain united by their common language together with those ties of blood and history that have always made us brothers across the sea."

The second visitor was Franklin Delano Roosevelt, greeted by an estimated 200,000 people — the largest crowd in Atlanta's history. Only two months after his inauguration, Roosevelt appointed Tech alumnus L.W. "Chip" Robert Jr., Assistant Secretary of the Treasury. Robert's duties included administration of public works.

Roosevelt declared a "bank holiday," brought an end to Prohibition and inaugurated the New Deal. Tech profited from Roosevelt's promises: CWA, PWA and WPA projects dotted the campus with new construction, the first of which was the Naval Armory in 1932. Thirteen other projects followed.

The Techwood Homes Project, which included Techwood Dormitory, was the federal government's first slum-clearance and low-rent housing project. Harold Ickes, Secretary of the Interior, attended the 1933 dynamiting of slum houses in a 10-block area south of Tech. Flippen Burge and P.D. Stevens were the architects for what the President, on hand for its dedication, called a "tribute to useful work under government supervision."

In 1931 the state, partly because of Brittain's recommendation, formed the Board of Regents, a central governing body for the University System, and Tech's Board of Trustees was disbanded. To Brittain's dismay, one of the first acts of the new Regents was to transfer to Tech the civil and electrical engineering work at the University of Georgia and transfer to Georgia the commerce courses at Tech. It was an uneven trade. The University of Georgia's engineering program had never been substantial, but Tech's School of Commerce had grown to 447 students in the day program and 716 in the night division. In 1935 Tech responded by inventing an administrative fiction — a business school by another name. The new program in "industrial management" soon became the largest department on campus. Brittain,

The Varsity has been an Atlanta landmark since 1928, one year after Frank Gordy decided to serve Tech students rather than be one. He built a small two-room building just east of the campus on North Avenue to provide an alternative to institutional food. During the early 1920's a drugstore at North Avenue and Luckie was the central gathering place, but by 1930 The Varsity was so well established that "Gordy" was regarded as the underclassmen's counselor. In the late 1920's the carhop sections bore the names of women's colleges such as Agnes Scott, NAPS (North Avenue Presbyterian School) and Washington Seminary. In 1984, Manager Ed Minix estimated as many as 17,000 people were served each day, with the number swelling to more than 35,000 on football days.

A page of advertisements with Tech's 1931 football schedule tells it like it was five decades ago.

Mechanical engineering students ran performance tests on this two-stage air compressor driven by a steam engine. It was one of only a few made in the early 1920's by the Worthington Company of Atlanta. Now placed on the site of the first Shops Building, it is a mute reminder of change.

who opposed the Regents' plan to pull the commerce program out of Atlanta, warned that such a program would have to be replaced. As he predicted, a new unit of the system — the Georgia State College of Business Administration — soon began offering courses that "duplicated" those offered in Athens.

It was not until 1934 that funds were appropriated for Tech's Engineering Experiment Station, 15 years after the Georgia Assembly had authorized forming a state engineering research agency. The Station began its first year of operation with 13 part-time and two full-time workers.

When alumni recall the 1930's, few speak of momentous events. Rather, they seem to remember everyday scenes: Fred Ajax coming into his sophomore English class chuckling about the jokes he had just censored for *The Yellow Jacket*; "Taxi" Smith, who got tired during the cake race and took a taxi to the finish line; an episode when student pranksters moved a steel beam into the northeast corner room of the Electrical Engineering Building, a beam so massive it eventually had to be cut in two to remove it; and Earle Edgar Bortell, Physics Professor for 41 years, writing on the blackboard with one hand and erasing with the other. When Bortell submitted his resignation in his 41st year, he observed: "My father advised me, if you've been at a place forty years and don't own it, you might as well quit." Arthur Armstrong in Social Sciences was so devoted to Tech sports that when Tech lost a game he took to his bed or retreated to the mountains. Armstrong also insisted that his students wear ties to class. Marion Metcalf is convinced his "B" resulted from his failure to wear a tie on a scorching May day. "You were doing well," Armstrong explained to him, "until this last month, when you slacked off."

The list could continue with such names as the first Dean of Men, Floyd "Bo Cat" or "Billy Goat" Fields; English Professor and "immensely popular" speaker Glenn Rainey; Chemistry Professor Gilbert Hillhouse Boggs; Director of the Cooperative Division J.E. McDaniel, who owned a big Pierce-Arrow and lived in the attic at 133 North Avenue; Ceramic Engineering Head and later Director of EES, W. Harry Vaughan; Dean

The wedding party of Arthur B. Edge Jr. and Florence West in May 1930 includes Frank Edwards, Louise Lewis, Fuller E. Callaway Jr., Julia Sherman and Helen Byrd Daniel. "Skin" achieved a 4.0 GPA in Textiles and was active in Phi Delta Theta, honor societies and the Glee Club — both as President and as baritone in the Yellow Jacket Four. The Arthur B. Edge Jr. Intercollegiate Athletic Center, opened in 1982, is a tribute from the Callaway Foundation, which he served as trustee and as one of its presidents.

Feared by those in academic trouble and revered by all, Dean William Vernon Skiles was "a friend who saw two points of view."

William Gilmer Perry taught in the English Department for 48 years. Students remember his "Hour of Charm" and his favorite lines, "'Tis a beautiful thought; let us dwell upon it." The Perry Award given each spring to the best freshman writer commemorates his contribution to Tech, as does Perry Dormitory.

Chemical engineering graduate Sidney Goldin was captain of the 1930 basketball team and president of Anak.

"Froggie" Morton, a sharpshooter with blackboard chalk; Civil Engineering Professor R.P. "Rip" Black, everybody's friend; wood shop foreman "Uncle Heinie" Henika, creator of museum-quality inlaid mahogany pieces; and mathematics professor and basketball coach Roy M. Mundorff, whose 1937-38 squad remains the only Tech basketball team to win the Southeastern Conference championship.

And of course there was Dean William Skiles, the scholar and administrator so instrumental in setting Tech's standards and establishing its reputation. In his later years Skiles would occasionally turn off his hearing aid, effectively ending unwanted conversations. *The Atlanta Journal* called Skiles "Tech's Mr. Chips."

Meanwhile, students struggled to complete their requirements in the fewest quarters and professors continued to provide them with raw material for their highly embellished stories. Dean of Engineering D.P. Savant was one of them. Upperclassmen were willing to sit three straight hours in a classroom just to study under the bright, highly practical man who had once worked in the laboratory of Charles P. Steinmetz. "We're not here," he often said, "to teach you to be engineers. We are here to teach you to think." Savant was in the tradition of "Uncle Si" Coon, who was fond of saying "College education is no good for anything but to get a man started thinking along the right lines."

Phil Narmore, Professor of Mechanics and Strength of Materials, once gave students an "A" for going to Loew's Theater and watching a 10-minute newsreel on the collapse of a poorly designed mile-long bridge. Students described the experience as a "cheap A" — costing just 35 cents. Through successive years a student tradition in Narmore's classes was to caution each other not to answer any verbal or written question without first checking to see if, in one student's words, "You haven't exceeded the strength of the material." After receiving a perfect score on a written quiz, Marion Metcalf was asked by Narmore, "Why did you write that answer?" His response, "My roommate last year had you." Turning to another student, Narmore queried, "And why did you?" With no hesitation the student replied, "Mr. Metcalf's my roommate this year."

The Board of Trustees appointed
Mathematics Head Floyd Field to be the
first Dean of Men, an office created in
June 1922. Students remember Field as
"Bo Cat" or "Billy Goat" because of his
fierce approach to teaching and his
distinctive goatee. Dean Field led the first
Ramblin' Wreck parade.

Harry F. Guggenheim, a World War I
aviator, was President of the Daniel F.
Guggenheim Fund for the Promotion of
Aeronautics when Tech received the
$300,000 award in 1930. At the June 8,
1930, commencement he was awarded *in
absentia* the honorary degree of Doctor of
Science. On the same day students,
faculty and visitors gathered for the
formal dedication of the Guggenheim
Building.

In 1918 the President of the Chamber of Commerce spoke of the importance of having a landing field ready when the war ended: "The cities which have built their landing fields will naturally be the first to get this mail service. We want to start early, keeping pace with our famous slogan, 'Atlanta Always Ahead.'" In 1927 the field was provided with lights under the supervision of Alderman W.B. Hartsfield. In 1930 Fuller E. Callaway Jr. flew with Eddie Rickenbacker from Atlanta to Newark airport on one of Eastern's first passenger flights. In the canvas and wood plane with windows that opened, they sat on straw-webbed seats that ran the length of the fuselage facing each other. Because other cities had no lights, they left at daybreak, flying low and following the railroad. Before landing at Newark, the pilot flew just above the streetcar lines on Fifth Avenue from the north end of Manhattan to the Battery. When the group at last got out of the plane to drive to New York, Rickenbacker commented, "Now begins the dangerous part of the trip."

Students in 1938 could buy a rat cap at the "Robbery" for a dollar and in-state tuition was still only $50 a semester. Streetcar fare was a dime. Frank Gordy, whom students sometimes called the "King of Grease," was just beginning to accumulate a fortune selling hamburgers at The Varsity for a nickel. Parking on campus was no problem. Students could arrive as late as 7:55 a.m. and make it to an 8:00 a.m. class.

In October 1938, Tech celebrated its first 50 years with two days of events, speeches, luncheons, a tea dance, dinner and an evening dance. Tech played Notre Dame that year, in keeping with the big-time intercollegiate tradition begun by Heisman and Alexander, and lost 6 to 14.

This group of the Evening School Carolers in 1932 had three women officers: Juliet Dowling, President; Grace Wooley, Vice President; and Mettie McDavid, Secretary-Treasurer. At the 1932 graduation the seniors selected Dowling, front row, fifth from the left, to lead the class in the academic procession. She also received the Loving Cup as "Miss Student Activities of the Evening School."

Tech and Georgia have fought many fierce battles on the turf of Sanford Stadium. As many as four special trains would carry loyal Tech fans the 60 miles to Athens. Students also used any transportation available and labeled it accordingly.

The first Ramblin' Wreck Parade was held in 1932. For more than 50 years such vehicles have displayed the latest technological advances.

The 1940's began with a long-remembered 10-inch snowstorm in January that brought Tech and the city of 302,288 to a complete halt. Pictures of the crippling blizzard cover the pages of *The Blue Print.* The night before, students had walked to The Varsity in shirt sleeves, but they awoke the next morning to find a city blanketed in a quiet soft covering of white. On this rare Tech holiday, the ATO's and dormitory residents engaged in a "battle royal" at the North Avenue-Techwood intersection. When traffic stopped, "rats" were ordered to open the rear doors of cars and fill the

Hazard Reeves, upon graduating from Tech in 1928, set out for New York City because he felt "where there were that many lights, there must be activity and opportunity." Reeves formed a company that eventually developed the Oscar-winning Cinerama process. Reeves later returned to the campus for sessions with students and faculty.

cars with shovelsful of snow before the hapless motorists could escape. The snow also furnished the warriors with portable ammunition. Otho Perritt owned a 1929 Model A Ford touring car called "Rambler." He and four friends ordered "rats" to fill it with snowballs. They donned formal attire, complete with top hats, and cruised the streets of Atlanta spoiling for a fight. When the first snowballs flew their way, Perritt recalls they let go a "return salvo that was something to behold." After they exhausted their stock of snowballs, they returned to the ATO house to rearm and set forth again.

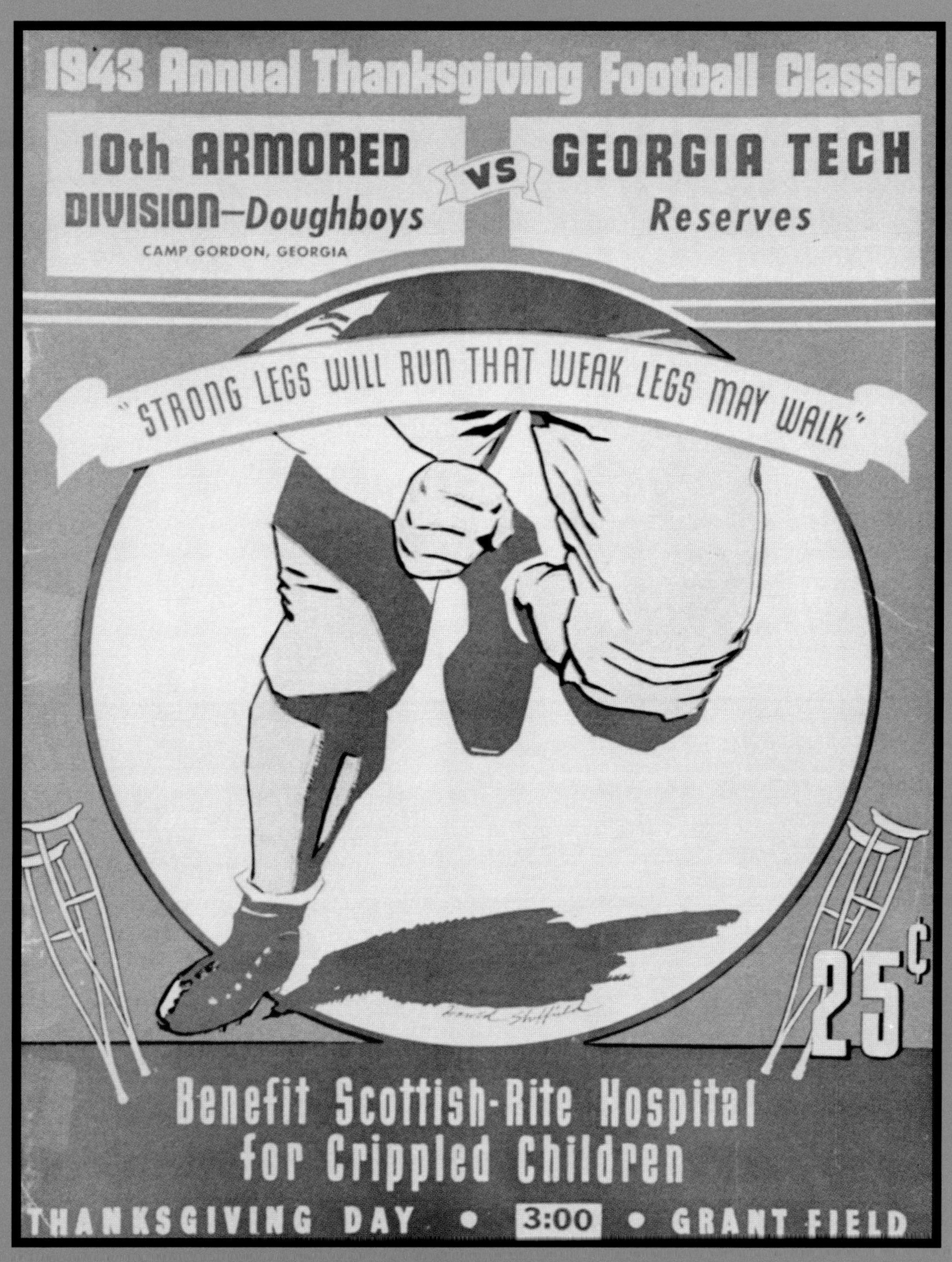

The first Scottish Rite Tech-Georgia Freshman game was played on Thanksgiving Day in 1933. The phrase "Strong Legs Will Run That Weak Legs May Walk," now also used in the East-West Shrine game, was first proposed by Ralph McGill for the Atlanta classic. During World War II, substitute teams kept the project going.

In 1930 the Daniel Guggenheim School of Aeronautics opened its doors with Montgomery Knight, whom President Brittain had recruited from Langley Field, as its Head. Rotors were on Knight's mind and, within months after arriving in Atlanta, the school was the proud owner of a used Pitcairn PCA-2 three-place autogiro the Coca-Cola Company had donated.

The autogiro, invented in Spain in 1923, had fixed wings, a propeller and a rotor, but it could not hover. It could, however, fly very slowly and land on short landing strips.

Unfortunately, Tech's autogiro died in a ditch in 1935 at the end of Candler Field's runway. On that fateful day, T. Edward Moodie, who invented the Roadplane, had already made several successful flights and was set for a demonstration flight from Candler Field to the Tech campus where he planned to land the plane on Rose Bowl Field. But the autogiro had other ideas. Moodie cranked up the motor, then went inside for a cup of coffee. When he returned, he walked to the front of the plane and adjusted the motor. Without warning the autogiro began to taxi down the runway — with Moodie hanging on. The autogiro swept gracefully in a wide loop around the field and then resolutely dove off the runway. Fortunately, Moodie was not seriously injured.

Despite this incident, helicopter research continued in the lab. Professor Donnell W. Dutton, who later became Director of the school, and E.I. Bricker worked on a hollow-blade that was to become the rotor of a jet-powered helicopter. And Dr. Robin Gray, now Regents' Professor of Aerospace Engineering, conducted theoretical research on the "hover" state of helicopters.

Successful lift tests were conducted with Tech's jet-powered helicopter, but when Knight died in 1943 that project was abandoned. Tests of all kinds continued in the wind tunnel and Professor Walter Castles Jr., Knight's successor, and his colleagues kept the rotorcraft tradition alive. In 1982 the Army chose Tech as a Center of Excellence for Rotary Wing Aircraft Technology, one of only three in the nation.

RESEARCH AUTOGIRO
DANIEL GUGGENHEIM SCHOOL OF AERONAUTICS
GEORGIA SCHOOL OF TECHNOLOGY

Meanwhile winds from a different storm were blowing. In Europe armies were marching, and ominous signals were coming from the Pacific. October brought the first peacetime draft, Fort McPherson became the Army induction center for the area and work began on the Naval Air Station in Chamblee.

Despite the storm warnings, the 1940 *Blue Print* looked to the future with confidence. Its theme was "The Beating Heart of the South, The Treasureland of Potentiality." Inside were color pictures and lengthy descriptions of different industries important to Georgia — vegetable oil, ceramics, textiles, pine forests, and iron and steel. Robert Gregg, President of Tennessee Coal, Iron and Railroad Company, and past-President of Atlantic Steel Company, was lauded for his brilliant career in Southern industry and for his civic leadership. It recorded the visit of film stars Mary Pickford and Buddy Rogers, the coming of the "jitterbug" and swing music, and a dance in the new gymnasium at mid-term with Eddy Duchin and his orchestra. Arthur Murray selected the beauties for the publication. There was mention of technical training programs on campus that attracted 57 students from 14 countries, including 27 from Cuba, six from Canada and one refugee from Germany. That year the Co-op Club Plan made its first 10 student loans and the M.L. Brittain Debating Society had as its stated topic for the March 12, 1940, meeting: "Resolved: That the United States shall fortify Guam."

The war was still 18 months away when Tech naval units sailed to New York, saw the World's Fair and then set off for Boston and Guantanamo Naval Base — "Gitmo" — in Cuba. That year they carried away all the prizes in gunnery competition with Harvard, Yale, Northwestern and Tulane. The teams, Dean Griffin recalls, consisted of athletes who were used to working together and simply transferred their efforts to a different medium.

In June, Griffin himself was called into service "for three months but remained on duty six years." Fred Ajax took over his work at the Placement Office, where he served until 1958, developing a program that has been the envy of schools

T. Edward Moodie, one of Tech's first graduate students in aeronautics and later an Associate Professor in the school, did his master's research in 1934 on a "streamlined road vehicle" he called the Roadplane. Moodie admitted that the contraption, which predated the Batmobile by several decades, would experience "aerodynamic moments" if it exceeded 100 mph. But Moodie contended the Roadplane "offered considerable promise as a high-speed land vehicle." The three-wheel craft was steered by means of an air rudder and individual wheel brakes, not conventional steering. Students who rode in the car remember road tests as hair-raising, especially when they encountered cross-turbulence from passing trucks. Moodie himself complained of headaches caused by banging his head against the cockpit's low roof.

Atomic research was the nation's most closely-guarded secret when, on February 15, 1942, *The Atlanta Constitution* carried this article predicting the development of the atomic bomb. Montgomery Knight, wide-ranging head of Tech's Aeronautical Engineering program, based his comments on his knowledge of characteristics of the then little-known U-235. Dr. John Harper, then one of Knight's students, remembers FBI agents descending on the campus shortly after the article appeared. They closeted themselves with Knight for a long session in his office.

History's Most Destructive Missile Seen

New Element, U-235, May Prove Answer to Alchemists' Prayers.

By LAMAR Q. BALL.

Give the scientists 25 years more, according to Professor Montgomery Knight, director of the Guggenheim School of Aeronautics at Georgia Tech, let them work with the tools and the elements and the knowledge they now have, and War—the No. 1 man-made means of settling international disputes—will be out, laid on the shelf, just a convenient memory for poets and romantic writers to revive occasionally as their setting for stories of man's brutality and heroism during the grim, old gunpowder days of the past.

Just one little element that scientists are now peering at through their microscopes, an existing element that they touch off occasionally in their outdoor laboratories, will be developed within those next 25 years as a swift boot in the pants for the whole game of war.

Let the little element be developed into a practical weapon that man can control and direct, says Professor Knight, and all nations will be on an equal footing as far as tests of power and equipment are concerned.

Not Practical.

War no longer will be practical. Yawning soldiers will be able to assemble at some given points within their own national boundaries and pour death and destruction into the capitals and cities and continents on the other side of the world. All this, without worrying about mobilizing frantically for a swift invasion of the enemy's country.

And as soon as the enemy is aware he is being attacked, he can assemble his soldiers on his own ground and hurl blast after blast of the self-same death and destruction into his assailant's territory with the same ease and minimum effort.

And, then—with hostile nations levelling one another, destroying cities and farms and industries with no object other than malicious and unjustified destruction —man will awaken to the realization that war by explosives is getting nowhere and man will be forced to resort to a power that has been long neglected i. the settlement of disputes — reason and intellect.

"In just about 25 years," said Professor Knight yesterday, "the forces of the world equipped with machines that will accomplish nothing but the destruction of the world."

No Visionary.

No idealistic, dreaming visionary is Professor Knight. He is a cold, hard, practical scientist, the director of a school that teaches technological facts to students countize for the soundness of their education.

He is not talking after the manner of an H. G. Wells, or an Orson Welles or an Edwin Balmer or any of those other visionaries who ...

BOMBS OUT OF THE BLUE—And from far away, thousands of miles distant, may some day strike the state capitol building in a manner depicted in this conception by John Williamson, of The Constitution's art staff. That's the vision of 25 years hence seen by an Atlanta scientist, Professor Montgomery Knight, who says that wars will be forever over when man perfects the most destructive of all elements—a thing known to science as U-235.

without warning as she did in those blitzkriegs, 25 or 30 years ago.

"We retaliate. We fire the same sort of projectile at Berlin or Hamburg or any of the other German cities. A new type of war has been evolved.

Not Impossible.

"All this is not so far from possible."

The armies of the world, in the not far distant future, says Professor Knight, will be utilizing the destructive element known to science as U-235.

The chemists know today that one pound of U-235 has the same amount of energy as 10,000,000 pounds of coal.

All this U-235 needs is a few more years of study before it will be utilized as the most destructive force that man has ever discovered.

Disintegrated today under properly-controlled conditions, U-235 gives off an enormous amount of energy. Today, the element is available in only minute quantities. That will soon be corrected. It was discovered when scientists were trying to shatter atoms or molecules. Its enormous force knocks parts off an atom and can change the characteristics of the atom.

"It won't be very long before we find that U-235 may be answer to the alchemists' prayers of the olden days," said Professor Knight.

Scientists, such as Professor Knight, can go into deeper and, to the layman, less understandable explanations of the discovery and the development of U-235; its present standing in the scientific world and its future. But the best a layman can under-

THE END TO ALL WARS—No idle, dreaming visionary is Professor Montgomery Knight, director of the Georgia Tech Aeronautical School. He is a cold, practical scientist who says that man already has discovered material that will make war no longer practical means of settling quarrels.

the nations allied against the Axis powers $500,000,000 a day.

Vicious System.

Students waked in January 1940 to find eight inches of snow and more falling. The ATO's showed unusual ingenuity. Motorists who stopped at the North Avenue light were stunned to have pledges open the back doors and shovel in snow. Other brothers lined up in front of the house and had snowball fights with passing pedestrians and residents of nearby dormitories.

Professor Gilbert H. Boggs measures the amount of heat generated in an acid-base reaction. The son of a former Chancellor of the University of Georgia, Boggs became Head of the Chemistry Department following the death of Dean William Henry Emerson in 1924.

throughout the nation and the delight of interviewers. In the Engineering Experiment Station, Gerald Rosselot became Director with a young assistant, Paul Weber, who was doing research for the Georgia naval stores industry. "Chip" Robert, now back in construction, was building military installations all over the world.

As the nation edged closer to war, the lines in Georgia were being drawn for a brutal battle over control of the state's colleges and universities. Eugene Talmadge, an admirer of Louisiana's Huey Long, had been elected Governor in 1940 and he soon showed his intention to follow Long's example in dealing with state universities. Talmadge proposed naming David Irenus "Red" Barron, one of Tech's most illustrious football stars and an ardent Talmadge supporter, Vice President of Georgia Tech. At the time, Barron was Head of Monroe A&M. Instantly, resistance formed among Monroe. Instantly, resistance formed among faculty and students. For although Tech people admired Barron personally and cherished his contributions on the gridiron, they resented Talmadge's interference in the administration of the School and feared what such action, if successful, might mean for the future. On May 29, students began to march toward the state Capitol but were halted by police after two blocks. However, the aborted march and organized protest was successful. Barron decided to remain at Monroe.

Talmadge's next sally into the educational arena did not end as peacefully or as quickly. He had apparently become upset by reports that certain prominent educators in the University System, some of them "furriners," were a bit soft on the doctrine of racial segregation. When Talmadge sought to have two of them fired — Dr. Walter D. Cocking, Dean of Education at the University of Georgia, and Dr. Marvin Pittman, President of the Georgia Teachers College at Statesboro — the Board of Regents failed to comply with the Governor's wishes. Temporarily frustrated, Talmadge managed to oust three Regents who opposed him and named his own followers to take their places. The revamped Board of Regents then voted to fire Cocking and Pittman.

Streetcars were an important feature of Tech life in the 1940's. Here they are lined up during the five o'clock rush hour at the intersection of Forsyth, Peachtree and Pryor.

The "Robbery" in the early 1940's served as drugstore, bookstore and soda fountain, with 15-cent cold fudge sundaes on a "pay when served" basis.

Jack Griffin "Stumpy" Thomason, younger brother of Ernest K. "Tommy" Thomason, has at least two claims to fame: the famous fumble that led to the Rose Bowl victory January 1, 1929, and his bear cub from California. Here "Bruin," when he was still manageable, eats from Thomason's hand.

Stories abound about Stumpy's bear. Once he got loose and wandered onto the porch of a nearby residence. The wife and daughter both fainted and the husband had difficulty convincing the police that a bear was trying to get into his refrigerator.

Dean George C. Griffin recalls that Coach Alex hired Mike Chambers of Ohio State as trainer, telling him to go directly to the training room when he arrived on campus. After waiting two hours, Chambers remarked to a friend, "I believe we've made a mistake; nothing has happened here since 1864." Just then Stumpy's bear walked in ready for his afternoon shower. One man got in a trunk and the other in a closet. The bear went from one to the other scratching to get someone to turn on his water or at least give him his favorite refreshment, a bottle of Coke. Rescued later, Chambers vowed, "Never will I say nothing ever happens in Atlanta!"

In the mid-1930's, the bear broke glass doors and generally wreaked havoc at the Fox Theater. The playful cub had outgrown both the Tech campus and the athletic gear trunk in which he rode to games. Peters Park was too small for his prowling. He was sent to be mascot of the Buffalo, N.Y., football team where Thomason was then playing. Eventually too big even for them, he was given to the zoo in Crystal Springs, Canada.

Clint Castleberry, one of Tech's all-time great performers, played only one season and led the 1942 squad to a 9-1 record and the Cotton Bowl. In 1943 he enlisted in the Army Air Corps and a year later died in a plane crash in North Africa. L.W. "Chip" Robert Jr. and President Brittain retired his jersey in 1944. Serving as a symbol for all Tech men who died in World War II, the jersey was used to raise $4,079,100 in war bond sales.

As soon as this happened, opposition arose on all sides. The Southern Association of Colleges and Secondary Schools — the official accrediting organization for all schools in the region — recommended the suspension of schools in the University System. Its reason: the Governor had used dictator tactics.

Tech, though not directly involved in the firings, nevertheless lost its accreditation. In response, Bill Clearman, a Tech senior, organized a coalition of students, called the Student Political League, to resist Talmadge's interference and restore accreditation to the state schools. Students throughout the state got involved. Even when they went home for holidays, they campaigned for the cause, talking to legislators and other influential people about the problem. When Ellis Arnall announced he would challenge Talmadge in the next election, the League supported him. Brittain, now 75 years old, decided not to retire but to stay until the dispute was over. In 1942, Ellis Arnall defeated Talmadge. That same year the Southern Association of Colleges and Secondary Schools restored the accreditation of the entire University System of Georgia. Bill Clearman, who had helped organize the League, received the ODK Citation of Honor for his part in the crucial victory for higher education.

Amid the bad news of those darkening years, there was some good news. John E. Smith, who had attended Tech under the administrations of its first two Presidents, Hopkins and Hall, presented a tract of land on 10th Street to be used as the site for the President's home. "You, my dear Dr. Brittain," Smith wrote, "have been president for 19 years and have inspired this gift. Under your guidance Tech has made wonderful strides in growth, in reputation and in character. The luster reflected by Tech since you have been its president will always be a great source of pride and satisfaction to its alumni."

One event in 1941 did more than any other to shape Georgia Tech's future — Pearl Harbor. Soon, there were new programs and an influx of students, and Tech professors were sent for intensive training throughout the country. Research projects burgeoned, with one year's funding for EES from both industry and the government rising

NAVAL ROTC   --1943

The Navy ROTC had been at Tech 15 years when war came
in 1941. One of the midshipmen sitting on the gun barrel
holds the unit's mascot.

The 1944 *Blue Print* bears the mark of
the war years.

After Pearl Harbor the federal government urged compulsory physical training. Large contingents of Navy V-12 students trained in a program called one of the best in the country.

to an unprecedented $155,000. The armed forces needed men trained in the fields Tech stressed — aeronautics, physics, chemistry, mechanical and electrical engineering. The government asked Tech and other major colleges and universities to accelerate their work and operate year-round, to make physical training compulsory, to stress mathematics and science, and to emphasize the values of the democratic way of life. Evening courses provided instruction in vocational education and the Ordnance Department brought women to the campus to be trained as inspectors in factories. Two hundred SPARS (the U.S. Coast Guard Women's Auxiliary whose name is derived from the Coast Guard motto, *Semper Paratus)* attended, living at the Biltmore Hotel and eating at Brittain Dining Hall. Graduation in 1942 was held two weeks early, and more than 90 percent of the graduates received commissions and orders with their diplomas. The class of 1943 graduated in February instead of June and the class of 1944 graduated in October. Faculty remember the heavy loads and different calendars: quarter, semester, 10-weeks, 5-weeks. It was always final exam week for someone.

As early as 1937 Army ROTC Commander Tommy Jones had attended high-level military meetings in Washington and reported confidentially to Brittain that in the event of war, Tech would be designated a major center for naval training. Shortly after Pearl Harbor Brittain learned that by July 1942, he should prepare for 1,050 incoming naval students rather than the usual 250. The ROTC program, already compulsory for the first two years, was enlarged with other units. Tech eventually trained 17,500 people during the war years.

Prior to Pearl Harbor, few students had taken ROTC seriously. In fact, most of them thought of it as "a joke, a nuisance." That all changed on December 7, 1941. When Major John B. Day told Tech's ROTC students the following day that "ROTC is the most important course you have," his message was suddenly believable. Later he used miniature guns and shells to teach gunnery to the Coast Artillery units. Students fired the guns on Rose Bowl Field, spending much of their time retrieving their total arsenal of eight projectiles.

Research at the Engineering Experiment Station in the 1930's focused primarily on ceramics and textiles. Harold Bunger, Chief of the Chemical Engineering Division and Director of EES, gained prominence for his work on a machine to process flax for commercial purposes. With relatively few changes in the regular cotton mill machinery, the Tech laboratory wove cloth from flax, flax-cotton and flax-cotton-rayon to use for suiting, toweling, parachute webbing and other items. In this photograph, ME Professor Dean Smith examines flax fibers.

Librarian Dorothy Crosland, Vice Chancellor Mario Goglia and Harry L. Baker Jr. at the installation of Tech's UNIVAC 1108 II system in 1967. Baker directed the Georgia Tech Research Institute for 16 years after it replaced the Industrial Development Council. Fuller E. Callaway Jr. helped develop the idea for this contractual arm of the Engineering Experiment Station; and he, Monie Ferst and Robert H. "Bob" White contributed $1,000 each. Baker often mentioned that he was hired between the Terminal and Brookwood Station as Callaway passed through on the train to New York. "You're a smart boy," Baker was told. "You know enough math to know how long $3,000 and your job will last at $500 a month unless you raise more." The Baker Building testifies that he did.

161

Thomas Buchanan McGuire Jr. is one of three Tech men to receive the Medal of Honor. McGuire, AE class of 1942, left Tech in February 1941 to join the Army Air Corps, serving in the Aleutians and then the South Pacific as a P-38 fighter pilot. Before he was killed on January 7, 1945, he had shot down 38 Japanese planes, two short of the World War II record. In 1949 the Air Force base at the Fort Dix Military Reservation in New Jersey was named in his honor. A memorial to him was designed by 1980 graduate Kenneth M. Gardner, architect with the 438th Civil Engineering Squadron at McGuire Air Force Base. It includes a park and a P-38 painted to duplicate McGuire's plane. McGuire's fraternity, Beta Theta Pi, placed a memorial plaque on the Tech campus, and each pledge learns his history.

John McGaughey remembers that a bit too much powder sent some of the shells over the 10th Street fence.

One program brought to the campus was the intensive Army Specialized Training Program (A.S.T.P.), designed to train "high grade technicians and specialists." The program lasted only a year, but those "wearers of the golden lamp" left Tech, in the words of *The Blue Print,* "a different school, a wiser school, a more appreciative school." The V-12 program, designed to train Navy and Marine officers, arrived in July 1943 with more than 1,000 cadets.

Entries in the Ramblin' Wreck parade in 1942 had to be pushed or pulled around the course because of gasoline rationing. During this period, the band director, Ben Sisk, made an unsuccessful attempt to secure majorettes. When he explained their function, Coach Alex tersely replied, "No girls."

In the fall of 1942 a high school football star entered Tech and went out for the team that was ranked eighth in the 12-team SEC after a disastrous 3-6 season in 1941. Only 5'9" and 145 pounds, Clinton Dillard Castleberry Jr. substituted in the first game against an Auburn team ranked eighth in the nation. Tech won, 15-0. A match-up with Notre Dame followed. John McGaughey and five others drove to South Bend, stopping in Chicago to go to NBC's "Breakfast Club." A roving reporter brought his mike and questioned John and his brother Roy about the outcome of the game. "Sure, we're gonna win because we have this freshman sensation in the backfield." Host Don McNeil and the rest of the audience chuckled at the idea, since Notre Dame was number two in the nation. About 50 June graduates stationed at nearby Wright-Patterson Field came to the game. Castleberry did indeed lead his team to a 13-6 victory, the first Tech win on Notre Dame turf. Coach Alexander's "destiny squad" and its freshman star could not be stopped for nine games, but finally lost — first to Georgia and then to Texas in the Cotton Bowl. Castleberry was selected for the All-SEC team. Coach Bobby Dodd proclaimed him the halfback with the most potential of any he had ever coached. The potential went unrealized, for

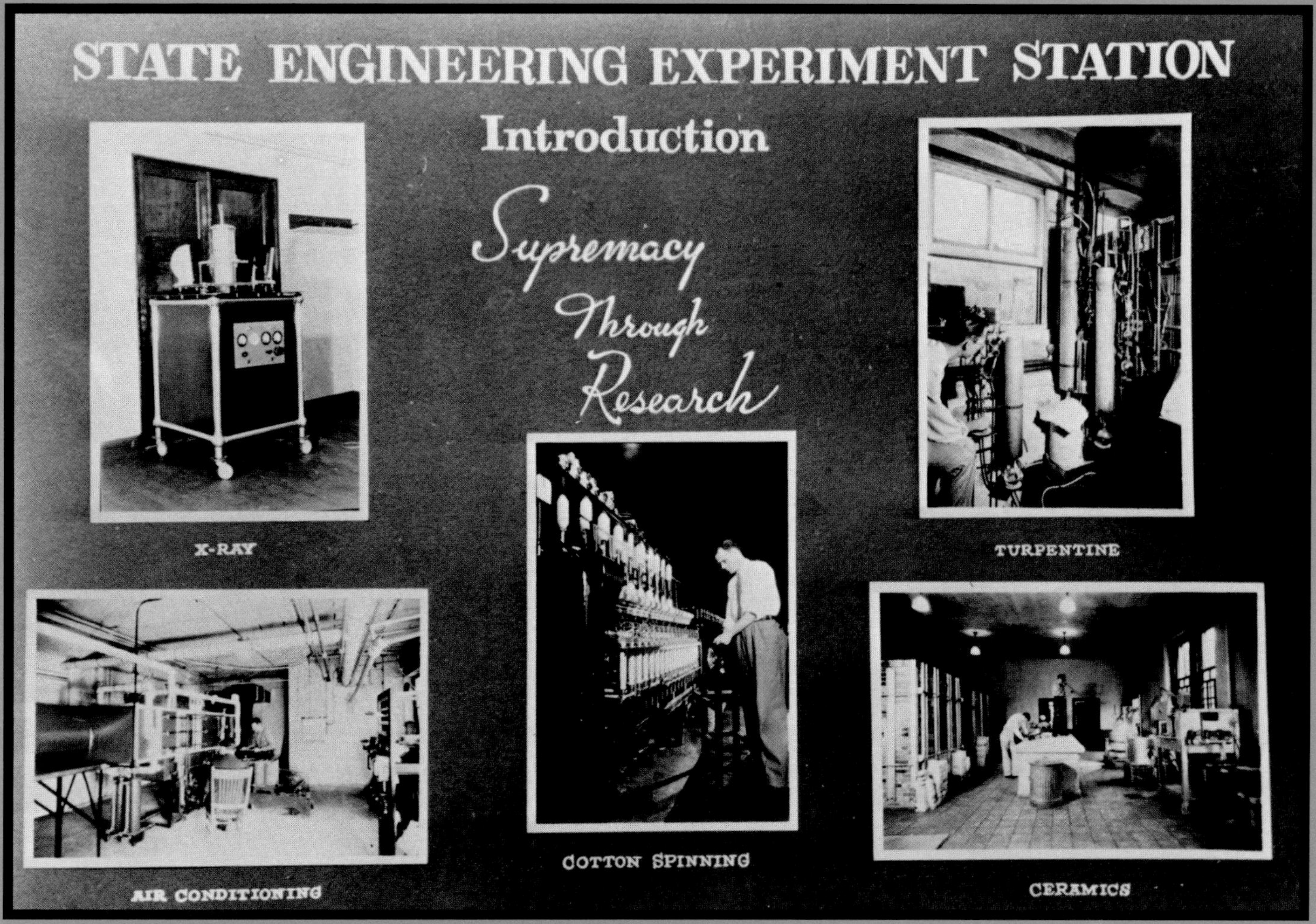

STATE ENGINEERING EXPERIMENT STATION

Introduction

Supremacy Through Research

X-RAY

TURPENTINE

COTTON SPINNING

CERAMICS

AIR CONDITIONING

Authorized in 1919, the concept of an Engineering Experiment Station languished for more than a decade. But the State Legislature in 1934 at last provided funding. Harry Vaughan, Ceramic Engineering Head and Director of the Station, oversaw many research projects. A young Paul Weber, later Acting President of Tech for 17 months, conducts turpentine experiments; and Herman Dickert, later Director of the A. French School of Textiles, observes cotton spinning.

The Navy ROTC cadets embark for Mayport, Florida, for their summer cruise in 1942. Supplies and equipment indicate Atlanta's involvement in the war effort. Seabags came from the George Muse Clothing Company in the city. George Muse Jr. had been a student at Tech in the 1890's.

In the early 1940's the education of
engineers still required "hands-on"
experience in the shops and foundry.

Castleberry joined the Army Air Corps in February 1943 and less than two years later died in the crash of a B-26 in North Africa. "He was here," teammate Jim Luck said, "he made [good] things happen and then he was gone."

That year the football coaches of the nation selected Alexander "Coach of the Year," and Tech students dedicated their yearbook "not only to Alexander, the coach, but Alexander, the man, as well."

The football fortunes of Tech rose during the war years, with students coming from across the nation to enter the V-12 program. Students like Phil Tinsley, Bill Chambers and John Steber, who had played against Tech in previous seasons, now became staunch Yellow Jackets. Graduating groups soon joined the ranks of a body of alumni known for its outstanding support of the Institute.

During the war these Tech men traveled around the globe and back, taking their traditions with them. Allan Matthews and his B-26 crew made numerous missions over Germany in the "Ramblin' Wreck." George P. Burdell harassed Harvard's Naval Unit before joining the 8th Air Force, and then fought valiantly in both theaters of the war.

Tech men in the Pacific returning to Honolulu for rest and recreation found a welcome face — George C. Griffin, who welded them into a cohesive group. Jack Spears' account has it that Commander Griffin was in Hawaii mainly "to look up Tech students and be a morale booster." Lewis C. Radford Jr., a Hellcat pilot, knew he could go to the submarine base Officers Club and always find Griffin telling tall tales at the head of a table full of Tech men.

Initiation activities designed to humiliate
and embarrass the initiates and amuse the
initiators led to coveted membership in
the Skull and Key Society. Established at
Tech in 1916 to recognize outstanding
sophomores, the society flourished until
the early 1940's.

John E. Smith, Hal L. Smith and John E. Smith II attended the dedication of Smith Dormitory in 1948. The building commemorates the financial assistance John M. Smith gave Tech in the 1880's. He was one of the those men who gave their money and their sons to a dream. In Smith's case, three generations followed that dream and made it their own. In 1941 John E. Smith gave land on 10th Street for the President's home, built in 1949. His regard for President Brittain is evident in his letter announcing the gift: "You, my dear Dr. Brittain, have been president for 19 years and have inspired this gift."

Radford was eventually shot down and drifted in a small rubber boat until a destroyer came in sight. Underestimating the distance, he leapt into the water and reached the ship utterly exhausted. The hands that grabbed him and pulled him aboard were the hands of classmate Austin Thies, who later became Vice President of Duke Power Company.

Classmates of James T. "Jimmy" Andrews tell how he won the Navy Cross: "He got lost in the clouds somewhere in the South Pacific. Breaking into the open, he found a detachment of the Japanese fleet immediately below and made repeated devastating bombing runs." Locke Trigg, another Tech man, shot down the Japanese plane that had just bombed the USS *Franklin*.

But there were many brave men who did not return.

By the mid-1940's, ivy covered a number
of buildings. President Van Leer ordered
the ivy sandblasted away.

Section Four
The Van Leer Years: 1944-1956

On July 1, 1944, M.L. Brittain ended the longest tenure of any Tech President — 22 years — and became President Emeritus by official act of the Board of Regents. Brittain, 78, had fought and won his last battle for higher education: Tech had returned to full accreditation and, for the immediate future, the whole University System seemed safer from political interference.

His successor, Blake Ragsdale Van Leer, was born in 1893 in Mangum, Texas (now Oklahoma). Educated in electrical engineering at Purdue University and in mechanical engineering at the University of California at Berkeley, he served as a captain in the 316th Engineers during World War I, then worked briefly as an engineer with the Southern Pacific Railroad and the Bryan-Jackson Pump Company. He next became Assistant Secretary of the American Engineering Council and, in 1932, became Dean of Engineering at the University of Florida. After five years he moved to Raleigh, North Carolina, as Dean of Engineering at North Carolina State until he was recalled to active duty in 1942, becoming Chief of the Facilities Branch of the Army Specialized Training Division. Van Leer was promoted in 1943 to Colonel, a title he preferred to any other.

The Van Leers moved to Atlanta in the summer of 1944, just a few months before thousands of war veterans began to stream home. During the early 1940's, many of Tech's programs had been modified to meet the needs of a nation at war, and now curriculum changes were necessary to meet the needs of a post-war society and to exploit the scientific and technological advances that had been made during the war. Administrative changes were also required. William Vernon Skiles retired as Executive Dean and was succeeded by Dr. Phil Blasier Narmore. Temporary Vice President Cherry Emerson was appointed new Dean of Engineering. Cherry Emerson, incidentally, was the son of W.H. Emerson, first Head of the Chemistry Department, and was associate editor of the first *Blue Print* when he was a student at Tech. Dr. Robert Sarbacher, another noted engineer, became Dean of the Graduate Division; and Bobby Dodd, Alexander's assistant for 13 years, was named Head Football Coach. Van Leer established

President Van Leer in formal academic
dress, a portrait that now hangs in the
Alumni-Faculty House.

faculty committees to help run the School, tightened the academic structure to deal with a projected enrollment of 5,000 students, sought funds for new facilities and mounted a campaign to recruit top faculty members for the classrooms.

Housing was a top priority. Two off-campus apartment complexes were found for returning veterans: the Lawson Apartments and units built for Tech students at the Naval Air Station in Chamblee, Georgia, both over 12 miles from campus. But those plans were only for the immediate future.

According to the long-range plan, housing would be on the eastern side of campus, athletic and physical training facilities would extend through campus from North Avenue to 10th Street, academic instructional units would be concentrated in the southwest corner so students could easily walk from one building to another between classes, and auxiliary buildings would be north of Eighth Street.

Planning was one thing, implementation another. In fact, state funds were not available,

President Emeritus M.L. Brittain holding a first edition copy of his history of Georgia Tech, published in 1948.

This charcoal-fired gas producer unit was designed and built by the Tech Engineering Experiment Station in 1943-44 and was attached to an automobile belonging to Paul Weber. The eight-cylinder Cadillac operated on gasoline or charcoal.

The crowd at Grant Field when the cadets came in uniform and the freshmen wore rat caps.

A rare picture taken by a student in 1944 of Mercer McCall "Mack" Tharpe, former player and legendary assistant coach who was killed during World War II, and Bobby Dodd. The Alexander-Tharpe Fund is named for Coach William Alexander and Lt. Commander Tharpe.

Built by RCA and given to Tech by the Rockefeller Foundation circa 1945, this was the first transmission electron microscope in the Southeast. Standing, left to right: Benjamin Weil and Dr. Gerald Rosselot (Director, EES). Seated, Robert W. Koza.

and two years passed before a single new building was in place. "Georgia Tech," Van Leer complained in his annual report, "is probably the truly unique institution in the United States in that it is privately supported but publicly controlled."

But better times were ahead. Fuller E. Callaway Jr. provided a then-anonymous gift of $100,000 to build a President's home to replace the old one on North Avenue. In 1949 the neoclassical building was dedicated and soon became the site of numerous parties, ceremonies and receptions.

That year the Harrison Hightower Textile Engineering Building was completed and furnished with more than $750,000 of equipment donated by the Textile Education Foundation. The vacated A. French Textile Building was then remodeled with a grant from the Rich Foundation and became the new home of the School of Industrial Engineering.

A project sometimes referred to as Van Leer's "baby" got its start in 1948 in nine buildings formerly occupied by the Naval Air Station in Chamblee. The Technical Institute, as it was first called, began with 166 students as an official unit of Tech's Engineering Extension Division. It grew

John Henry Henika came to Tech from Kalamazoo, Michigan, in 1892 to teach for one year. In 1901 he returned to Tech to stay and subsequently instructed thousands of students in the wood shop.

out of Van Leer's conviction that post-war America would desperately need trained technicians. From the beginning, the Technical Institute had a distinctive curriculum, mission and identity. Perhaps symbolically, its athletic teams were called Green Hornets, not Yellow Jackets.

On another front, planning began for a new library. The Carnegie Library, once the delight of President Matheson, was now so crowded that books and materials were stacked in every corner. Clearly something needed to be done.

Bob Ison, left, a 1940 graduate of the Naval ROTC program at Tech, served as Executive Officer on the submarine *Bergall* with Commanding Officer John M. Hyde, Captain U.S.N., right. After World War II, Ison's former Naval Science instructor at Tech, Tommy Dykers, produced 39 hour-long episodes for the television show *Silent Service,* two of them about Ison's experiences on the *Bergall.* While at Tech, Ison was a walk-on end on Coach Alex's 1939 Southeastern Conference co-champion team and was on the first string All-America team of the Hearst Newspapers and *The Chicago Sun.* Since then, he has been especially active as a board member of the Alexander-Tharpe Scholarship Fund, now serving as Trustee Emeritus.

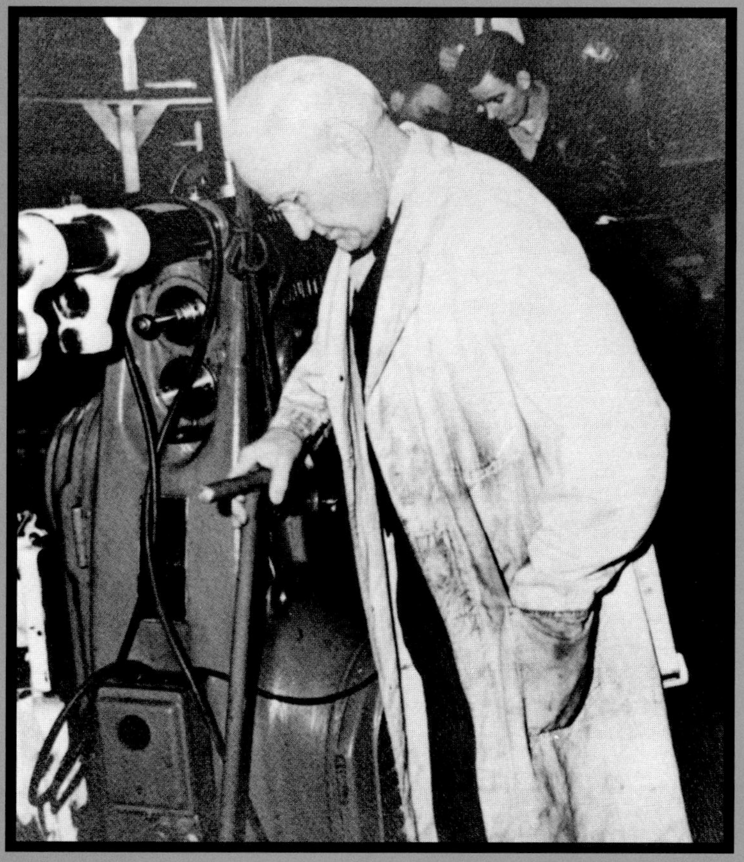

Major Allando A. Case believed a Tech engineer should be able to build a machine as well as design one, and for 27 years — from 1921 to 1948 — devoted himself to that task. Over the years he spent about $30,000 of his own money to equip the shop. When he reached age 70, the white-haired mechanical engineer refused to retire and became Chief Engineer of the Southwire Company in Carrollton, where he remained until his death at age 82.

David M. Smith came to Tech as a mathematics instructor in 1913, where he spent the next 41 years. "Dr. D.M." was Director of the School of Mathematics when he retired in 1954. The old Physics Building, dedicated in 1923 and built with funds from the Carnegie Corporation, is named in honor of the man *The Atlanta Constitution* called "Tech's irascible, beloved math professor."

Tech students pose before a replica of the ODK key in September 1945. From left to right, standing: George B. Hills Jr., B.D. Smith, Jack Wilson, Earle Holliday; kneeling, left to right: Eddie David and Ross Oliver.

For almost three decades, Dorothy Murray Crosland, the librarian, had waged a frequently frustrating campaign for a new facility and an expanded collection. Now she had support in high places and, in the fall of 1946, was commissioned to travel to Europe to obtain rare scientific journals and books. She returned to Atlanta laden with treasures, more determined than ever to see a facility built that would serve the School well. Seven years later, in 1953, the vision was realized and the new library was dedicated — named for its chief benefactor, Judge Price Gilbert.

The move from the old library to the new was an enormous, sometimes chaotic, campus-wide undertaking. Assistance was required from freshmen, requested from fraternities and demanded from those who needed to atone for misdemeanors.

Meanwhile, another building was in place — the Architecture Building. Ironically, this school which had graduated so many architects renowned for producing homes for others had no adequate home of its own until 1952. For years the architecture program had been housed in makeshift quarters, so the new building, comprising auditorium, library and classrooms, was a boon. This building, along with the Price Gilbert Memorial

From Luke Bowen's scrapbook: "Here is a priceless picture of 1945. The time was V E Day when the Germans surrendered during World War II. I am the one in the middle holding the girl. My roomies were Tommy Curtner, George Cummings, Don Ross and Malcolm Stamper. The Soldier is the wise guy that I found with my date in the Owl Room at the Dinkler Hotel." This picture appeared in *The Atlanta Constitution* the morning after.

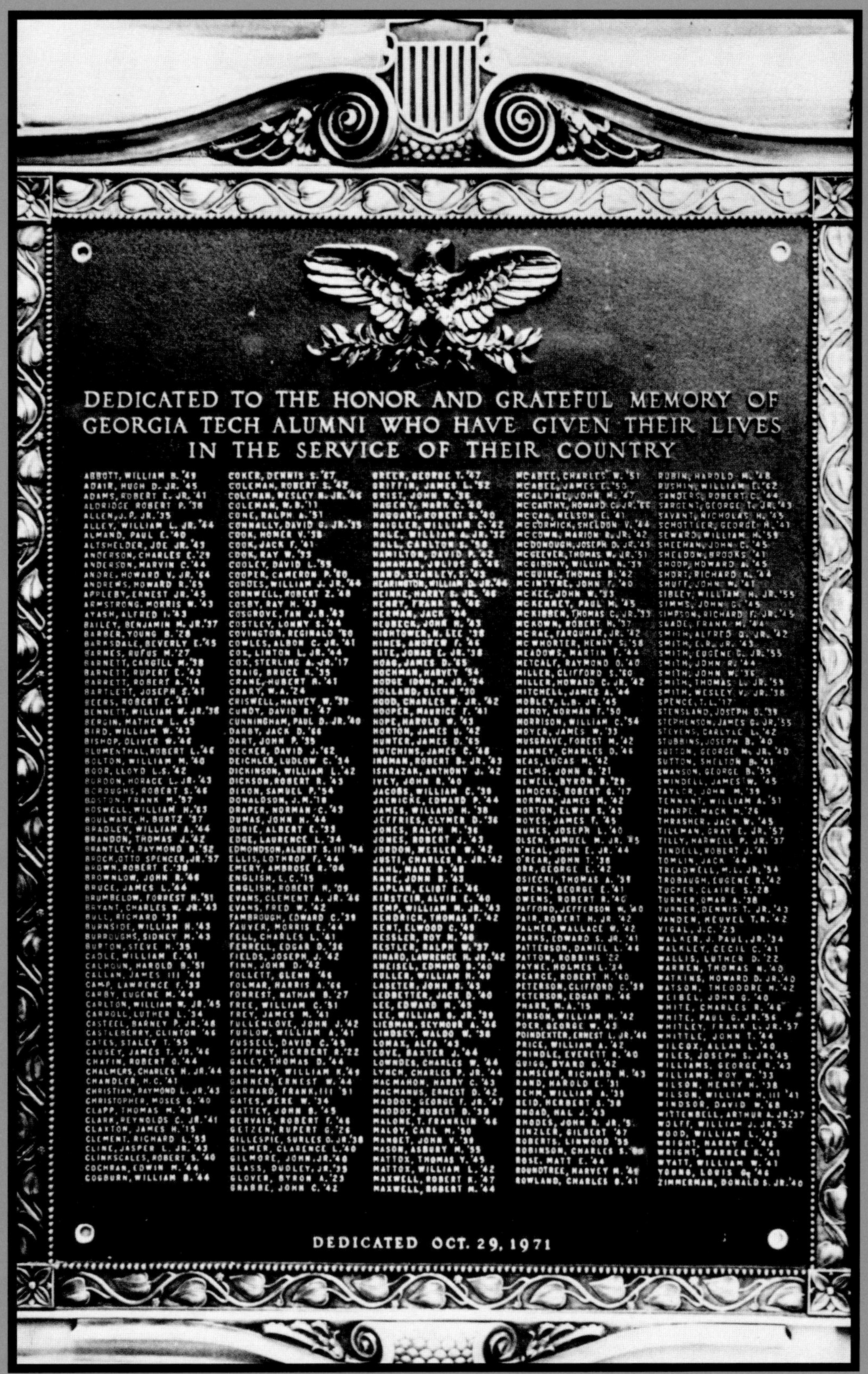

This plaque, dedicated in 1971 and
located in the Student Center Plaza,
honors Tech alumni who gave their lives
for their country.

Library and the Harrison Hightower Textile Engineering Building, formed a triangle around which the central campus was evolving. In each of these projects, state-appropriated funds were matched and multiplied by funds from a bond issue as well as by generous gifts from Tech's loyal supporters.

Another of Van Leer's interests was the Engineering Experiment Station. Although the Station had been growing before Van Leer came, he relentlessly pursued the goal of raising the quality and quantity of its research to that of other scientific and technological institutions around the country. In addition, the Georgia Tech Research Institute, chartered in 1946, enabled Tech faculty to do contract research for outside

As the 1940's ended, many Tech students who were veterans were still part of the ROTC program. Pictured here are eight Tech NROTC seniors on their final cruise in 1949. The students are enjoying liberty in "Gitmo," Guantanamo Bay, Cuba. From left to right: Ed Montague, Jack Sheffield, Tommy Towles, unidentified student, John Hiles, Jim Gray, Lamar Oglesby and Charles Quarles.

Tech provided housing to accommodate married students after World War II. "Many of the students after the war were married and some had children," John Portman Jr., a veteran, recalls. "They seemed to be highly motivated, more interested in self preparation and less interested in the typical college life with fraternities and parties."

The Peters Park Monument with Van Leer and three generations of the Peters family. This area is now used for parking facilities, tennis courts and basketball courts.

entities in an efficient manner. Under the aegis of GTRI, help was given in administering patents for the inventions of Tech's faculty and staff.

Research was now more important than ever. In 1952 a new wing was added to the Hinman Research Building, and in 1955 Van Leer presided at the dedication of the Rich Electronic Computer Center, a facility made possible by a grant from the Rich Foundation.

By the late 1940's the student body had surged beyond the projected 5,000 mark to over 6,000 students, with thousands more enrolled in the Evening School and the Technical Institute. Many of these students had returned to school as veterans under the G.I. Bill. This influx of veterans profoundly affected the attitudes and values prevailing on campus. "We were not the typical students who go directly from high school to college," John Portman Jr. recalls. "Our lives had been interrupted by the war, and we were in a hurry to get on with our future. There was a deep sense of seriousness about the campus." According to Portman, the Tech student was highly motivated and interested in self-preparation. He remembers "makeshift classrooms, long hours and a helluva lot of hard work."

Long-time Tech Registrar William L. Carmichael. A 1926 graduate of the A. French Textile School with the highest average then on record, Carmichael began his 46-year career at the Institute as an instructor in the Textile Department. He was Director of Admissions from 1945 to 1948 and, in 1948, became Registrar as well. He retired in 1968. During his tenure, he admitted 37,145 students and signed 23,500 diplomas.

In 1947 Tech built the Research Annex Building to house a facility that was called "the world's largest and most complete A.C. Network Calculator Laboratory." Herbert P. Peters, a special research engineer, is shown here with the calculator.

Tech students performed their first card tricks on October 12, 1948, at the Tech-Washington and Lee game. The Jackets blanked the Generals 27-0.

First known as the Technical Institute, Southern Technical Institute started in 1948 with 166 students who attended classes in nine abandoned buildings at the Naval Air Station in Chamblee. The Technical Institute was known as Colonel Van Leer's "baby" because he vigorously supported the project.

In 1952, women were officially admitted to Tech's main campus as full-time students — a decision many decades in coming. But there was opposition. The *Technique* announced: "When they show they have the ability, then they'll be accepted as one of us." The President of the senior class made the modest observation: "If they come here to study engineers instead of engineering, they won't stay long." But they came, they stayed and they excelled.

In September the first two arrived — Elizabeth Herndon, a World War II widow, and Diane Michel, a young woman from Houston, Texas. At her graduation four years later, Diane Michel recalled that time:

"At first, it was plenty tough. We definitely weren't accepted like we are now. And the great publicity fuss made over the two of us sure didn't

Tech's first graduate, Henry L. Smith (1890), and other old-timers returned for the 1948 Homecoming. Left to right, front row: Smith, J.B. McCrary (1891); J.A. McCrary (1894); back row: C.J. Kamper (1903) and H.O. Ball (1903).

Julian Hoke "Judy" Harris in 1949 at work on the plaque for the Harrison Hightower Textile Engineering Building. Harris is the only sculptor in the United States to be elected a Fellow in both the American Institute of Architects and the National Sculpture Society. Harris also created the Georgia Tech Thousand Club Medallion and the Centennial Medallion for his alma mater.

In 1949 the Department of Architecture had no place to call its own, so instructor D.J. Edwards gave the students in course 403 the assignment of redesigning a house at 661 Plum St. for classroom use. John Portman Jr., who headed the project, is shown here with Harry Porter and George Phillips.

HOW TO LOWER CEILINGS

Architecture Students At Tech 'Do Over' House

Take an old house with small drab rooms, add 20 Georgia Tech students and 72 hours, and what do you have? Bright, pleasant classrooms for architecture students.

Tech's School of Architecture, unlike other parts of the institution, has no building it can call its own. Classrooms spread over much of the campus, stuck away in old residences taken over by the school.

Friday, the students of architectural course 403 were given an assignment to fix over their house at 661 Plum St., without major structural changes.

They did it. Contributions of materials from several Atlanta businesses helped out. Yesterday afternoon, with a punch bowl on the ...

side showing. No two walls in a room are one color. On one, a pattern was made by using the separating paper from egg crates. In another, an abstract mural shows the approximate size of sitting and standing men and women.

The operation wasn't difficult, the student said, just needed a ...

help. The fear that somehow we might change Tech infected the boys. And although they were never nasty to us, they didn't go out of their way to ease our situation."

Even though the students who attended the "new" Tech were more diverse than ever, there were still rules to be followed, some of them quite old. For example, the rule book stated: "Tardiness in excess of fifteen minutes is counted as an absence," and the definition of "cuts," "excused" and "unexcused" absences were explained in detail. Unexcused absences could affect students'

Receptions were frequently held for students and their families. Here the Van Leers welcome guests at June 1949 graduation time. The student at the far right is L. Travis Brannon Jr., Secretary-Treasurer of the senior class.

When World War II ended, 32 B-29s remained on the assembly line at Bell Bomber Plant in Marietta. One entire plane was given to Tech — which remained in the B-4 Building in Marietta — plus this nose section that was placed on campus. When the Lockheed-Georgia Company moved into the plant in 1951 to recondition B-29s for the Korean War, Tech returned the B-29 to Lockheed. The plane was used as a mock-up to check out harnessing, wiring and hydraulic systems so that when B-29s were flown in from mothball in the West, Lockheed was ready for them.

In 1949 Judge S. Price Gilbert gave Tech $9,000 for library plans, and the following year an additional $11,000. The next year, he donated more than $28,000 for library plans and furniture. On July 5, 1951, Judge Gilbert made his final appearance on the Tech campus — at the ground breaking. On August 28 of that year, the Judge died. In his will he left another $50,000 for the library that bears his name. After his death, his widow (now deceased) and his son continued to support the library. With the Judge is Herman Talmadge, then Governor, and Dorothy Crosland, Director of Libraries.

grades in such a way that their class-standing was in jeopardy. Moreover, students could not come and go as they pleased. The regulation read: "No student will be allowed to leave the city — except to visit suburban places reached by electric cars — unless he has filed with the President or Dean a letter of consent from his parents or guardian."

The "Y" remained the center of extracurricular activities, and "Y camps" were still popular. The "Y" even provided lodging for a few students, and the rooms for photography, study and games were in constant use.

A set of letters kept by a mother as future heritage for grandchildren tracks one student — Houston Welch of Hattiesburg, Mississippi —

Y. Frank Freeman Jr. majored in EE and played baseball for John Heisman. In 1910, while a senior, Tech's EE Department Head, Henry P. Wood, told him: "I am confident you will make a success in life. Not in electrical engineering but in another field. You've made a good record in school. You deserve a diploma. I will certify you a diploma in, heaven forbid, electrical engineering, if you promise never to be one and show the world how wrong I was." Freeman graduated, purchased the telephone company in Ocilla, Ga., then the tiny Amusu Theater in Fitzgerald, Ga. He eventually took a job with Paramount and subsequently became boss of the company's Hollywood studio where he was sometimes referred to as "God." Freeman was the first President of Tech's Alumni Association and received the Alumni Distinguished Service Award in 1939. Freeman Residence Hall is named in his honor.

President Blake Van Leer presents a diploma to William Lloyd Carter, Tech's first student to earn the doctorate, at the June 1950 commencement exercises. Dr. R.L. Sweigert, Dean of the Graduate Division, has just hooded Dr. Carter. Oscar Davis, President of Tech's Alumni Association, is seated to the left.

Van Leer awarding degrees at a ceremony held in Grant Field. Since June 1970 the ceremony has been held in the Alexander Memorial Coliseum at the end of each term.

The Atlanta Weekly ran this feature article on 1927 graduate Carter Barron, who began his career as manager of an East Point neighborhood theater. Barron later managed Atlanta's Fabulous Fox and then moved to Washington, D.C., where he managed the Loew interests. His idea for an amphitheater in Washington reached fruition in 1950 shortly before his death, and in 1951 President Harry S. Truman dedicated this first federal monument named for a showman.

from enrollment in 1954 to graduation in EE in 1957 and provides an illustration of student life. Welch attended "Y camp" as a freshman, had three roommates and was a drummer in the Tech band. That first year, his books, ROTC uniform, drawing equipment and meal tickets came to the grand total of $290.

He took English 102 and was assigned a 400-word theme on his opinion of comic books. We do not know if he approved or disapproved, but one of his next assignments was Orwell's *1984*. Welch and his English professor got into a "heavy" discussion about the Tennessee Valley Authority. Evidently the professor approved of government-sponsored business and Welch did not.

His senior year, money was still on his mind. "I have cut down on my everyday spending a lot," he wrote, "to about $20.00 a week instead of $25.00."

During the 1950's, Tech students were especially fond of dancing to the beat of the "Big Bands" that frequently came to Atlanta. Sometimes these dances were sponsored by the Interfraternity Council; sometimes students visited neighboring schools. And always there were parties and dances traditional to various fraternities — the Kappa Alpha Old South Ball, for example, and the Fiji

A woman in class was something of a
novelty in the early 1950's.

The Y.M.C.A. World Student Fund
(WSF), one of Tech's unique
contributions to international
understanding, began in 1949. Students
raised money to bring to Tech Max
Bächer from Stuttgart, West Germany,
and Juhani Waris from Finland. Arthur
Franklin Beckum Jr., a graduate student
in architecture, became the first of 157
Tech students to receive appointments as
WSF Scholars abroad. Beckum,
incidentally, returned from Stuttgart to
join the faculty of the School of
Architecture, where he continues to
teach.

Leadership of the program has always
rested primarily with Tech students,
whose fund drives are as unique as the
group itself. Each fall, during the halftime
of one football game, six minutes are
allotted to WSF for solicitation. Student
volunteers swarm over the Grant Field
stands and pass their cups down the rows.
During 1984-85, 11 Tech WSF Scholars
were in three countries and 19 scholars
from abroad studied at Tech. An
experiment has become a tradition.

In 1945, soon after the veterans started returning as students, a small black-and-white dog appeared on campus. Because of an accident, she walked with a list and acquired the name "Sideways." According to one account, she had once resided in a house on the corner of North Avenue and Williams Street. When it was torn down and the owner and Sideways moved away, she became homesick. Her owner persuaded students to adopt her, and she spent the rest of her days visiting classes and labs and running around campus with her peculiar gait.

Georgia Tech Thousand Club Medallion.

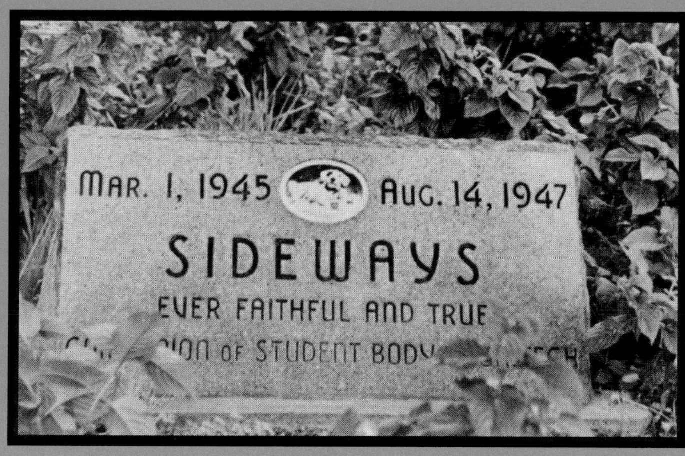

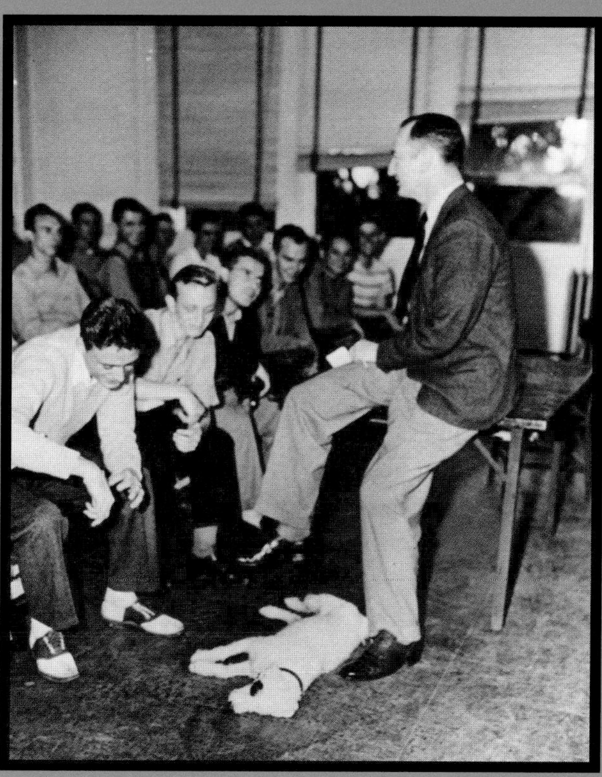

On November 24, 1952, Marine Lieutenant Colonel Raymond G. Davis was awarded the Medal of Honor, the nation's highest award. President Truman presented the award at the White House ceremony while the family of Colonel Davis looked on. The medal was awarded for Davis' heroism in leading his battalion in a four-day attack at a vital mountain pass in Korea. Davis was the third Tech man to receive the Medal of Honor. (The previous two were General Leonard Wood and Major Thomas B. McGuire Jr.)

party for Phi Gamma Delta. There were also special social traditions at Tech. For several years the co-op students sponsored a "Miss Perfect Lips Dance." At first formal, it gradually became more relaxed, especially since it was sometimes held in the hot summer months.

Stan Kenton played in the Alexander Memorial Coliseum and the crowd set a new indoor attendance record for the state. Louis Armstrong visited the University of Georgia in the spring of 1957, and a large number of Tech students and their dates went over to hear him.

A student writing about his social activities reported that he and his date went to hear Mantovani and his orchestra. "It was," he said, "a grand concert." Afterward they drove to the Plantation House for "supper." The following weekend they attended a Les Elgart dance in Conyers and the next weekend, the Navy Ball. That weekend they also went ice skating with a group from the North Avenue Presbyterian Church.

Another student of the 1950's, Jerry Comer, remembers his years at Tech as hard work and hard play. He feels that too many people today think of college students in the 1950's as apathetic, non-involved and materialistic. "It is true that the students of the fifties did not drop out," Comer says, "and they did not have riots for great noble causes. But there was a great pride in America, in American culture, and especially in Georgia Tech." He remembers that the "Y" was the center of student activities and that religious organizations on campus were especially important in student affairs.

During the 1950's the *Technique* prospered under a series of vigorous editors. However, *The Yellow Jacket,* Tech's humor magazine, ended its long and checkered history on a dramatic note in 1955. That year *The Yellow Jacket* published a highly controversial parody that included unflattering comments about Dean Griffin's secretary. The Dean, who had often been the publication's only champion in the past, had had enough. *The Yellow Jacket* was published no more. The *Technique* reported in its June 3 edition: "The Georgia Tech YELLOW JACKET, the orphan child of the publications family passed away quietly Tuesday morning at 11 o'clock, May 31, 1955.

In the fall of 1950 Tech was still an all-male school. Enrollment was increasing and the lines at registration didn't just seem longer each year — they were.

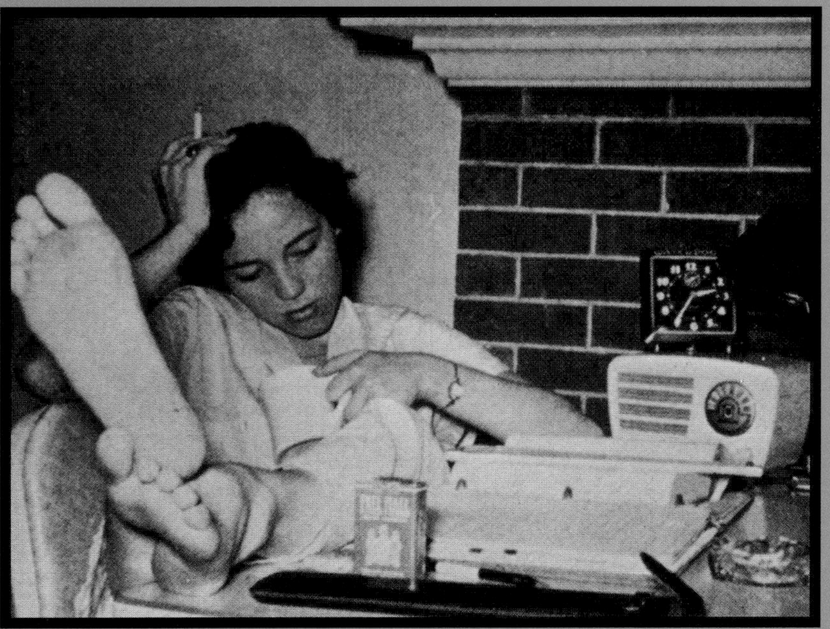

Shirley Clements, one of Tech's early "coeds," found she needed the usual student "helpers": a slide rule, a radio, a clock, coffee and cigarettes to help with late-night studying.

In the 1950's all freshmen celebrated Homecoming by rallying around a bonfire the night before the game. The only way freshmen were permitted to remove the required rat caps was for Tech to beat Georgia.

After 46 years of ill health — sometimes on the brink of death — the YELLOW JACKET was laid to rest by the Faculty Senate."

There were other publications: *The Georgia Tech Engineer*, an essay periodical for student work, and *The Rambler*, a feature magazine that reflected student life and opinions, and included some humor.

In the 1950's, on crisp fall Saturday afternoons, Atlanta was jammed with fans who came to cheer the white and gold. Those who could not get tickets had to settle for radio coverage on WGST or wait until the Thanksgiving Day game between the Tech-Georgia freshmen. Even the freshman game drew tens of thousands. Bobby Dodd, whose first season in 1945 was an uninspiring 4-6-0 record, had gradually built a program that was the envy of the nation. From 1951 to 1956, the Yellow Jackets won six straight major bowl games. (Dodd had two assistant coaches during those six years who later went on to football fame in their own right — Frank Broyles and Ray Graves.) Fans held Dodd in such high esteem that a common saying of the period was, "In Dodd We Trust."

However, for one bowl game the Jackets needed all the Dodd luck they could get. In 1955 the team had completed a highly successful season and

Tech halfback Bill Teas scoring the winning touchdown against Duke at Grant Field in 1953. With Duke leading 10-6 (note scoreboard) and about four minutes left to play, Teas took a punt on the Blue Devils' 48-yard line and returned it, with the help of great blocking, for the score. Other Tech men in the picture are end Henry Hair (No. 55), quarterback Pepper Rodgers (No. 29), tackle Ben Daugherty (No. 67), halfback Leon Hardeman (No. 11, behind official) and guard Jake Shoemaker (No. 53, on ground after throwing a block near the goal line). Georgia Tech won 13-10.

In 1952 Georgia Tech placed six players on the All-America first team. Left to right: standing — end Buck Martin, linebacker George Morris, off-tackle Hal Miller; kneeling — halfback Leon Hardeman, center Peter Brown and defensive halfback Bobby Moorhead. George Morris has an extra honor: Bobby Dodd has often said Morris was the best player he ever coached.

agreed to meet Pittsburgh in the Sugar Bowl. Pitt, however, had a black player — a back named Bobby Grier. "As soon as the Sugar Bowl officials contacted me," Dodd recalls, "I knew the red necks and bigots would jump all over me if I accepted a bid to play a team with a black. I talked with President Van Leer, who told me he would back me to the hilt, and with Governor Marvin Griffin, who said he would support me too, but not publicly because of political pressure." As it turned out, the Citizens' Council of Augusta heard about the contract and contacted the Governor, who requested the Board of Regents not to permit Tech "to engage in contests with other teams where the races are mixed...."

The Governor's request was news from coast to coast, as was the student response. That night Tech students marched on the state capitol,

The Third Street tunnel was built to give students access to the Varsity and Spring Street after Interstate 75 was built.

Cecil Jesse "Pete" Silas, an outstanding center and All-SEC (1953), is in Tech's Hall of Fame. Silas is President and Chief Executive Officer of Phillip's Petroleum Inc. and, in 1985, was awarded the Georgia Tech Alumni Exceptional Achievement Award.

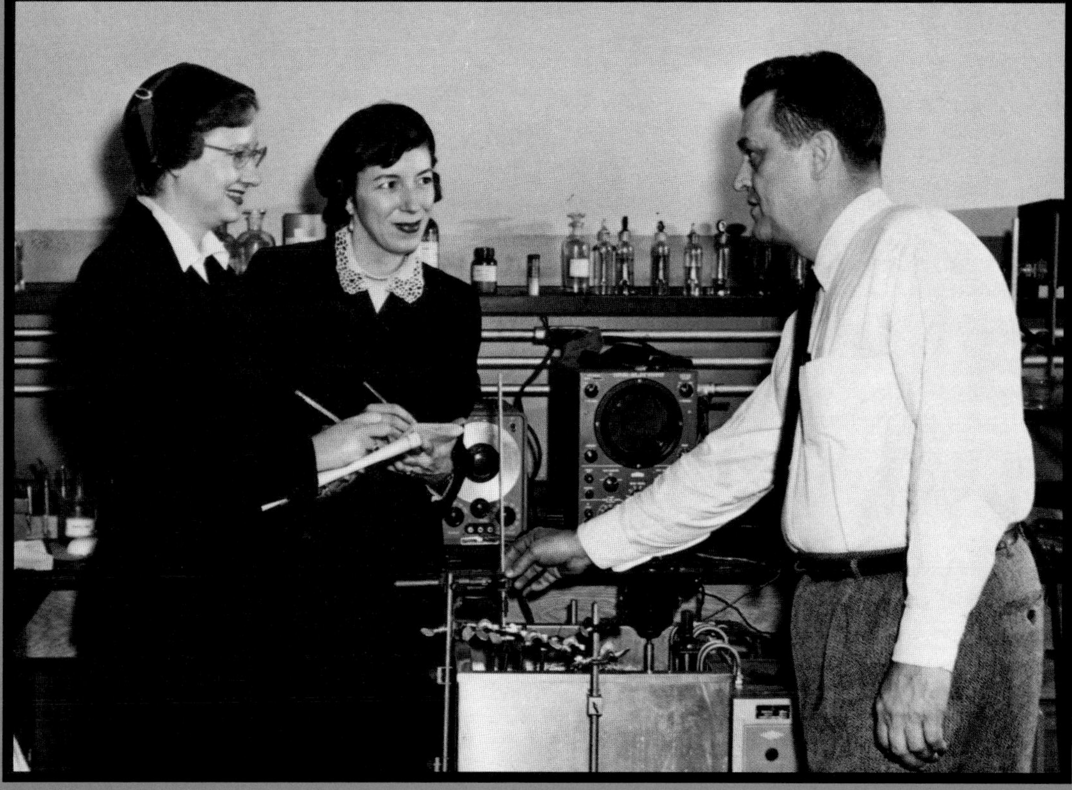

Dr. Paul K. Calaway, Acting Director of the Engineering Experiment Station (now GTRI) in 1954, demonstrates a constant temperature bath in the chemistry laboratory to the science writers of the Atlanta newspapers. Left to right: Miss Edwina Davis (*The Atlanta Journal*) and Miss Katherine Barnwell (*The Atlanta Constitution*).

The Rich family, owners of the famed Atlanta department store, contributed to the Computer Center, which opened in 1956. The "s" was later dropped and the building, now known as the Rich Electronic Computer Center, has been modified and expanded.

hanged the Governor in effigy and then turned toward the Governor's Mansion. They carried placards, hooted and sang at the Mansion, then disbanded.

When the Regents met to thrash out the issue, President Van Leer stated that he would resign if Tech broke its contract with the Sugar Bowl. Finally, after long debate, Tech was permitted to play and the Regents said that future contests played outside the state would abide by the laws and customs of the host state. However, strict segregation would be the rule for all games played in Georgia.

So, it was settled. Van Leer stood firm, the game was played and Tech won 7-0. The Governor subsequently recommended that three Tech students arrested during the demonstration be released.

The *Technique,* which earlier had supported segregation, now advocated change. "One Negro in the middle of many white players did not compromise integrity," readers were told. When desegregation came to the Institute five years later, and three black students enrolled peacefully, the Sugar Bowl incident was remembered by many as an event that helped make the transition smoother.

Meanwhile basketball was growing in importance. For years the sport languished, drawing small crowds and little publicity. A turning point occurred in 1951 when Dodd hired John "Whack" Hyder as basketball coach, but it was not until

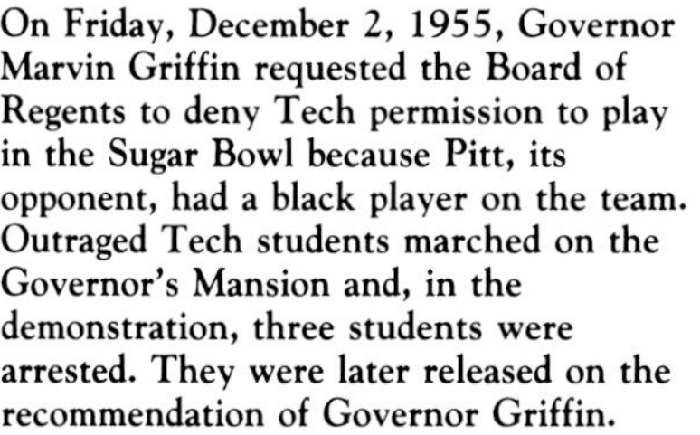

On Friday, December 2, 1955, Governor Marvin Griffin requested the Board of Regents to deny Tech permission to play in the Sugar Bowl because Pitt, its opponent, had a black player on the team. Outraged Tech students marched on the Governor's Mansion and, in the demonstration, three students were arrested. They were later released on the recommendation of Governor Griffin.

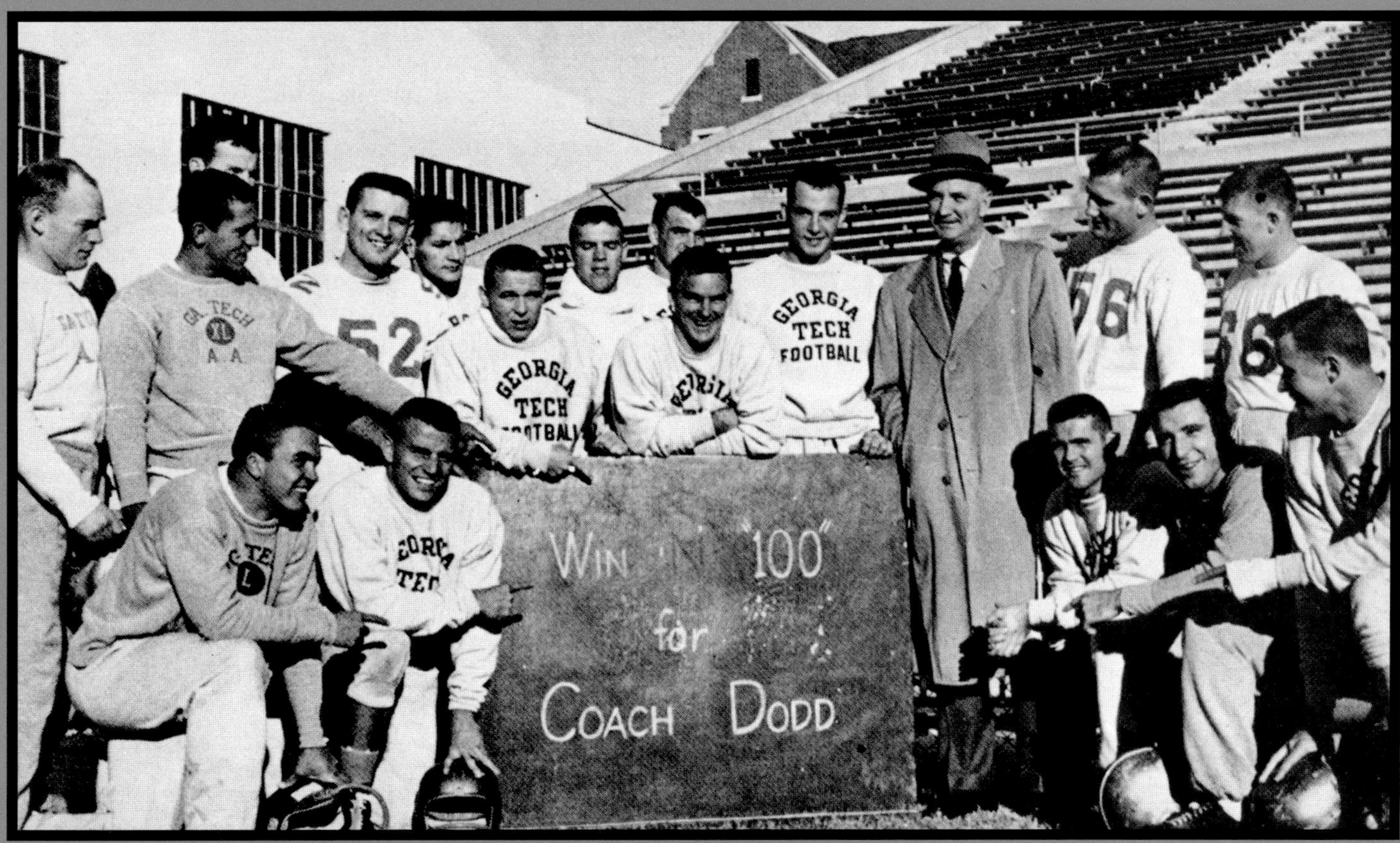

Two milestones were reached in 1956: A Dodd-coached team won its 100th game, and Tech won its sixth straight major bowl game. Bear Bryant equaled that record with a streak that began in 1975, but no coach has ever bettered it. Coach Dodd was asked to recall those victories for *The New York Times* in 1984, (Dec. 30, p. 2S) from which the following excerpts are taken:

"The streak began in 1951. I had a strong crop of young players and a new coaching staff. Two of my assistant coaches later went on to bigger things — Frank Broyles and Ray Graves — but they stayed with me through the entire six years. In 1951 we were undefeated, with one tie, and we played a strong Baylor team in the Orange Bowl. We trailed most of the game, but in the closing seconds of the game, Pepper Rodgers kicked a field goal that enabled us to win, 17-14.

In 1952 we had essentially the same team and went untied and undefeated. At year's end The Associated Press ranked us No. 2, some lists ranked us No. 1, and we drew a powerful Ole Miss team as our opponent in the Sugar Bowl. Ole Miss started out strong. But we got stronger as the game went along and we finally beat them 24-7.

In 1953 we were invited back to the Sugar Bowl to play West Virginia. We just had the stronger team, and we won handily, 42-19.

In 1954 the Yellow Jackets were strong again, and at the end of the season we received a bid to play Arkansas, champion of the Southwest Conference, in the Cotton Bowl. The Arkansas coach, Bowden Wyatt, had the same coaching philosophy I did, so it turned out to be a hard-fought defensive battle. We finally prevailed, 14-6.

In 1955, we had a terrific team and were invited to play a tough Pitt squad in the Sugar Bowl. This was a special game for the South because we broke a racial barrier. One of Pitt's backs was a black player named Bobby Grier. The Regents finally gave us permission to go to New Orleans — Colonel Van Leer threatened to resign if they didn't — and we won 7-0. Grier played throughout the game.

We had another good year in 1956 and lost only one game. Pitt hadn't been satisfied about the outcome of the previous Sugar Bowl and was hankering for revenge. We seemed not to have convinced them we had the better team. I hated to tangle with Pitt again because I knew they were tough, but I wanted to help the Gator Bowl and finally agreed. It was another battle royal, and we won again 21-14."

When the Coliseum was first conceived, Coach Alexander said it would be "the most glorious field house ever built." But funds were short and 15 years after plans were announced, construction began on a scaled-down version. The Coliseum is named in honor of the coach who dreamed of it.

Friday, January 7, 1955, that the results of Hyder's uphill battle were clearly evident. That evening Tech ended first-ranked Kentucky's incredible record of 129 consecutive wins on their home court. At the half, Hyder's Jackets were down 26-23, but at the final buzzer the scoreboard read Tech 59, Kentucky 58. From that day forward, Hyder became known as the "Adolph Rupp killer." In 22 seasons at Tech he beat Rupp-coached teams more frequently than any coach and, overall, logged a 292-271 record.

Hyder is proudest of another accomplishment: during his tenure as coach more than 80 percent of his players received their degrees.

It was during Hyder's tenure and Van Leer's presidency that Tech finally moved its basketball program into the Coliseum. The idea of a multi-purpose house for concerts, assemblies and sports had been introduced by Coach Alexander in the 1940's.

As originally conceived, the Coliseum was to have been a magnificent creation — "the most glorious field house ever built," Alexander said of the original plans. And it would be expensive, very expensive. Therein lay the problem. Alexander, who died in 1950, never saw the building he dreamed about. That may be just as well, because financial realities gradually and inexorably narrowed the vision and many of the facilities in the original concept were dropped. On April 23, 1955, the fifth anniversary of Coach Alexander's death, Van Leer announced that the contract had finally been signed. Eighteen months later, the 7,000-seat Alexander Memorial Coliseum was completed at a cost of $1.5 million.

By 1956, Van Leer's last year at Tech, much had been accomplished. Housing had been provided for veterans and their families, the campus was larger and three major buildings were in place — Textile Engineering, Architecture and the Price Gilbert Memorial Library. Tech had kept its Sugar Bowl commitment. The Technical Institute, now known as Southern Technical Institute, was a reality with almost 700 students enrolled. Women were enrolled as full-time, on-campus students. The school's official name was now the Georgia Institute of Technology, a name better known and more highly respected than ever.

On the afternoon of January 23, 1956, Colonel Van Leer suffered a massive heart attack and died with his wife at his bedside. The entire Institute was shocked and grieved by his death.

Section Five
The Changed World of Tech: 1956-1969

On the afternoon of January 23, 1956, President Van Leer, then in his 11th year as head of Tech and in declining health, suffered a massive heart attack and died almost immediately. At his funeral students and friends stood together to mourn their loss. Like President Brittain before him, Van Leer had totally committed himself to the administration of Tech. Dr. Paul Weber, who only a few days earlier had been named Dean of Faculties, was appointed Acting President, a post he held for the next 18 months.

Weber, who had come to Tech as a chemistry instructor in 1927, was a good administrator who attended to details and had a reputation for working at tasks until they were completed. He also had a sure sense of what Tech needed. In his report to the Board of Regents, Weber emphasized the need to raise salaries in order to keep and recruit high-quality faculty members. The response was positive. The Board of Regents added $300,000 to Tech's operational budget, and that same year the Georgia Tech Foundation began a salary supplementation program for faculty that has continued to the present.

In June 1957, the search committee selected Dr. Edwin D. Harrison, Dean of Engineering at the University of Toledo (Ohio), as Tech's sixth President. Two months later he assumed presidential duties on the hill, and Paul Weber returned to the post he said he preferred — Tech's Dean of Faculties.

Harrison was born in 1916 in Evadale, Arkansas, received a B.S. degree from the United States Naval Academy in 1939, and served in the Navy through 1945, rising to the rank of lieutenant commander. Both his graduate degrees were in mechanical engineering — an M.S. from Virginia Polytechnic Institute in 1948 and a Ph.D. from Purdue University in 1952.

Eisenhower was still President when the Harrisons arrived in Atlanta. Vietnam was a small dark thundercloud in Southeast Asia, Tech students were largely concerned with getting a degree, and college life typically was viewed as a time to study hard for predictable careers in a predictable world, go to football games, Agnes Scott and movies at the Fox. Administrators enforced rigid regulations

Dr. Edwin D. Harrison, President of
Tech from 1957 to 1969, presided over
"the biggest building boom" in the
Institute's history.

from the Van Leer period; classes met on Saturdays and attendance was checked. Even though students no longer had to sign out to leave campus, as the regulations of 1940 had required, the Dean of Students had disciplinary powers he was not loath to use.

However, not many months passed before the civil rights movement reached full tide, the space age began and the storm in Vietnam became a full-blown gale. Flower children burst into bloom and, in Atlanta, hippies and runaways camped along Peachtree and 10th. Campuses across the nation were convulsed by anti-war and student-power demonstrations, and at many universities the president had less job security than the football coach. Seemingly nothing about the quiet and steady days of the Eisenhower years foretold the explosion that occurred in the 1960's.

What happened on North Avenue was more evolutionary than revolutionary, occurring largely without confrontations or violence. But by the end of the sixties, substantial changes were

In the late 1940's and 1950's, fans were treated to halftime performances by a Yellow Jacket mascot that performed aerial acrobatics. Here, Billy Millar and companion make a last-minute adjustment. "During four football seasons, we never failed to get a model Yellow Jacket airborne to both thunderous applause and drowning jeers," remembers Stuart L. Richmond, a pilot from 1948 to 1952.

This photograph was taken before the
Student Center, the Fuller E. Callaway
III Student Athletic Complex and the
west campus were built.

evident in many areas: new buildings dotted the campus, the student body was desegregated, the curriculum was larger and more diverse, graduate study was a new priority, the push was on for funded research and, in intercollegiate sports, Tech was an independent.

One of the most obvious changes was in the campus itself. Harrison presided over the biggest building boom in the school's history, which culminated earlier efforts and continued throughout his presidency. During Harrison's tenure these buildings were begun or completed: the new classroom building (Skiles), the Electrical Engineering Building (Van Leer), Southern Technical Institute's new campus in Marietta, five new dormitories, the new infirmary, the Chemical Engineering/Ceramic Engineering Building (Bunger-Henry), the Student Center — begun in 1967 and dedicated in 1970, the Radioisotopes and Bioengineering Laboratory, the Neely Nuclear Research Center, the Electronics Research Building and the Baker Building.

The student body changed. For years Georgia Tech had attracted many students from other states and, in this sense, was already more heterogeneous than most state universities in the South. But during the Harrison years the school became even more diverse. Increasing numbers of women came to Tech and enrolled in courses leading to fields once regarded as exclusive male domains. Graduate students also began to make their presence felt, especially in the classrooms and labs where they often served as instructors and assistants.

Until 1961 blacks were not part of Tech's student body because of legal barriers and social norms. However, by the end of the Eisenhower administration, legal barriers had begun to fall. A full-scale assault was launched — law suits, boycotts, sit-ins, the Freedom Rides and marches — and one by one the bastions of segregation crumbled. College campuses were the sites of many confrontations, some ugly and dangerous. One such incident occurred in 1961 in Athens just after a Tech-Georgia basketball game. Demonstrators gathered in front of the dormitory of Charlayne Hunter, the first black woman to attend any formerly all-white school in the University System.

Jim Heard and his wife, Mary, were familiar figures on the Tech campus for years, but few knew their last name. He was known as "Apple Jim" and she as "Apple Mary." They had a white and tan dog that students called "Apple Joe." The Apple era spanned three decades, from the early days of President Brittain to the 1950's.

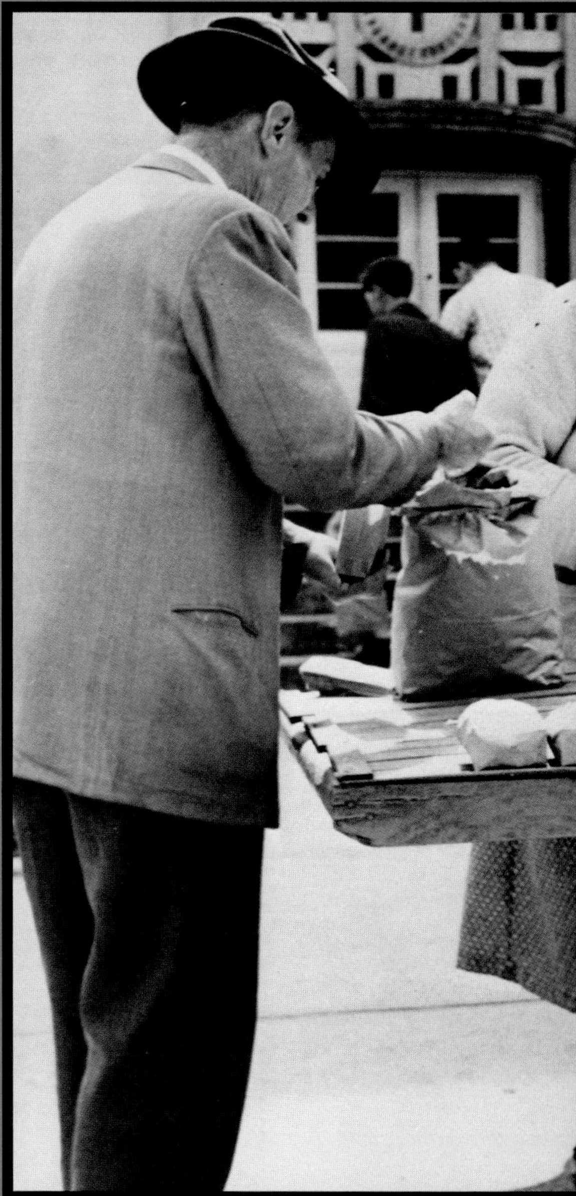

At graduation in June 1956, Barbara Diane Michel and Shirley V. Clements became the first women to receive degrees from Georgia Tech since the early days of the century when women attended the School of Commerce. Acting President Paul Weber is shown here congratulating Michel.

In the 1950's rat caps were worn everywhere, not just to football games. Freshmen who failed to produce the cap on demand were given "T" cuts. One such infraction seems to have taken place.

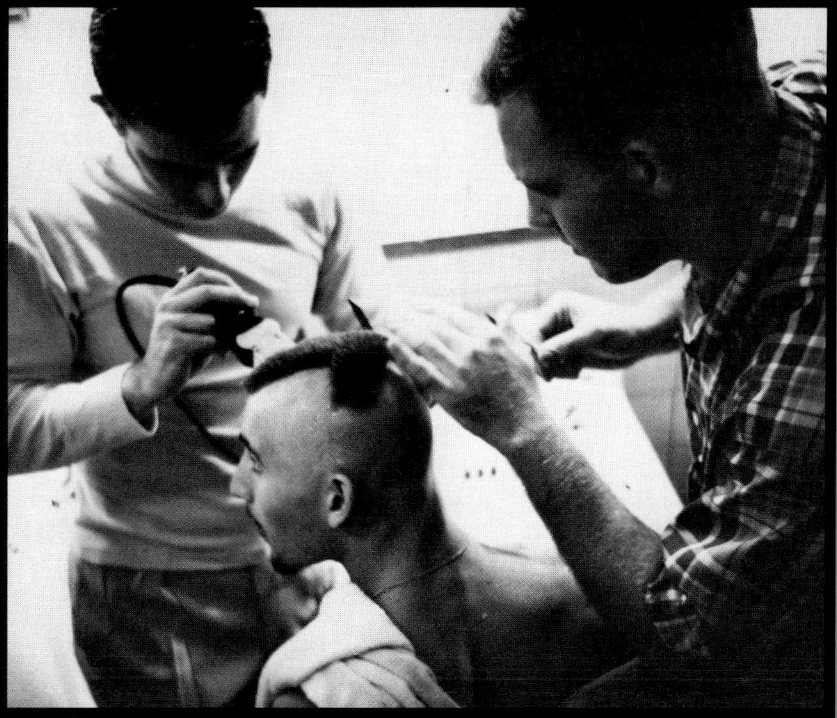

Robert B. "Bob" Wallace Jr., a 1949 IM Tech graduate and highly decorated bombardier-navigator-radio operator during World War II. Wallace returned to Tech in 1952 as editor of the *Georgia Tech Alumnus.* In 1955 he was named Publicity Director. As part of Tech's 75th Anniversary, Wallace wrote *Dress Her In White And Gold.* Here he listens to Anita Wall, who has just been elected the 1956 Homecoming Queen.

"I was there and almost got mobbed," Ray Moore, then News Director with WSB-TV and now Director of Tech's Research Communications Office, remembers. "Tear gas saved me. The demonstration was anticipated — regardless of the outcome of the game. Many non-students as well as students were there."

The next week President Harrison, in a meeting with Tech students, fielded questions about Tech's policy on demonstrations. His reply: "Georgia Tech does not condone or permit participation in such disturbances likely to become riots. Any participation in such disturbances will be grounds for immediate dismissal."

Harrison then asked how many students would openly resist desegregation. About 30 students raised their hands.

Later in the year, three black students — Ford Greene, Ralph Long Jr. and Lawrence Williams — were accepted for fall admission. And on September 18 the three went together to the infirmary for the required freshman physicals. The examining physician sent them "straight down the hall to x-ray" as he had done all morning with other freshmen. On September 27, 1961, they began classes without incident and Tech became the first major state university in the Deep South to desegregate peacefully without court order.

Television crews had been forbidden to come on campus, but they gathered across from the Armory on Third Street. Deloye Burrell, then a

At the 1956 Homecoming, Sam Nunn won the cake race and was awarded a kiss from Anita Wall, Homecoming Queen.

Double parking under The Varsity night lights was a favorite sport for Tech men in the late 1950's.

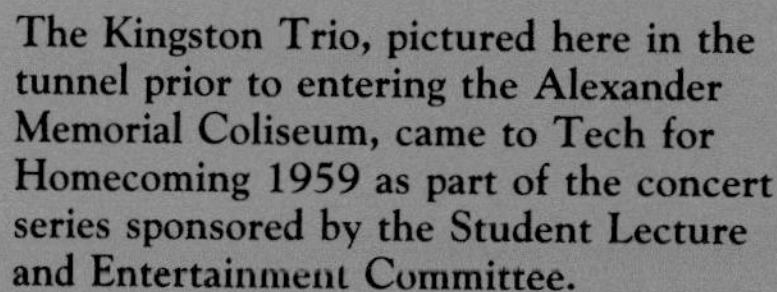

The Kingston Trio, pictured here in the tunnel prior to entering the Alexander Memorial Coliseum, came to Tech for Homecoming 1959 as part of the concert series sponsored by the Student Lecture and Entertainment Committee.

Anak tapping is always a special occasion.
This tapping was in 1959; the new
members are being escorted by their
sponsors, who are dressed in academic
robes.

freshman and later sports editor and photographer
for the *Technique,* remembers television crews asking students to do something dramatic. Burrell and
his buddies responded, "Hi, Mom." Predictably,
they did not appear on the evening news.

The space age began during Harrison's administration and Tech became a leading player in that
drama, partly because of its programs in science
and technology and more specifically because of its
well-known program in Aerospace Engineering.
Ruth Hale, Tech librarian, remembers the mood
on campus during those years:

"The Russian launching of Sputnik caught the
general public by surprise, and there was a feeling
of hurry-up so we wouldn't forever be in second
place. JFK promised that within a decade we
would put a man on the moon and return him
safely, and it became a matter of national pride
that we do so.

"I felt a general sense of enthusiasm throughout
the Institute....We were the closest large scientific and engineering library to Cape Canaveral,
and their library relied on ours heavily for books
and journal articles. When Grissom, White and

Dave "Duke" Denton (No. 41), a native
of Kentucky, played some of his greatest
games against the University of
Kentucky. He was All-SEC and
Honorable Mention All-America in
1959-60.

This creation was put together by Pi
Kappa Alpha.

For many years, Georgia Tech's
Y.M.C.A.-sponsored Freshman Camp was
the largest in the nation. Upperclassmen
and faculty counselors explained Tech
life, and freshmen "got the word" on
Tech professors.

Chaffee burned to death on the launching pad in 1967, the NASA librarian discussed sending a plane to pick up several large boxes of books in their anxiety to determine the cause of the accident. They did not, in fact, send the plane but we supplied them with large numbers of usually non-circulating materials, no questions asked, because we felt such a stake in the space program."

Partly because of the space race, with its emphasis on innovation, and partly because of general trends already underway in science and technology, noticeable changes began to occur in Tech's classrooms and labs. Formerly, Tech students spent long hours in the foundry, machine shop and wood shop, but gradually these requirements were modified or dropped. Now, a solid foundation in the fundamentals of science and mathematics was emphasized. Tech's goal, Harrison said in his first presidential report, was to produce a "new type of engineer and scientist, one able to adapt himself readily to new concepts and new fields as they are developed, yet possessed of enough so-called 'practical' knowledge that, with a reasonable period of orientation, he is able to serve capably at the operating level." Consistent with that view, the Harrison administration supported the humanities and social sciences and implemented new interdisciplinary approaches to traditional academic problems.

Fred Berman and Carl Vereen were two
of the best weight men in Tech track
history, and both are in Tech's Hall of
Fame. Berman has continued his
association with Tech in another way —
as a part-time instructor in Tech's
College of Management.

James Marion McAvoy Jr. earned an M.S.
in Aerospace Engineering for his research
in 1963 on this human-powered aircraft.
McAvoy, with his back to the camera, is
making last-minute adjustments to the
120-pound plane — its wingspan was 54
feet — while pilot Dewey Ransom
prepares for takeoff. Ransom got it off
the ground briefly, but a downdraft
crumpled the plane's wings.

Coach "Marse Joe" Pittard is pictured with Doug Veazy, who was also starting quarterback in football. From 1946 to 1961, Pittard compiled a 169-170-7 record.

Tech also began to raise its entrance requirements so that students admitted would have a good chance of graduating. By the early 1960's, a high school graduate needed one unit each of chemistry and physics, four units of English, plus trigonometry, algebra and plane geometry to gain admittance. And increasingly more of Tech's courses were graduate-level. Although Tech had started relatively late, by 1969-70 the Institute offered the M.S. in 27 fields and the Ph.D. in 13 fields.

The Engineering Experiment Station underwent considerable expansion and diversification, growing to almost 500 research projects annually by the end of the decade. Electronics research continued to be a major emphasis, with work mainly in communications and radar. In 1959 EES erected the Radioisotopes and Bioengineering Laboratory, and the next year the Legislature broadened the Station's charter, authorizing it to develop a statewide industrial extension service. Its first field office opened in 1961 in Rome, Georgia, and by the end of the decade the number of field offices had grown to seven (12 in 1985).

Coach Earle Bortell and Edgar A. "Ned" Neely. Bortell, tennis coach from 1934 to 1961, compiled a 215-107-2 record. The Tech Tennis Center is named for him. Neely, captain of the 1960 squad, is one of four All-Americas in Tech tennis history.

Roger Kaiser, an All-America in 1960
and 1961, was also an outstanding
member of the Tech baseball team. After
graduating from Tech, Kaiser became
nationally known as a basketball coach,
directing West Georgia College to the
NAIA Championship in 1973-74.

Tech's first woman teacher, Dr. Mary Katherine Cabell, began teaching in the School of Mathematics in 1960. On the left is Marvin B. Sledd, Director.

Many of the academic departments were starting new programs or adapting to new and growing fields of knowledge. For example, Industrial Engineering became Industrial and Systems Engineering, Chemistry revised its curriculum to compete successfully for NSF equipment grants and Electrical Engineering became heavily involved in microwave research.

These and many other developments created funding demands for which traditional sources of state and federal support proved inadequate. So, again, Tech turned to loyal alumni and friends for help. This time the campaigns were led by Joe Guthridge, who had come to Tech from VPI and headed the placement system from 1958 to 1960, and who subsequently became Vice President, Development and Public Relations.

Students themselves were changing, not just in the way they looked and partied — that was obvious — but in what they thought and felt. "When I came to Atlanta," Lance Ozier, who attended Tech from 1967 to 1971, recalls, "Lester Maddox was Governor of Georgia. Four years later, Governor Jimmy Carter was the speaker at my commencement. In between, Martin Luther King and Bobby Kennedy were assassinated; Neil

Students gathered in the gym for a meeting with President Harrison before campus desegregation. "I told them if they didn't behave, they couldn't stay in school," Harrison recalls.

Elaborate preparations preceded the September 1961 entrance of Tech's first black students: Ford Greene, Ralph A. Long Jr. and Lawrence Michael Williams, three friends from Atlanta. In 1985, Greene was a computer specialist with IBM in Baltimore, Long was in data processing with AT&T in Atlanta and Williams was employed by Atlanta's WAGA-TV in master control, air operations.

The 1930 Ford Model A cabriolet sport coupe became the official Ramblin' Wreck of Georgia Tech in 1961. Not only in the song but in the minds of Tech students everywhere, it visually represents the school. It leads the Ramblin' Wreck parade each year at Homecoming and at each football game it leads the team onto the field. For significant campus events it is the official car and VIP's occupy its rumble seat.

The Ramblin' Wreck Club cares for the "Wreck," taking it in a van to all the "away" games and electing an official driver each year. Lisa Volmar, driver for 1984-85, has the distinction of being the first woman to occupy the coveted position.

The "Wreck" has an interesting history. Captain Ted Johnson, Chief Pilot, Delta Air Lines, bought the "sorry rusty mess" in 1956 and with his son, Craig, spent more than $1,800 and two years restoring it to its original splendor. He found original parts in junkyards

and other spots throughout the country. The mahogany in the top framework he brought from Caracas, Venezuela; welded steel served as flooring in the rumble seat; and honeycomb aluminum flooring from a discarded Convair 440 aircraft replaced other flooring.

When son Craig, a student at Florida State University, ran in a track meet at Tech, Dean James E. Dull saw the car and left a note for the owner to call him. Captain Johnson was reluctant to part with the car; but after much pleading, he relented, selling his prize for $1,000. In 1984 he returned the money to the Alexander-Tharpe Fund, and a plaque on the dashboard lists him and his son as sole contributors of the little car.

Earlier cars had been rambling wrecks, with the most famous the 1914 Ford of Mathematics Professor Floyd Field, Dean of Men. The *Technique* for September 28, 1928, duly noted its passing. The Ramblin' Wreck Parade began four years later in 1932.

The Campus Police in 1961. (In 1985 there were 52 employees in the department, including 35 sworn officers.) Captain Melvin Coppenger is remembered as a friend to students.

Dr. Homer S. Weber, Director of the School of Mechanical Engineering from 1946-62. In the insert, Dr. Weber (right) is standing at the sundial with Joe Davis Brown.

Dr. Demetrius T. Paris, one of the early doctoral candidates in Tech's electrical engineering program, is shown shortly after earning his degree in 1962. Paris has served as Director of the School of Electrical Engineering since August 1969.

In the late 1950's and early 1960's, the "Robbery" was the place for a "Coke" and conversation — conversation frequently about profs, quizzes and the GPA problems of Tech.

Mary Nell (Ivey) Santacroce giving directions at a Drama Tech play rehearsal. First called the Engineer's Theater, the group was officially named Drama Tech in 1946. "Mary Nell Santacroce is to Drama Tech what Bobby Dodd is to the Yellow Jackets," Terry Kay wrote in *The Atlanta Journal* in 1965. "She is the unquestioned leader, the catalyst that turns common drama into a living experience, both for her players and those played to."

Drama Tech performed classical plays as well as modern drama. "We did *Oedipus Rex* to appease the English faculty," Santacroce recalls. "They had been upset by some of the plays we were producing...so I agreed to do it but on condition that the faculty take parts in the chorus. They agreed, although one of them took a tranquilizer before every performance."

In the last game coached by Bobby Dodd, the 1967 Orange Bowl, left-handed Kim King (no. 18) passes to Lenny Snow (no. 41).

Armstrong walked on the moon; the Vietnam War became widely unpopular; and students were killed at Kent State University."

Ozier, who edited *Erato*, Tech's literary magazine, remembers the impact of these events. "In the beginning, it seemed to me that at Tech the prevailing attitude toward anything happening off-campus was to ignore it. The faculty never let up on the homework....In the spring of 1968, we had to cut classes to march in Martin Luther King's funeral procession from Ebenezer Baptist Church to Morehouse College. But inevitably the tide of massive societal changes managed to seep into campus life and eventually the outside world could not be ignored."

Rush S. Smith Jr., now an Atlanta attorney, was a World Student Fund exchange student who lived in Stuttgart, West Germany, during the 1969-70 academic year. He writes: "I left Tech, which had just participated in a rally entitled 'Affirmation Vietnam' that was supportive of our presence in Vietnam. Upon my arrival in West Germany, newspapers told the stories of U.S.

This cover of a special issue of *The Atlanta Journal and Constitution Magazine* marked Georgia Tech's 75th Anniversary. The celebration began on May 17, 1962, with a convocation at which President Harrison spoke on "Scientific and Technological Education: Our Nation's Strength."

Chief Justice Earl Warren was one of the speakers invited to Tech's campus as part of the Institute's 75th Anniversary events.

Dean Griffin's picture wall tells of his long involvement with Tech.

embassies being mobbed. German students were in the street, all in violent protest of that same U.S. involvement that had been sanctioned in Atlanta. Needless to say, it led to some interesting political discussions over a few beers."

Even though the political winds changed at Tech, the thrust of change was reformist, not revolutionary. "The way the sixties touched Tech was in community-based idealism — not counter-culture and not violent anti-war protest," says Dr. Robert McMath, Tech historian.

It was the time of the "we" generation. Tech faculty and students got involved in a number of projects that formed connections between Tech and the people of Atlanta. Members of the English Department coordinated a community fair in the Bass community and developed a series of seminars on the humanities for the Atlanta Police Academy. The Techwood Tutorial, developed by Harwood "Woody" Bartlett, an honor graduate at Georgia Tech and at that time the Episcopal chaplain at Tech and Agnes Scott, brought

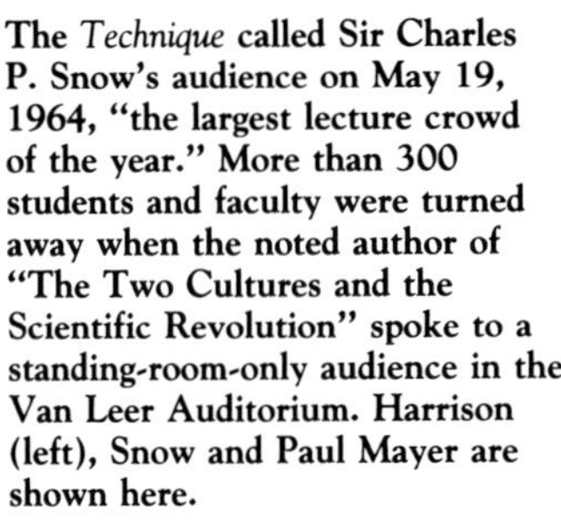

The *Technique* called Sir Charles P. Snow's audience on May 19, 1964, "the largest lecture crowd of the year." More than 300 students and faculty were turned away when the noted author of "The Two Cultures and the Scientific Revolution" spoke to a standing-room-only audience in the Van Leer Auditorium. Harrison (left), Snow and Paul Mayer are shown here.

William Johnson "Johnny" Gresham Jr. was a halfback on Tech's 1962, 1963 and 1964 teams. After graduating, he became a realtor and developer in the Atlanta area.

Douglas L. "Buddy" Fowlkes, a 1952 IM graduate, set the world record in the 100-yard dash for 34-year-olds in 1962 (9.5 seconds), a tenth of a second faster than he ran it as a student more than a decade earlier. Fowlkes has been Tech's track coach since 1964. During his tenure at Tech he has coached 13 All-Americas. Fowlkes also has been on Atlanta's City Council since 1961.

A feature in the 1963-64 student spoof, the *Techlique*, showed a student crucified on a slide rule in a parody of William Jennings Bryan's "Cross of Gold" speech. Unfortunately for Editor Guinn O. Leverett Jr. and his colleagues, the administration was not amused. Leverett was relieved as editor of the *Technique*, and his colleagues were reprimanded.

together Tech volunteers — "long-hairs and short-hairs," Rush Smith remembers — and youngsters from the Techwood-Clark Housing Project. Tech students tutored their "friends" and took them to movies, the zoo and the General Motors plant in Doraville. The program still exists but, during the late sixties and early seventies, was exceptionally strong.

Dr. Vernon D. Crawford, Dean of the General College, remembers an incident in which a student from another university came to the Tech campus to sell copies of *The Great Speckled Bird* and raise "student consciousness." He gave a rousing speech against the Vietnam War and for draft card burning until a Tech student who was passing by interrupted him: "If what you want to do is confront us and change matters, here is a shovel.

The following words on a bronze plaque
near the pool in SAC help keep the
memory of Freddie Lanoue alive:

1908-1965
Frederick R. "Freddy" Lanoue
Teacher, Coach, Friend
Creater of Drown Proofing
Georgia Tech Swimming Coach
1936-1965
This Plaque is Dedicated to His Memory
By Anak 1977

Lyle Welser, Tech's first gymnastics coach from 1947 to 1970, has become known both as "the father of gymnastics in the South" and as the "father of the U.S. Gymnastics Clinics."

When the post office burned in 1965, its postmaster, Asa M. Barber, organized a temporary post office that was open for business the following morning. ODK later gave Barber a watch for the feat.

Come help us. We are digging a ditch across the street into the Techwood project to help provide a better drainage system." The speaker declined, retrieved his newspapers and left.

During the Vietnam War, students needed to maintain high grade-point averages to avoid the draft, and the attendant stress created problems for students and faculty alike. But there seems to have been little grade inflation and little overt pressure from students to demand grades in order to stay in school.

The course was steady for most students. At a time when fraternities and sororities were abandoned entirely at many universities, those at Tech declined in popularity but survived. The ROTC remained strong, and religious and service organizations increased rather than diminished in membership.

Students heard a wide range of speakers — some conservative, some liberal — who constituted a who's who of the sixties and seventies: Robert Penn Warren, Al Capp, François Mitterrand, John Kenneth Galbraith, Hosea Williams, Julian Bond, Margaret Mead, Ralph Nader, Ralph McGill and perhaps the most controversial of all, the Chief Justice of the U.S. Supreme Court, Earl Warren.

George Griffin, then Dean of Students, wrote the following note to Harrison, dated January 28, 1968, that reflects the mood of those days as well as Griffin's administrative style: "I hate to mention things like this to you, but I received a call from one of our alumni stating that he was representing some group which is protesting the appearance of Chief Justice Warren on our campus. I don't think this is anything to worry about, but I thought I'd better pass the information along. They seem to think that since Mr. McGill has already appeared here, and now Chief Justice Warren, that we are trying to brainwash the boys. So maybe to smooth over the situation we might invite old brother Goldwater to appear on our 75th Anniversary program."

Goldwater never came to Tech, but the school continued to invite speakers with widely varying views. Tech also had a Free University for several years that offered courses ranging from automobile repair to classical music. "It was a kind of cultural

Dr. James L. Taylor came to Tech in 1936 and taught first in the School of Chemistry. Dr. William M. Spicer also joined the faculty that year, and he and Taylor shared the same office for two years. Taylor began research on the chemistry of fibers and later became Head of Tech's Textile Chemistry program. He subsequently served as Director of Textile Engineering from 1959 until he retired in 1972.

Officials taking part in the 1965 ground breaking of the Joseph H. Howey Physics Building are (left to right) Chancellor George L. Simpson Jr., Dr. Howard Page (NSF) and Dr. Vernon Crawford, then Director of the School of Physics.

Bud Carson, Head Coach 1967-71, stands with Coach Tom Moore (in background with headset), Gary Wingo (No. 31) and Eddie Hughes (No. 20).

supplement students could identify as a part of their own educational needs," recalls English Professor James D. Young, who taught a course in French cooking for the Free University. Motivation for class attendance depended entirely upon student interest, with the result that nine-week courses sometimes became six-week courses because students simply quit attending.

Many of the old traditions remained, such as Homecoming — still the most important fall celebration — and fraternity parties in the spring. But by the end of the sixties, the parties had different themes and sounds. The big band music of the fifties was replaced by the sounds of groups like the Fifth Dimension. They came to the Coliseum in 1968, began the concert with "Stoned Soul Picnic," and by intermission had the Coliseum floor jammed with impromptu dancers. Al Hirt, Glenn Yarbrough and Neil Diamond also received warm Atlanta welcomes. Tastes were clearly eclectic.

By the late sixties rat caps had all but disappeared. George P. Burdell's name still appeared on class rolls, though less frequently. Tech's male/female ratio was still a staggering 70:1, but three women were on the staff of the *Technique* — Linda Williamson, the Feature Editor, Cindy Hilton, Assistant Feature Editor and Sheilah Luckett, Staff Cartoonist. And blacks were making their presence felt, too. The Editor of the *Technique* in 1967 was a black, John Thomas Gill III. On one occasion, Gill was asked how Tech students "treated" him, to which he replied, "They don't treat me. I pay my own way." The Afro-American Association was organized in 1968 and is still active in student life.

The influence of the Y.M.C.A., which for seven decades had been led by strong and popular secretaries, had begun to wane. Charlie Commander, one of its notable leaders, died in 1967, the year construction started on the new student center building. From Commander's death onward, the "Y" never again played the role of quasi-official student union — not just because of the change of leadership but because the times were changing. Gradually the Student Government Association and the Student Center Governing Board assumed control over student activities.

For 23 years, from 1927 to 1950, there was always a Ziegler enrolled at Tech. In 1977 the seven Ziegler brothers gathered for their mother's 90th birthday. (One daughter, Betty, attended Agnes Scott.) Dr. Waldemar T. Ziegler (front, left) served as a physical chemist on the Manhattan Project, then joined the Tech Chemical Engineering faculty in 1946, remaining until he retired in 1978.

Staff of the 1967 *Technique* crank out another edition. John Thomas Gill III (left) was the first black editor of the *Technique*.

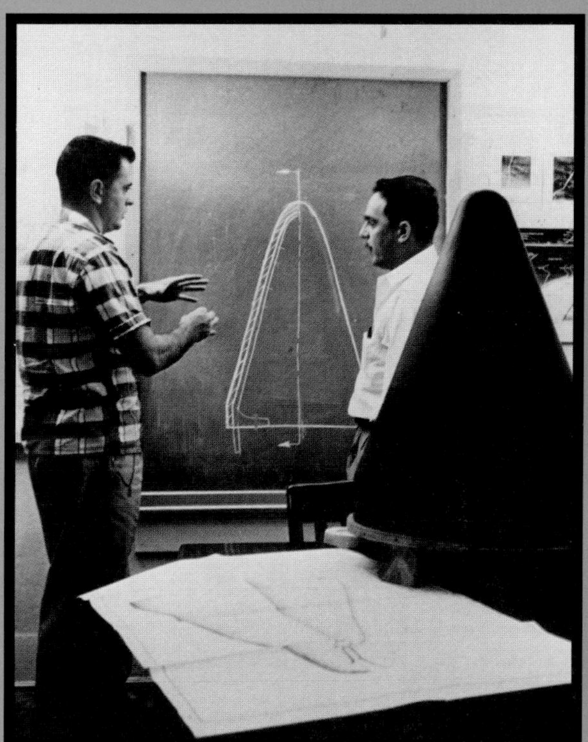

A picture in 1967 of Tech's High Temperature Materials Laboratory, where fused silica nose cones are formed and then heat-treated for the extremes of space travel. Pictured here are, left to right, J.D. Walton and Nick Poulos.

The Civil Engineering Building is named in honor of long-time Dean of Engineering and Regents' Professor, Jesse W. Mason.

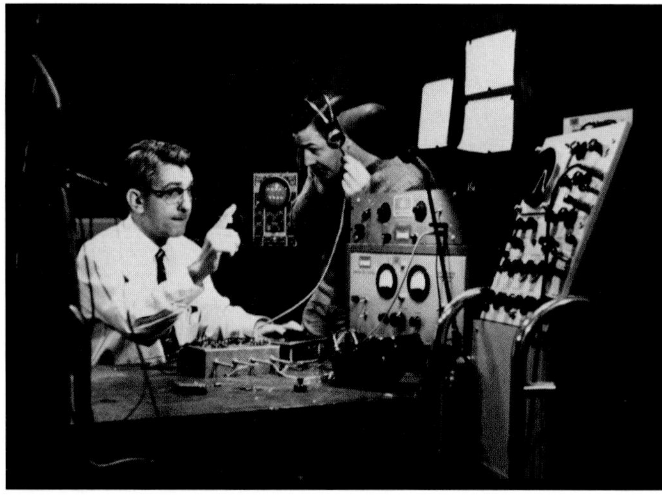

Dr. Benjamin J. Dasher, a member of the Tech faculty from 1939 until his death in 1971, served as Professor and as Director of the School of Electrical Engineering, Acting Head of the School of Nuclear Physics and Associate Dean of the College of Engineering.

One of the most controversial changes that took place during the Harrison years involved Tech's decision to leave the Southeastern Conference (SEC). The issue that led to Tech's withdrawal was the 140 Rule, a regulation that limited member schools to no more than 140 grant-in-aid athletes at one time. Tech objected because the rule meant that athletes who stayed on a few quarters in order to graduate used up the School's available slots for new talent. Thus, Tech's philosophy of keeping players in school until they graduated was in danger. The SEC chose to stay with the rule and Harrison, on the recommendation of the Athletic Board, took Tech out of the conference.

There were advantages in being an independent besides maintaining a stay-till-you-graduate policy. Tech was a football powerhouse and, in its new status, could keep all television revenues instead of dividing them with member schools. This was wonderful as long as Tech remained powerful, but when the poor seasons came, as they later did, the decision came under fire.

One change in Tech's athletic program saddened virtually everyone, except perhaps the teams that played the Jackets. In 1967, after 22 years as Head Coach, Bobby Dodd retired. Even though he remained as Director of Athletics, it was unmistakably the end of an era.

A letter from one of Dodd's boys, J. Foster Watkins, captain of the 1958 team, describes what players felt during those years: "My reflections on Georgia Tech are highly influenced by the Pygmalion-type approach to the student-athlete taken by Coach Bobby Dodd and his coaching staff and the high expectations that existed in the classrooms at Tech. They impacted on a rather impressionable young fellow from Columbus, Georgia, and assisted him in becoming more than he might have been." Watkins chose a career in higher education, earned a doctorate and is now President of Gainesville Junior College.

Leon Hadden "Bud" Carson, Dodd's successor and Tech's fourth head football coach, did not get off to an auspicious start. During his first year, the Jackets struggled through a 4-6-0 season. The next year's win-loss record was identical and so was the next. Tech fans were becoming restive.

Dr. William Monroe Spicer, who came to Tech as an instructor in 1936, served as Director of the School of Chemistry from 1955 to 1973. Soon after his death in 1981 at the age of 72, the W.M. Spicer Memorial Lecture series was inaugurated with Nobel Prize Laureate Herbert C. Brown as the first lecturer.

John Oran Eichler, shown in this prize-winning photo, taught surveying at Tech for many years. He came to Tech in 1956 and retired in 1973.

All four men who served as Director of Placement posed for this photo shortly before A.P. De Rosa's death in 1969. De Rosa died in Leningrad, escorting a group of Tech students on an exchange tour. The Directors are (left to right) Joe W. Guthridge, De Rosa, Fred Wesley Ajax and George C. Griffin.

But this was one issue Harrison would not have to resolve, for on July 4, 1968, *The Atlanta Journal* announced: "Tech President Resigns In Row With Regents: Policies Reported as Issues." Harrison's resignation, which surprised many people, was effective June 30, 1969. Some speculated that it was the outcome of a conflict with Chancellor George L. Simpson Jr., but Harrison refused comment other than to say he had been President long enough. Later that academic year, J.P. Stevens and Company announced that Harrison had accepted a vice presidential post with them — a position he held until he retired in 1976.

In the spring, Tech students, faculty and staff held a "Wonderful Ed's Day" proclaimed by Mayor Ivan Allen Jr., himself a 1933 Tech graduate. The students gave Harrison a surprise gift for "the man who has everything": a "T" taken from the Tech tower.

During the closing days of his administration, Harrison told how he wanted to be remembered:

"Those who review the changes in Tech during my tenure will no doubt comment on the number of new buildings and the expanded area of the campus. But essential as facilities are to an educational institution, they are still not the major ingredients of a college education. I am grateful that the new facilities and added space were made available, but I am much more pleased with the steady progress that has brought about a unification of direction and purpose, more interdisciplinary activities and a broader dialogue between you [students] and us."

Incidentally, Harrison returned the "T" to Tech's Physical Plant after he moved to Charlotte, N.C. "At no expense to Tech — in a J.P. Stevens truck," he is quick to add.

When Shanghai-born C.S. Kiang arrived in Atlanta in 1962 to begin graduate work, Dr. Vernon D. Crawford, who was then in charge of graduate programs for the School of Physics, met Kiang at the Greyhound Bus Station. In 1964 Kiang learned that he had tuberculosis and was hospitalized for 50 days. When he was discharged from the hospital, the Crawfords took him into their home for an entire year and patiently nursed him back to health. Mrs. Crawford, incidentally, is the daughter of a distinguished missionary to Korea and spent her early years in the Orient. Kiang now jokingly says the Crawfords took him in because he blended in with the decor of the house. When Kiang married Marilyn Maisel in 1968, neither family attended the wedding, so Vernon Crawford took part in the ceremony. "Vernon gave me away," Kiang says. Not until 10 years later did Kiang learn the whole story of his hospital and medical expenses. The Crawfords had paid them. Dr. Kiang has been Director of the School of Geophysical Sciences since 1982.

On "Wonderful Ed's Day" in 1969, students staged a mock takeover of Harrison's office, tied up his secretary Janice Gosdin and "kidnapped" Harrison, taking him to the square subsequently named for him. There the "T," which had been lifted from the tower the previous night, was presented to "the man who has everything." In this photo, Student Body President Carey Brown holds the whistle while Harrison (left) and Atlanta Mayor Ivan Allen Jr. look on. Seven students, "The Magnificent Seven," had stolen the whistle and asked the Student Government Association to present it to Harrison as their parting gift.

As the 1960's ended, there was considerable disarray on the hill. Administrators were coming and going and, for the first time, Tech would soon fire a head football coach. All this in a school that had long prided itself on its deliberate and unflappable ways.

In 1969 President Harrison left Tech ahead of his announced departure date and Chancellor George L. Simpson Jr. named Dr. Vernon D. Crawford Acting President. Crawford was a physicist who had held several important posts at Tech, but his tenure as Tech's fourth Acting President was brief. After just three months, Dr. Arthur G. Hansen, Tech's Dean of Engineering since 1966, was named the school's seventh President.

The choice of Hansen surprised many people. But the decision was popular with students, who found the 44-year-old, pipe-smoking engineer and mathematician willing, like Harrison, to discuss issues and problems with them. Hansen also had already been initiated into Tech culture and did not need to be freshly introduced to many features of Tech life.

Hansen was born in 1925 in Sturgeon Bay, Wisconsin. He earned a B.S. degree in electrical engineering in 1946 and an M.S. degree in mathematics in 1948 from Purdue University, and received his doctorate in mathematics from Case Western Reserve University in 1959. Faculty members present at his doctoral defense said afterward that it was "super...one of the best."

Hansen, who assumed the office of the presidency on August 1, 1969, implemented major administrative changes and moved Tech toward a more formalized organizational structure. The building boom continued during his presidency: new dorms and the Student Center; new homes for the Schools of Chemistry, Physics and Civil Engineering; a new facility for the Engineering Experiment Station; and an addition to the Library Building. Many Tech departments recognized new opportunities in the seventies and started carefully planning expansions. Hansen's successor as Dean of Engineering, Dr. Thomas E. Stelson, began pushing "mission-oriented" research in earnest.

Dr. Hansen on his first day as President. The ceremonies of moving, of beginning the day's work and of lunch at his desk were duly recorded.

Col. Frank Groseclose, Director of Tech's School of Industrial Engineering, with Dr. Lillian Moller Gilbreth, noted authority on technical and human relations problems in management. The book, *Cheaper by the Dozen,* written by two of Gilbreth's children, Frank B. Gilbreth Jr. and Ernestine Gilbreth Carey, was made into the well-known movie by the same name. Both the movie and book are based on experiences of the Gilbreth family. And yes, Dr. Gilbreth did rear 12 children.

The "Ramblin' Raft Race" was called a "Watery Woodstock" by *Newsweek; The Atlanta Journal* called it the "largest participation sport in the world." At the height of its popularity, the race attracted an estimated 200,000 spectators and participants.

The late Fuller E. Callaway III, for whom the Student Athletic Complex is named, on board his yacht *Morning Star* in San Francisco about 1965.

Despite this activity, Hansen's administration was brief. He resigned from Tech effective July 1, 1971, to become President of Purdue, a position he would hold until 1982, when he became Chancellor of the Texas A & M University System — a position involving the administration of four universities and various state agencies.

One of Hansen's last memories of Tech is a fond one. The students sponsored a "Day" as they had for Harrison, but this time called it "Good Ol' Art's Day." A crowd of students and faculty assembled in Harrison Square near the Tech Tower, where the departing President was given a bronzed rat cap. Lieutenant Governor Lester Maddox represented the state and Hansen was declared a "true Ramblin' Wreck."

After Hansen's departure, Dr. James E. Boyd, who had been a member of Tech's Department of Physics from 1936 to 1961 and Director of the Engineering Experiment Station from 1957 to 1969, became Acting President. Boyd had served as President of West Georgia College from 1961 to 1971 and later served as Vice Chancellor for Academic Development for the University System. High on his agenda were topics such as the pass/fail proposal, financing the Student Athletic Complex and developing a viable relationship between the Engineering Experiment Station and Tech's other units. Progress was made on each agenda item. One of the most visible problems involved parking. The "Stinger" campus bus service, which made its debut during the Boyd administration, was one of the more successful attempts to deal with this vexing part of campus life.

Boyd presided over two graduation ceremonies, one of which was especially memorable. On graduation day in the fall quarter of 1971, Atlanta had another of its disruptive snowfalls which, this time, prevented the ceremony from taking place. Some students received their diplomas that day in the President's office, but about 200 graduates received theirs by mail.

Well-known speakers continued to visit the campus: Ralph Abernathy, Julian Bond, Andrew Young, U.S. Senators Charles Percy and Herman Talmadge, General Motors President Ed Cole and Vance Packard, the author. In the early seventies,

Dr. Joseph Mayo Pettit in academic robe.

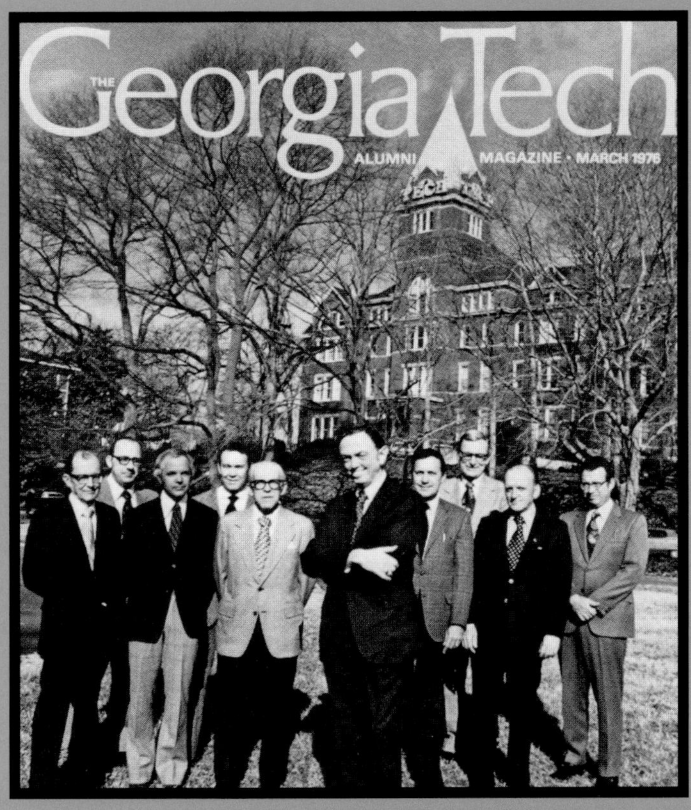

"All the President's Men" — *The Georgia Tech Alumni Magazine*, **March 1976. Left to right: Ewell Barnes, Vice President, Business and Finance; James E. Dull, Dean of Students; Dr. Clyde D. Robbins, Vice President, Planning; Forrester C. Auman, Campus Safety Director; Joe Guthridge, Vice President, Development and Public Relations; Dr. Richard Fuller Jr., Assistant to the President; Dr. Walter Carlson, Dean and Executive Director of Southern Technical Institute; Dr. Vernon D. Crawford, Vice President, Academic Affairs; Dr. Thomas E. Stelson, Vice President, Research.**

The Deans. Left to right: Vice President Henry C. Bourne Jr.; William L. Fash, College of Architecture; Dr. Les A. Karlovitz, College of Sciences and Liberal Studies; Dr. Gerald J. Day, College of Management; Dr. William M. Sangster, College of Engineering.

The President's staff — 1985. Front row, left to right: Dr. Henry C. Bourne Jr., Vice President, Academic Affairs; President Pettit; Janice Gosdin-Sangster, Assistant to the President. Second row, left to right: Warren Heemann, Vice President, Development; Dr. Richard Fuller Jr., Vice President, Business and Finance; Dr. Thomas E. Stelson, Vice President, Research; John P. Culver, Assistant Vice President, Special Events; John H. Gibson, Assistant to the President; Dr. James R. Stevenson, Executive Assistant to the President. Third row, left to right: Dr. Homer Rice, Athletic Director and Assistant to the President; Dr. Jesse Poore, Associate Vice President, Academic Affairs/Information Technology; Dr. Clyde D. Robbins, Vice President, Planning; James E. Dull, Vice President/Dean of Student Affairs.

Georgia Tech Research Institute. Standing, left to right: Howard G. Dean Jr., Associate Director; Dr. Donald J. Grace, Director; Robert G. Shackelford, Associate Director. Seated, left to right: Gerald J. Carey, Associate Director; Dr. James C. Wiltse, Associate Director.

A meeting of the Centennial Campaign Executive Committee — J. Erskine Love Jr., Chairman; Lawrence L. Gellerstedt Jr. and Charles R. Yates, Vice Chairmen.

Eight Presidents of the Georgia Tech Alumni Association were present for this 1985 photograph. First row, left to right: J. Frank Smith, 1979-80; Joe Westbrook, 1947-49; Richard B. Bell, 1980-81. Second row, left to right: E. Rembert DuBose, 1984-85; Charles R. Simons, 1957-58; John E. Aderhold, 1976-77; Madison F. Cole, 1965-66; Don L. Chapman, 1982-83.

thousands of students trooped into the Coliseum to hear the Allman Brothers, Bread and Steppenwolf. Chicago played at Homecoming, and Judy Collins performed during Greek Week.

Tech was in the process of adding another tradition to its rich repertoire — the Ramblin' Raft Race. The event began in 1969, when Larry Patrick and several fraternity brothers of Delta Sigma Phi challenged local disc jockeys to a 34-mile race down the Chattahoochee River. It gradually grew from 55 entrants in the first race into what the *Guinness Book of World Records* recognizes as one of the world's largest participation events. The last race in Atlanta was held in 1979, but Ramblin' Raft Races are held in other cities annually in the summer.

Another competition ended in 1971, this one for Tech's presidency. On October 5, *The Atlanta Journal* announced: "Stanford Dean Gets Georgia Tech Helm." Paul Weber, who had served with all but the first three Tech presidents, commented on the choice: "This man tops them all in experience and eminence in engineering education before coming to Tech." Tech's new helmsman, Dr. Joseph Mayo Pettit, was a member of the National Academy of Engineering — at the time there were no other members of this prestigious organization in Georgia — and President-Elect of the American Society for Engineering Education.

Pettit was born in 1916 in Rochester, Minnesota, but spent much of his youth in Portland, Oregon. After graduating from the University of California at Berkeley in 1938, he attended Stanford University for graduate study in electrical engineering and worked under the legendary Frederick Terman. Pettit received his doctorate in 1942. During World War II, he joined his former advisor at Harvard's Radio Research Laboratory and, after the war and a brief stint at the Airborne Instruments Laboratory in New York, became a faculty member, then Dean of Stanford University's School of Engineering.

In one of Pettit's first public statements after coming to Tech, he said: "Society's problems aren't all technical, but they can be solved by teams of the best people in all fields — engineers, economists, politicians. In addition, an academic

Al Ciraldo and Kim King, Tech announcers. King, "the young left-hander," is a Georgia Tech graduate and former quarterback. Ciraldo, who began announcing Tech games in the early 1950's, was the first to cover Tech's basketball games — in the Old Gym.

In this 1971 photograph, Tech linebacker Gary Carden confers with Maxie Baughan, Defensive Coordinator, and Jerry Glanville, Assistant Coach. Baughan, an All-America center on Tech's 1959 team, is now Head Football Coach at Cornell University, and Glanville is Defensive Coordinator with the Houston Oilers.

Eddie McAshan, the first black quarterback at Georgia Tech.

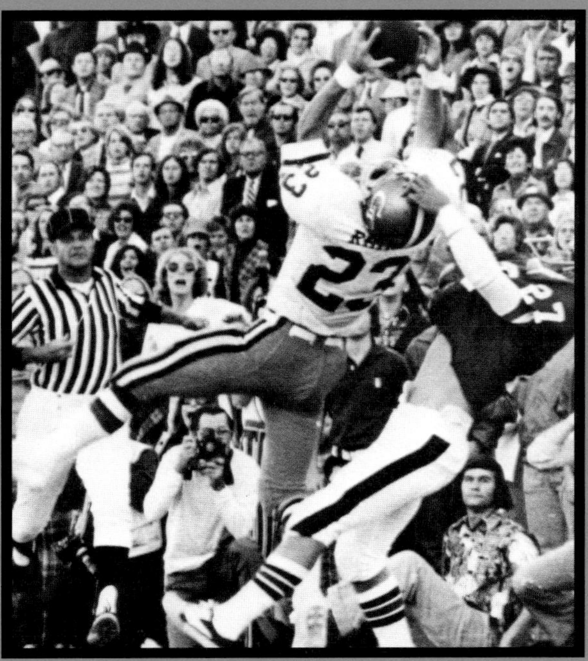

Randy Rhino, an All-America defensive back in 1972, 1973 and 1974, intercepts a Georgia pass.

William M. "Bill" Fulcher was Tech's head football coach in 1972 and 1973.

Jim Robinson gallops for one of his record-breaking touchdowns after catching a pass, while Tech cheerleader Wayne Kerr shouts encouragement.

institution can take the time necessary for basic research that develops new knowledge rather than putting Band-aids on existing techniques." Pettit's reference to "the best people" working together on research problems stated his administration's priorities.

Although graduate-level research and teaching had not been heavily emphasized during Tech's early years — the first doctorate was awarded in 1950 to W.L. Carter in chemical engineering — Pettit immediately began to emphasize and upgrade graduate programs. And from the beginning of his tenure, he encouraged recruiting the best students and faculty members available.

Pettit's insistence on recruiting top-quality faculty members was implemented by Dr. Vernon D. Crawford, Tech's Vice President, Academic Affairs until 1979. That year Crawford became Acting Chancellor of the University System of Georgia and was named Chancellor in 1980. When he resigned from Tech, a man equally committed to quality was recruited from the National Science Foundation — Dr. Henry C. Bourne Jr. While at NSF, Bourne had helped pioneer programs in microelectronics that brought the government, universities and industry together as partners. This background was ideal for Tech's new initiatives.

Prior to the Pettit years, annual research funding at Georgia Tech had reached the $12 million range. Pettit came to Tech convinced that research is vital to higher education, primarily because it·keeps faculty and students at the cutting edge of knowledge. To make research a Tech priority, he elevated Stelson from Dean of Engineering to the newly-created post of Vice President, Research, helping Tech climb to its high ranking among the nation's top research universities. In fiscal 1985, Tech's research and development projects exceeded $90 million, with funding for more than 1,500 projects involving over 1,100 faculty members and 2,000 students.

The man with the ball is Eddie Lee Ivery.
Ivery set the all-time Tech and NCAA
single-game rushing record of 356 yards
against Air Force in 1978.

The Carters and the Pettits at the 1977 Tech-Navy game in Annapolis. President Jimmy Carter, who
attended Tech from 1942 to 1943 before transferring to the U.S. Naval Academy, sat with Tech fans
during the first half, then switched sides at halftime. Tech lost 16-20.

Richard A. "Rich" Yunkus set more
Tech scoring records than any previous
player in Yellow Jacket history. He was
academic All-America in 1969, 1970 and
1971. In 1970, a Yunkus-led Tech team
beat North Carolina in the North-South
Doubleheader, a feat not repeated until
January 28, 1985.

National Science Foundation figures show that from fiscal 1972 to fiscal 1982, Georgia Tech had the largest percentage increase in federal research and development funding of any of the leading 100 institutions in the nation — 603 percent.

This research also benefits the private sector. An example is GTSTRUDL — a structural-design language software program for architectural engineering firms developed by Dr. Leroy Z. Emkin and his colleagues at the Georgia Tech Integrated Computer Engineering Systems Laboratory (GTICES). GTSTRUDL earned more than $5 million from 1979 to 1985 and is expected to earn more than $1 million a year into the late 1980's.

Another example is Tech's Microelectronics Research Center — a selling point whenever city and state officials woo industry to the area. "We can do classified research, we can do proprietary research, and we can do traditional research," says Dr. John W. Hooper, Director.

Mainstream engineering is still the big-ticket item at Tech, but visitors are constantly surprised at the breadth of engineering research underway and the vigor and prestige of Tech's other programs. A few examples are programs in city planning and rehabilitation technology in the College of Architecture; the Center for Work Performance Problems, in the College of Management, that investigates problems associated with alcoholism in the work place; biotechnology — including genetic engineering and microbiology; health systems research and community outreach; research in fields as diverse as nuclear fusion, fish hearing and underwater communication, improved hearing aids for the elderly, acid rain, radiation and cancer, and blood-flow disorders in premature babies; a program administered in Tech's English Department that guides the development of technology

Director of Tech's College of
Architecture from 1956 to 1976, Paul
Malcolm Heffernan was a designer with
Bush-Brown, Gailey and Heffernan —
developers of master plans and building
plans for the Institute in the late 1940's.
Heffernan became Professor Emeritus in
1976.

Team captain and first Tech gymnast ever
to qualify for the NCAA championships,
Jeff Morrison was recipient of the ACC
Scholar-Athlete Award in 1978. In this
photograph, Jeff performs while his twin
brother, Jerry, one of Tech's all-time
great gymnasts, "spots" him. The brothers
were known as the "Magnificent
Morrisons."

Graduation ceremonies used to be
conducted in the Fox Theater and at
Grant Field. Today they are held at the
end of each quarter in the Alexander
Memorial Coliseum.

The first woman graduate of Georgia Tech AFROTC to become an Air Force pilot, Captain Cathy Caseman, daughter of Dr. Austin B. Caseman of Civil Engineering, is shown at the controls of a KC-135 Stratotanker refueling aircraft. Since receiving her pilot wings in 1979, she has served as pilot and aircraft commander of the KC-135 at Wurtsmith Air Force Base, Michigan, with assignments in Alaska, England and Spain, and in 1985 was a research pilot at Wright-Patterson Air Force Base.

Named in honor of a Tech alumnus and late President of the Callaway Foundation, the Arthur B. Edge Jr. Intercollegiate Athletic Center is one of the finest athletic facilities in the nation. Pictured at the 1980 ground breaking are, left to right: Fuller E. Callaway Jr., Bobby Dodd and Bill Curry.

modules for use in 18 historically black colleges in the Southeast; a doctoral program in psychology; course work in international relations taught by Sovietologist Dr. Daniel S. Papp; pioneering course work and research in computer law based in the School of Information and Computer Science; graduate-level work in Technology Assessment and Social Policy (TASP), a center for nuclear fusion, and courses on the history of science and technology taught by the pioneer in the field, Callaway Professor Melvin Kranzberg, founder of the Society for the History of Technology.

Disappointments, frustrations and occasional setbacks have marked the course to these achievements. In June 1975, for example, the General Assembly slashed the state budget, and Tech lost about $2.6 million. Another $300,000 was cut in December. But as in the days when Hall, Matheson and Brittain were at the helm, Tech's friends came to her aid. Tech survived the year because sponsored research increased and alumni and friends were generous.

Alumni and corporate gifts have meant the difference between quality and mediocrity. Under the leadership of Warren Heemann, Tech's Vice President, Development, total giving rose to $24.3 million in 1984-85 from $4.8 million in 1979-80; corporate giving increased to $11.9 million from $1.6 million during the same period and placed Tech fourth among the nation's larger public institutions in terms of gift revenue per enrolled student. Tech was awarded the prestigious Ford Motor Company Fund Grand Award from the Council for the Advancement and Support of Education (CASE) for Tech's fund-raising achievements in 1982-83. (In recognition of Heemann's leadership in fund-raising and development, CASE awarded him its coveted Frank L. Ashmore Award in Washington in July 1985.)

Dr. Homer C. Rice, Director of Athletics since 1980, has revolutionized Tech's athletic program. A highly successful high school football coach in Tennessee and Kentucky, Rice served as Assistant Coach at the University of Kentucky and the University of Oklahoma, and as Head Coach with the University of Cincinnati, Rice University and the Cincinnati Bengals of the National Football League. Rice was Director of Athletics at the University of North Carolina from 1969 to 1975, Director of Athletics at Rice University from 1976 to 1977 and an executive with the Cincinnati Bengals prior to coming to Tech in 1980.

Dr. Paul G. Mayer with a heliostat on the roof of the J.W. Mason Civil Engineering Building.

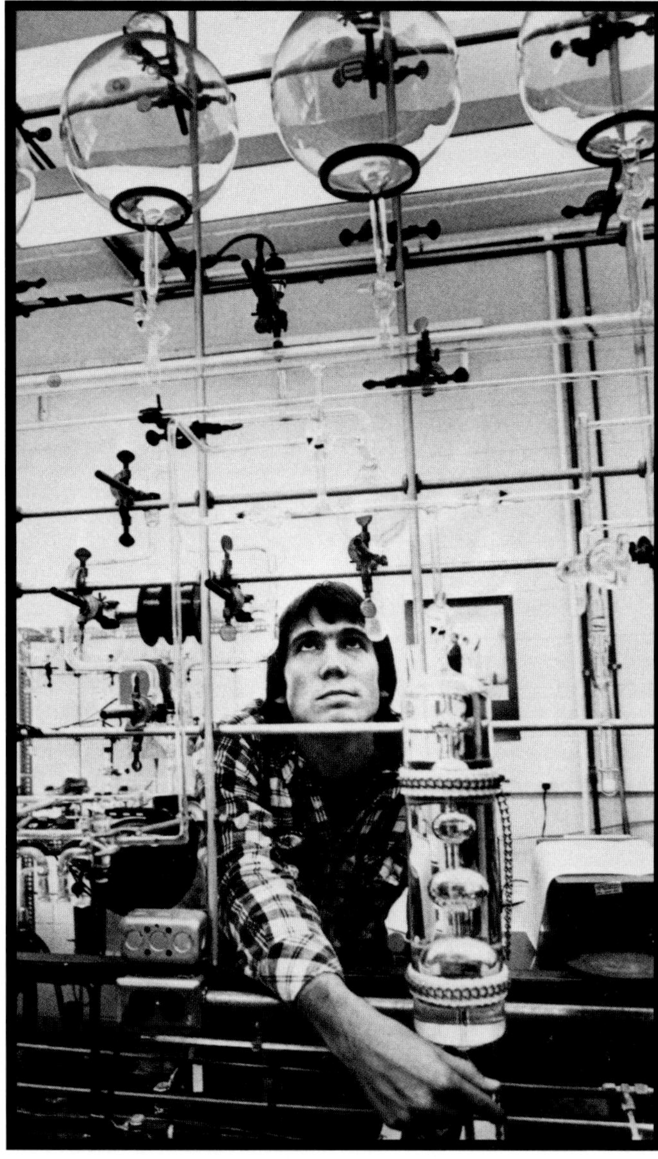

Steven Poehlein, son of Dr. Gary W. Poehlein, Director of the School of Chemical Engineering, in the Kinetics and Catalysis Laboratory. Steven received his M.S. degree in 1984 and is now in the doctoral program in chemical engineering.

In 1980, Tech's traditional card catalog was replaced with a COM (computer output microfiche) catalog. Director of Libraries Graham Roberts, who retired in 1984 after 25 years at Tech, is shown presiding over the disposal of 1.4 million cards. In 1983 the library became a member of the prestigious Association of Research Libraries.

And at a black-tie dinner at the Hyatt Regency Hotel (a creation of Tech graduate John Portman Jr.) on March 1, 1985, several hundred Tech alumni heard Dr. Pettit announce the goal for the Centennial Campaign — $100 million. Of that amount, $33 million had already been pledged the night the announcement was made, thanks to 18 months of hard work by members of the Centennial Campaign Executive Committee, chaired by J. Erskine Love Jr.

Also that evening, four Georgia Tech alumni received the first Alumni Exceptional Achievement Awards: Ivan Allen Jr., ('33), former Atlanta Mayor; John Portman Jr. ('50), world-renowned architect/developer; C.J. "Pete" Silas ('54), Chairman of the Board and Chief Executive Officer of Phillips Petroleum Company; and John W. Young ('52), Chief of the Astronaut Office of the National Aeronautics and Space Administration.

The Engineering Experiment Station (EES) greatly expanded during the Pettit years. Dr. Maurice Long headed the Station from 1969 until he retired in 1975; then after an interim period when Dr. Thomas E. Stelson served as the Station's Director, Dr. Donald J. Grace was selected for the post. Since 1976, Grace has presided over the Station's expansion as well as the celebration of its 50th anniversary in 1984. At that well-attended and happy birthday party, the EES received a new name — the Georgia Tech Research Institute (GTRI). The existing contracting agency of that name was changed to the Georgia Tech Research Corporation.

The Georgia Tech Alumni Distinguished
Service Award originated in 1934, and its
first recipient was Lawrence W. "Chip"
Robert Jr. It is one of the highest honors
an alumnus can receive from Georgia
Tech.

PREVIOUS AWARD RECIPIENTS

1934-Lawrence W. Robert Jr., 1908
1935-Ferd M. Kaufman, 1894
1936-William H. Glenn, 1891
1937-Robert Tyre Jones Jr., 1922
1938-Robert Gregg, 1905
1939-Y. Frank Freeman, 1910
1940-William A. Alexander, 1912
1941-Frank H. Neely, 1904
1942-James F. Towers, 1901
1944-William H. Hightower, 1909
1945-Frank M. Spratlin, 1906
1947-Cherry L. Emerson, 1908
1948-Robert B. Wilby, 1908
1949-Fuller E. Callaway Jr., 1926
1950-George W. McCarty, 1908
1951-Robert L. McDougall, 1925
1952-Howard T. Tellepsen, 1934
1953-Wayne J. Holman Jr., 1928
1954-David W. Harris, 1912
1955-George C. Griffin, 1922
1956-Monie A. Ferst, 1911
1957-Hazard E. Reeves, 1928
1958-Ivan Allen Jr., 1933
1959-Walter M. Mitchell, 1923
1960-Robert H. White, 1914
1961-George T. Marchmont, 1907

1962-John P. Baum, 1924
1963-George W. Woodruff, 1917
1964-John J. McDonough, 1923
1965-Julian T. Hightower, 1919
1966-Albert H. Staton, 1922
1966-John C. Staton, 1924
1967-William C. Wardlaw Jr., 1928
1968-Henry W. Grady, 1918
1969-William A. Parker, 1919
1970-Oscar G. Davis, 1922
1971-Jack F. Glenn, 1932
1972-John W. Young, 1952
1973-I.M. Sheffield Jr., 1920
1974-Edward B. Newill, 1915
1975-Ira H. Hardin, 1924
1976-Morris M. Bryan Jr., 1941
1977-Frederic Holloway, 1935
1978-Charles Tillman Oxford, 1930
1979-President Jimmy Carter, 1946
1979-Frederick G. Storey, 1933
1980-Daniel A. McKeever, 1932
1981-Lawrence L. Gellerstedt Jr., 1945
1982-Paul Anderson Duke, 1945
1983-Alvin M. Ferst Jr., 1943
1984-Charles R. Yates, 1935
1985-Andrew Jackson Mundy Jr., 1934
1985-Dr. Vernon D. Crawford, Hon.

Lawrence L. Gellerstedt Jr., a 1945 chemical engineering graduate, was President of Anak, Sigma Chi, his senior class and the Student Council during his student days. Since graduating, he has served both as President of the Alumni Association and as President of the Georgia Tech Foundation. Gellerstedt is shown here receiving the 1981 Alumni Distinguished Service Award.

President Pettit congratulating Alvin M. Ferst Jr. in 1983 after awarding Ferst the Alumni Distinguished Service Award.

GTRI's International Division has had particularly strong growth, turning rice into gas and charcoal in the Philippines, developing water pumps in Indonesia, implementing solar projects in Ghana and facilitating technology transfer projects in Latin America and Egypt.

In 1983 Tech entered into another international agreement, this one with the China Association for Science and Technology. The agreement, negotiated by Warren Heemann and C.S. Kiang, brought China's famed ancient technology exhibition, "China: 7,000 Years of Discovery," to Atlanta to inaugurate Tech's Centennial activities. And in 1985 the Chinese government and Georgia Tech officials formed a joint venture company to coordinate the development of new technology in that country.

Tech's growing reputation has attracted thousands of students from around the world. In 1985 more than 900 international students were enrolled at Tech, with the largest percentage coming from the Orient.

To help international students meet Tech's demanding requirements, the Department of Modern Languages developed a strong program in "intensive" English. Begun in 1958, the program features techniques that enable foreign students not only to become fluent in English, but also to participate effectively in the culture. Most beginning students in the program are not enrolled in Tech's degree programs, but many are admitted after successfully completing their language work.

A large number of Tech's international students return home to become national leaders. One such student, Ulrich Geldmacher, in 1985 Treasurer of Essochem Belgium, took industrial and systems engineering courses in 1971 and remained at Tech for five quarters. He says that his most vivid memories are of Tech's "unbureaucratic hospitality," its small classes (by European standards), the "Greek-lettered fraternities with funny rituals,"

Atlanta's general aviation airport is named for Tech's Charles M. "Charlie" Brown. Brown was a Fulton County Commissioner for 20 years, Chairman of the Commission for eight years and State Senator from 1957 to 1964. His book, *Charlie Brown Remembers Atlanta,* was published in 1982.

J. Erskine Love came to Tech during the waning months of World War II and graduated in December 1948. *The Blue Print,* which he edited that year, was the largest ever published prior to 1948 and received an All-American rating. Since graduating, he has accepted many responsibilities at his alma mater, including Chairman of the Centennial Campaign Executive Committee. In 1963 Anak chose Love as the Institute's "Outstanding Young Alumnus."

Philip Trammell Shutze graduated from Tech in 1912 and practiced in Atlanta until his death in 1982 at age 92. He designed many of Atlanta's grand buildings, including the Temple, the Villa in Ansley Park, the Swan House and the Academy of Medicine. Tech architecture students created the Philip Trammell Shutze Alumni Award in 1981 and awarded it that year to Shutze himself. Julian Harris, who designed the medal, received it in 1982; Preston S. Stevens, a graduate of Tech and founder of Stevens and Wilkinson Inc., in 1983; and P.M. Heffernan, former Dean of the College, in 1984.

Participants in Challenge II, 1981. The Challenge program is a six-week, non-credit summer program in mathematics, English and chemistry for entering freshmen. Sponsored by Tech's Office of Minority Educational Development (OMED), the program enrolled 40 blacks and Hispanics in 1984. Faculty advisors shown here are, from left to right, Dr. J. Aaron Bertrand, Dr. James W. Walker and Dr. Harold R. Hunt. Two students are wearing MITE T-shirts. Minority Introduction to Engineering (MITE) started at Tech in 1974.

The Varsity, an "easy-to-use" library, a "placement" office, and "that final disgrace — the University of Georgia." According to Geldmacher, "It was Tech with the missing T that most engulfed me and formed my high regard for such American education."

University research can be important to industry as well as to government. Pettit brought that conviction with him from Stanford, where he was instrumental in the development of Silicon Valley. And he has successfully implemented the concept in Georgia, with the Advanced Technology Development Center (ATDC) being just one example.

The concept was strongly supported by former Governor George Busbee and, in 1980, enabling legislation was passed that placed the ATDC facility on Tech's campus. Located first in the O'Keefe High School Building, then in its new facilities on 10th Street, the ATDC provides "incubator space" so that fledgling high-tech companies can use Tech's resources. Thanks to the ATDC and other joint efforts, NSF figures rank Tech second in the nation in both dollar volume and percentage of university research performed for business and industry.

The ATDC is just the latest in a long history of Tech organizations created to meet local, state and national needs. One organization — Georgia State University — evolved tortuously from the Georgia Tech Evening School and has long since gone its separate way. Another — Southern Technical Institute, now located in Marietta — became autonomous during the Pettit years.

During its 30-year relationship with Georgia Tech, Southern Tech grew from a small division, primarily concerned with training technicians, into a four-year college granting the bachelor's degree in various fields of engineering technology. Dr. Walter O. Carlson, now Georgia Tech's Associate Vice President, Graduate Studies and Research, served as Southern Tech's Dean and Executive Director during the 1970's and was its Acting President when the School became an independent unit of the University System of Georgia on July 1, 1980.

For many months after Pettit arrived, Tech's

This photograph shows John W. Young,
Commander of *Columbia,* prior to the
first space shuttle.

Astronauts Joe H. Engle, left, and
Richard H. Truly, a 1959 Tech graduate
in aeronautical engineering, are shown
still wearing their ejection/escape suits
following their flight aboard NASA's
second *Columbia* space shuttle.

Tech student Mike Brown donated this 1885 silver dollar that went aboard the space shuttle *Challenger* with Tech graduate Dick Truly in 1983. The 1885 silver dollar signifies Tech's Centennial.

President Pettit blows out the candles on his birthday cake at a surprise party in 1981 given to him by his office staff. Pictured from left to right are Aggie Morris, Bobbie Fowler, Dr. Pettit, Janice Gosdin-Sangster and Kathryn Thompson.

highly visible problems with athletics overshadowed its steady progress toward academic excellence. They were difficult to solve because they involved long-standing, deep emotions.

When Leon H. "Bud" Carson became Head Football Coach in 1967, he faced not only the daunting task of following Bobby Dodd but also of competing with the Atlanta Falcons who were, at the time, a novelty in a region unaccustomed to professional football. Carson compiled a 27-27-0 record in five seasons at Tech, but break-even football was not good enough to keep fans happy and coming to Grant Field. So in December 1971, Acting President James Boyd had the unpleasant task of presiding over Tech's first firing of a head football coach. Carson, incidentally, went on to a successful career with the Pittsburgh Steelers.

Tech's next Head Football Coach was Bill Fulcher, a 1957 Tech graduate in IM. "Somehow, sometime, I always knew I would be here," he said when chosen. Fulcher started well with a 7-4-1 season and a 31-30 victory over Iowa State in the 1972 Liberty Bowl. But during his second year Tech was 5-6. At the end of the season, he resigned and left the coaching field.

Franklin C. "Pepper" Rodgers, a 1954 Tech graduate, was already in Tech's record book before he became its sixth Head Football Coach. He had played under Dodd in the glory days of the fifties and then had become a coach. His first head-coaching job was at the University of Kansas, where during his second season he won the Big-Eight Co-championship and played in the Orange Bowl. Rodgers then moved to the head-coaching job at UCLA, where he was ensconced when his alma mater summoned him.

Rodgers drew attention in Atlanta, not just for his exploits on the gridiron but for his nonconformist lifestyle as well. "I've always been a firm believer in the 13th Commandment," said Rodgers, summing up his personal philosophy. "Thou shalt not take thyself too seriously."

But the members of Tech's Athletic Association apparently did not believe earnestly in that commandment, and a parting of the ways occurred in 1980. Rodgers' record after six years was 34-31-2. When he left, there was also disagreement about compensation. Tech offered to pay his remaining salary, but Rodgers claimed that

Dr. James R. Stevenson in his laboratory in 1975. Stevenson was Director of the School of Physics from 1968 to 1978 and was Acting Vice President, Academic Affairs from 1979 until he became Executive Assistant to the President in 1981.

Frank Gordy founded The Varsity Drive-In in 1928. According to his wife, Evelyn, he wanted to "give Tech students a place to eat besides the cafeteria." Gordy died June 18, 1983, at the age of 79.

Tech's Co-op Plan, begun in 1912, is still going strong with about 2,100 students enrolled in 1985. In this 1982 photo, David Patterson (left) and Marilyn Jones, both co-op students in aerospace engineering, and Director of Tech's Cooperative Division James G. Wohlford are overlooking the stress testing area of Lockheed Georgia Company's C-5A program.

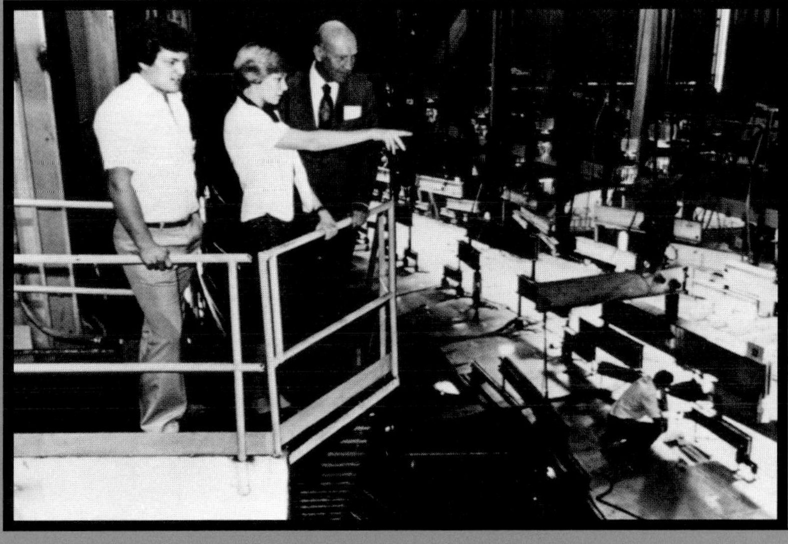

One of Tech's goals is recruiting the nation's finest academic prospects. The woman who heads that highly successful program is Dr. E. Jo Baker, Associate Vice President, Academic Affairs.

The Women's Student Association was dissolved in 1974, but in 1978-79 Amy Wepking was chosen President of the Student Government Association. In the 1982 elections, the three top positions of the SGA were won by women — from left to right: Ronda Ragsdale, President; Denise Ellis, Vice President; and Lisa Johnson, Secretary.

benefits such as a car, country club membership, and radio and television income came with the job. The dispute landed in court and was finally settled out of court three years after his termination. Rodgers later wrote a novel, *Fourth and Long Gone* (Peachtree Publishers, 1984), based on his coaching experiences. In 1985 he was Head Coach of the Memphis Showboats in the United States Football League.

In 1980, William Alexander "Bill" Curry (I.M. '65) was named Tech's seventh Head Football Coach. Like his two immediate predecessors, Curry played under Dodd, and was captain his senior year. He began his professional football career with the Green Bay Packers and played in the first Super Bowl in 1966, then went to the Baltimore Colts. Baltimore captured the World Championship in 1971, and Curry was All-Pro that season. He later played for the Houston Oilers and the Los Angeles Rams before retiring as a player in 1975. He spent a year as an assistant coach at Tech, then three seasons as Offensive Line Coach at Green Bay before returning to Tech as Head Coach.

Curry's first three seasons at Tech were disappointing, but in 1984 it finally happened. Tech capped a 6-4-1 season with a tremendous 35-18 win over a strong University of Georgia team for its first triumph in Athens in a decade. On that memorable Saturday afternoon in November, all the pent-up frustrations of many seasons came down on the hapless Dawgs.

A good season in addition to that victory made a significant difference in Tech's football program. "Now when I go out to a high school on a recruiting trip and I tell where I'm from," Coach Curry says, "I get a lot of respect."

Tech basketball has gotten respect too. Lots of it. But for many years basketball in Atlanta attracted little interest and few fans.

When John "Whack" Hyder retired as basketball coach at the end of the 1973 season after 22 seasons at Tech, he was known for regularly beating Kentucky when nobody else seemed able to. Hyder compiled a record of 292 wins and 271 losses. He was followed by Dwayne Morrison, who in eight seasons had a 91-122 record and made respectable showings as long as Tech played in the Metro Conference or as an independent. But the

Bernadette McGlade, Tech's first full-time female Women's Head Coach, is also Women's Sports Coordinator. While playing at the University of North Carolina, McGlade set 10 records and was captain of the team in 1979-80.

Corporate headquarters of Georgia Power Company, long-time employer of hundreds of Georgia Tech co-op students. This living laboratory for energy conservation and solar energy technology was designed by Georgia Tech graduate George T. Heery and his colleagues of Heery International Inc.

Paul Anderson Duke was a motivating force behind Technology Park and, in 1982, was awarded the Alumni Distinguished Service Award. He was on the first football team after Bobby Dodd became Head Coach and, in 1946, was named All-America center by both the Associated Press and the United Press International. He was also an AAU heavyweight wrestling champion.

George W. Woodruff in his downtown Atlanta office in 1983. A Tech alumnus and generous contributor, Woodruff received the Alumni Distinguished Service Award in 1963. Photos of his late wife, Irene, are on the credenza behind his desk. On September 14, 1984, George Woodruff personally dedicated the $8.5 million George and Irene Woodruff Residence Hall, Tech's 23rd and largest dormitory. The sculpture was done by Glen Acree. In September 1985, the School of Mechanical Engineering was named in Woodruff's honor.

Jackets' entry into the Atlantic Coast Conference in 1978 was disastrous, with Tech winning just one ACC game in the 1979-80 season and none the following year. Morrison left Tech after the 1980-81 season.

The reins of Tech's basketball program were then handed to Robert J. "Bobby" Cremins Jr., who transformed Tech from ACC also-ran into ACC champion. Prior to coming to Tech, Cremins was captain of the powerful 1970 University of South Carolina team and coached at Appalachian State University for six years. Three of those years, he was named Southern Conference "Coach of the Year." Cremins' success in Atlanta can be measured not just by the many honors showered upon him but by ticket sales as well. For the first time at Tech, every home game ticket for the 1984-85 season was sold before the season began — and thousands of requests were returned.

Those fortunate enough to get tickets were not disappointed. The Jackets warmed up by winning the Rainbow Classic in Hawaii and then methodically vanquished some of the mightiest teams in the nation. When the smoke had cleared, Tech had won the ACC regular season championship as well as the ACC Tournament and had advanced to Providence, Rhode Island, for the NCAA "Final Eight." There the Jackets defeated Illinois before losing to powerhouse Georgetown in the final seconds. 1984-85 was quite a season.

Tech's athletic programs for women do not have a long and rich heritage, but a start has been made. The intercollegiate program for women officially began in the 1973-74 academic year. Under the leadership of Bernadette McGlade, Coordinator of Women's Athletics and Women's Head Basketball Coach, women's sports now include varsity programs in basketball, tennis, volleyball and cross-country. Indoor and outdoor track were slated for 1985-86.

Jim Luck, Senior Assistant Athletic Director in 1985, and the first of two baseball coaches during the Pettit years, became Coach in 1962. During his 19 years of coaching at Tech, three teams were nationally ranked, and overall his record was 320-280-4.

Jim Morris, the second baseball coach during the Pettit years, became Tech's eighth head

Bobby Cremins and Mark Price in 1983, the year Cremins was named ACC Coach of the Year and Price ACC Rookie of the Year.

Jim Morris, Head Baseball Coach, with the 1983 Yellow Jackets. Morris, who came to Tech in 1982, compiled a 38-15 record in 1983 and was named ACC Coach of the Year. More than 60 of his players have been drafted by professional teams. In 1985 the Yellow Jackets were ACC Champions.

Recent Roll Calls have been highly successful. This "check" in 1983 is *prima facie* evidence of that support. From left to right, Don Chapman, Ben Dyer, Paul Smith and President Pettit hold the first Roll Call check to exceed $2 million.

Zeta Beta Tau's entry in the 1983 Ramblin' Wreck Parade.

baseball coach in 1982. He was named ACC Coach of the Year in 1983 after a record-breaking 38 wins. Coach Morris was instrumental in raising money for lighting Rose Bowl Field and, in 1983, Tech played a night game for the first time. But more is shining on Rose Bowl Field than lights. In 1985 Tech won its first ACC championship, going undefeated through the tournament and edging Clemson 7-5 at home in the finale. That game, incidentally, was played at night.

Athletic directors are usually not as visible as head coaches or players, but the decisions they make profoundly affect what happens on the playing fields and courts. When Bobby Dodd retired as Tech's Athletic Director in 1979, his successor, Doug Weaver, faced the problem of conference affiliation. Notre Dame and Penn State were thriving as independents, but the circumstances that favored those schools did not exist in Atlanta. Nor did Tech's affiliation with the Metropolitan Collegiate Athletic Conference, formed in 1975, prove entirely satisfactory. Consequently, in early 1978 Tech representatives met with the Atlantic Coast Conference and an ACC bid was duly offered. In 1978, Tech joined the conference.

Doug Weaver resigned in 1980 and Homer Rice, then an executive with the Cincinnati Bengals, accepted the Tech post. As a high school football coach, Rice compiled a phenomenal 102-9-7 record and then became the top assistant coach at Kentucky and Oklahoma. He went on to head-coaching jobs at the University of Cincinnati, Rice University and the Cincinnati Bengals. As Athletic Director at the University of North Carolina, Rice built a nationally acclaimed athletic program prior to coming to Tech.

Under his leadership, Tech's athletic fortunes have dramatically improved. Part of the story is the Arthur B. Edge Jr. Intercollegiate Athletic Center, made possible through a challenge grant from the Callaway Foundation and gifts from Tech alumni and friends. In addition, generous gifts made possible the George C. Griffin Track, the Earle Bortell Tennis Center and the Russ Chandler Stadium.

Also part of the story is balance. Sports like tennis, track and field, swimming and golf are on the upswing. Examples include William D. "Puggy" Blackmon's coaching the Tech golf team

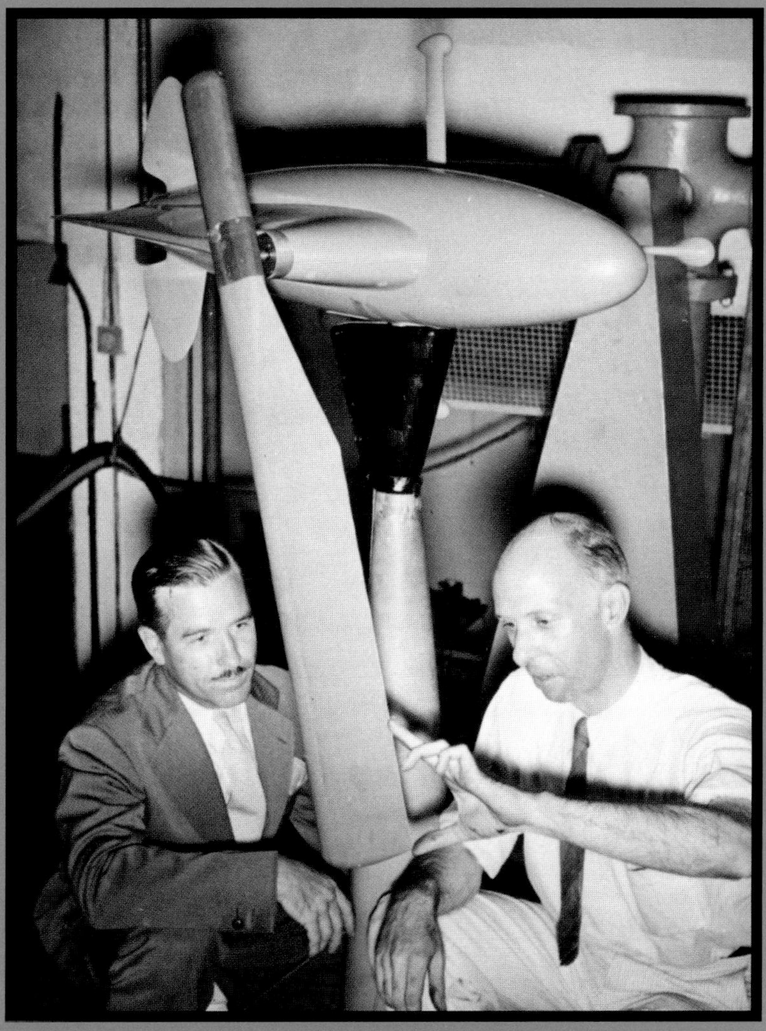

In this photo from the early forties, W. Harry Vaughan, left, is shown with Montgomery Knight, former Head of the Daniel Guggenheim School of Aeronautics. Vaughan graduated from Tech in 1923 with a degree in engineering chemistry. After receiving his master's degree from the University of Illinois, he returned to Tech as a member of the Ceramic Engineering Department and later became its Head. In 1934 Vaughan became the first Director of the Engineering Experiment Station. Dr. Donald J. Grace, below, became Director in 1976. Together they span more than six decades at Tech.

Jim Toler, right, who heads Tech's bioelectromagnetic research program, describes hyperthermia machines on CNN's "Daywatch" program.

President Joseph M. Pettit and Wang Shuntong, Executive Vice Chairman of the China Association for Science and Technology, sign the exchange agreement in June 1983. Other Tech administrators instrumental in the China-Tech accord are (left to right) C.S. Kiang, Director of Geophysical Sciences; Thomas E. Stelson, Vice President, Research; Henry C. Bourne Jr., Vice President, Academic Affairs; and Warren Heemann, Vice President, Development.

to the ACC championship in 1985. Led by Captain Bob McDonnell, the team beat Duke by five strokes.

Members of Tech's track team break records almost every time they compete — and not just local records. Antonio McKay set a world record in the 400 meters in 1984 and won gold and bronze medals in the 1984 Olympics; and in 1985 Mike Armour set a world's best indoor time in the 500 meters. Tennis coach Gery Groslimond was named 1984-85 ACC Coach of the Year; Bryan Shelton won the ACC championship, was named co-winner of the Player of the Year award and received the Sportsmanship Award. Shelton also was the first Yellow Jacket to play in the NCAA tennis tournament since 1972.

Tech even had a fencer in the 1984 Olympics — Dr. Mark Smith, an Assistant Professor in the School of Electrical Engineering. The 1984-85 school year will be remembered as one of the best overall success stories in the history of Tech athletics. "I'm just happy it came on our centennial year," Rice says, commenting on Tech's accomplishments.

Thus, the Centennial celebration has begun on an upbeat mood felt by students, faculty, administrators and alumni. "I think we're poised for a wonderful new century...we're poised for greatness," says Charles R. Yates, a former golf champion and Vice Chairman of Tech's Centennial Campaign Executive Committee.

"We've raised our horizons gradually to look at ourselves as more than a Georgian and Southeastern institution," says Pettit, reflecting on the progress made toward the goals he described when he arrived in 1972. Progress shows in the quality of faculty and students Tech attracts. By means of endowed chairs, Tech is bringing in and keeping scholars and teachers of the highest caliber.

Through grants and enrichment programs, the Institute is growing a fine crop of young scholars of its own. On a per capita basis Tech ranks first among state universities in National Merit Scholars and National Achievement Scholars, and its average Scholastic Aptitude Test score of 1,168 (1984-85) also places it near the top in that category. In 1985, 90 percent of Tech students

Professor L. Howard Olson and graduate
student Bill Manning watch textile
consultant Thomas R. Poole make
adjustments on the 65-year-old Draper
X-2 loom now being used to weave
tubular material for astronaut space suits.
The loom was located in a discard lot at
the Opelika Manufacturing Corporation
in Opelika, Alabama, and renovated at
Tech for about $500. A new loom with
the same capabilities would cost more
than $250,000.

On May 30, 1984, about 2,000 people
gathered in front of the Student Center to
witness an annular eclipse of the sun.
Buzz, who reportedly viewed an earlier
eclipse with the naked eye, is checking
the crowd's vision. Meanwhile, several
chickens donated for an experiment
actually settled down for a snooze during
the eclipse, confirming part of the
folklore surrounding eclipses.

The *Blue Print* and *Technique* staffs at the annual post-publications banquet party in June 1984. Past, present and future editors get together at these bashes.

"Visions of Ramblin' Robert [Lavette] will always be in Tech people's minds as long as they live," quarterback John Dewberry said at the end of the 1984 season. "In all the dim seasons and all the dreary weather, Robert was a ray of hope."

were in the top fifth of their high school graduating classes and even the remaining 10 percent had high school grade point averages of at least 3.0.

At the graduate level, recruiting top students has not been easy, due in part to the attractive salaries a student with a Tech undergraduate degree can command. But progress has been made. Graduate school enrollment has increased from 1,453 in 1972 to 2,228 in 1984. In 1983-84, 778 graduate degrees were awarded compared to just 463 in 1971-72. To strengthen industry participation in graduate education, the Graduate Cooperative Program was begun in December 1983 with Dr. Helen E. Grenga as its first Director. And two new doctoral programs were also recently started — applied biology in 1982 and architecture in 1983.

Student life is serious, says 1984-85 *Technique* Editor Robert Beauchamp, but Tech isn't about to become "some sort of black hole." "You will occasionally have to make sacrifices in your social life in order to maintain a reasonable GPA," Beauchamp says, "but at Tech we've got the best of both worlds: we have the satisfaction of knowing we're receiving a meaningful education, and we're having a helluva good time getting it."

When former President Jimmy Carter, who attended Tech one year, visited the campus in the spring of 1985, he left saying he could sense Tech's optimism. With good reason. Fund-raising for the Centennial Campaign is off to a running start, research is at an all-time high, Tech's athletic program is vigorous and the physical expansion of the campus has substantially increased. Already the ATDC has a new neighbor on 10th Street — the Centennial Research Building — joining others constructed during the Pettit years. These include the Fuller E. Callaway III Student Athletic Complex (SAC), buildings for the College of Management, the School of Industrial and Systems Engineering, the Instructional Center, the new Architecture Building, the Arthur B. Edge Jr. Intercollegiate Athletic Center, the renovation of the L.W. "Chip" Robert Jr. Alumni/Faculty House, the bookstore addition and the George and Irene Woodruff Residence Hall.

The U.S. men's 400-meter relay team leaves the site of its Olympic gold victory in Los Angeles on August 11, 1984. From left: Sunder Nix; Alonzo Babers; Tech's Antonio McKay; and Ray Armstead.

Dr. Mark Smith, an Assistant Professor in the School of Electrical Engineering, was a member of the American fencing team in the 1984 Olympics.

The first speaker of the Centennial
Lecture Series, U.S. Supreme Court
Justice Sandra Day O'Connor chats with
President Pettit prior to her lecture in the
Coliseum on October 15, 1984.

The first students at Georgia Tech — all 129 of them — found a small campus on the outskirts of Atlanta with seven faculty members, four shop foremen, slim resources and a provincial mission. The School was all-male, all-white, all-American. But it was a beginning in a city rising from the ashes of a recent and painfully remembered war. In 100 years "the Tech" of the 1880's has evolved into an institution that far surpasses the early plans of its founders. The size of its campus, the reputation of its graduates, the scope of its curriculum and research, the stature of its faculty and administrators, and the international flavor of its student body all attest to dreams that turned out well. Very well indeed.

Photograph Credits and Sources

School of Aerospace Engineering, 152, 153, 154, 155, 184, 213, 263, dust jacket; Alpha Tau Omega Fraternity, 16; Anak, 209; Atlanta Historical Society, Acknowledgements, 4, 11, 14, 17, 23, 51, 69; *The Atlanta Journal* and *The Atlanta Constitution*, 15, 32, 116, 117, 125, 141, 145, 155, 157, 176, 179, 188, 194, 196, 198, 200, 207, 216, 229, 253, 280; *The Atlanta Weekly*, 103, 109, 127, 131, 132, 133, 148, 149, 161, 179, 188, 224, 229; Mrs. Harry L. Baker Jr., 161; John P. Baum, 123, 130, 280; Bill D. Beavers, 247; Mrs. H.W. Beers Jr., 16; Luke Bowen, 176; L. Travis Brannon Jr., 184; Marion Luther Brittain, 158; Deloye R. Burrell, 223, 227, 228, 230, 231, 286, dust jacket; Fuller E. Callaway Jr., 121, 145, 240; G.E. Cantelou Jr., 27; Pete Casabonne, dust jacket; Dr. Austin B. Caseman, 248; Louis A. Cavalli, 173; Jerry Comer, 189, 207, 212, 216; Alan David, 84, 256, 260, 262, 263, 264, 265, 274, 279, 282, 287; Philip E. Davis, 280; General Raymond G. Davis, 192; John Dewberry, 280; James E. Dull, 139; John Dunn, 218, 219; Norman E. Elsas, 22; Emory University, Woodruff Library, Special Collections Department, 10; James Walter Estes, 50; Georgia Tech Alumni Association, 186, 187; Georgia Tech Alumni Magazine, 182, 241; Georgia Tech Alumni Publications, 150, 204, 218, 233, 241, 242, 250, 251, 252, 253, 258, dust jacket; Georgia Tech Archives, 9, 11, 12, 13, 18, 20, 23, 24, 25, 26, 27, 28, 30, 31, 33, 34, 36, 37, 41, 42, 43, 45, 46, 47, 48, 49, 50, 52, 53, 56, 58, 59, 60, 61, 62, 63, 65, 67, 68, 69, 70, 72, 73, 74, 75, 76, 86, 93, 94, 95, 96, 97, 99, 100, 101, 102, 104, 105, 112, 113, 115, 119, 120, 122, 125, 126, 129, 141, 143, 145, 146, 149, 155, 156, 158, 159, 160, 163, 167, 169, 170, 171, 172, 175, 177, 179, 180, 181, 183, 185, 187, 191, 193, 197, 199, 201, 203, 205, 206, 208, 210, 211, 220, 221, 222, 225, 229, 230, 231, 233, 234, 235, 236, 237, 239, 245, 247, 250, 256, 257, 258, 266, 268, 274, 275, 276, 277, 278, 279, 280, 281, 282, 283, dust jacket; Georgia Tech Athletic Association, 158, 195, 197, 211, 212, 214, 215, 227, 232, 243, 244, 246, 247, 248, 249, 259, 261, 266, dust jacket; Georgia Tech News Bureau, 190, 243, 245, 249, 253, 254, 256, 260, 262, 263, 264, 265, 269, 273, 274, 276, 277, 278, 279, 280, 281, 282, 283, 284, 285, 286, 287, 288, dust jacket; Georgia Tech Office of Financial Services, 141; Georgia Tech Publications, 7, 139, 147, 191, 251; Georgia Tech Research Institute, 161, 233; Georgia Tech Sports Information, 266, dust jacket; Joel Gilmore, dust jacket, 284, 285; Sidney Goldin, 146; Mrs. W. Frank Gordy, 142, 276; B. Eugene Griessman, 284, 285; George C. Griffin, 101, 111, 140, 162, 174; William E. Gross Jr., 99; The Harry Guggenheim Foundation, 147; Charles Haynes, 274, 275, dust jacket; George B. Hills Jr., 172, 176; Grey Hodges, 208; Billy Howard, 283; Mrs. Ernest Daniel Ivey, 75; David M. Kalish, 94; C.S. Kiang, 237; Lockheed Georgia Company, 257; James Herty Lucas, 107, 111; William Leckie Mattox Jr., 57, dust jacket; Paul Mayer, 225, 226; Frank Mayo, 118; E. Alan McGee, 259; School of Mechanical Engineering, 274; Gary Meek, 241, 242, 253, 263, 268, 269, 273, 276, 277, 278, 279, 280, 281, 282, 283, 284, 286, 287, 288, dust jacket; James C. Merrill Jr., 85; James Wayne Moore Jr., 33, 35, 128; Russ Moore, 285, 287; Mrs. Betty Thomason Mulkey, 157; Mr. and Mrs. John R. Murphy, 12; NASA, 255; Phil Narmore, 144; Noye Harland Nesbit, 64, 76, 77, 88, 91, 92, 98, 275; Lamar Oglesby, 178; Charlie Oldham, 227; Mrs. Nell Walthall Owen, 14; Frank C. "Hop" Owens, 110; William E. Palen, 85, 87; Dr. Demetrius T. Paris, 221; Larry Patrick, 239; Venable Patrick, 116, 124, 125, 127, 128; Mrs. Fred Patterson, 115; H. Wayne Patterson, 64, 66, 72, 73, 77, 79, 81, 82; Mrs. J.O. (Mary Matheson) Pearson, 55; Otho Perritt, 156, 173; Henry Phillips, 24; Mrs. John Portman Sr., 183; Lyman Hall Robertson, 32, 40; Al W. Rogers, 123; Mrs. Lillian Grant Rudolph, 86; Alfred R. and Emory B. Rumble, 124, 281; Scottish Rite Hospital for Crippled Children, 151; Chris Shine, 280, dust jacket; Forrest H. Shropshires, 39; Hal L. Smith, 166; Leroy Smith, 220; Mark Smith, 267; Muggsy Smith, 118; Patricia Stone, 263; William W. Sumits, 235; Keith Swindell, 218, 219; Richard Teach, 100; Jack G. Thomason, 157; Edward Van Voorhees, 157, 163, 164, 165, 277; Perrin Walker, dust jacket; Dr. Homer S. Weber, 220; Houston Longino Welch, 130; Joe Westbrook, 121, 137; Mrs. Lula Smith Westcott, 22; Richard K. Whitehead, 134; Randolph Whitfield, 134; Lawrence Michael Williams, 217; James G. Wohlford, 257; Clyde M. Wood, 90, 105; Worldwide Photos, 267.

Index

IMAGES

PARKING LOT
VARSITY
DRIVE IN
Coca-Cola
IN BOTTLES
Sold here
Ice Cold
ICE COLD
Coca-Cola
means below

ECHWOOD
MODESTY BLAISE IN COLOR
& THE FLIGHT OF THE PHOENIX
Junior's

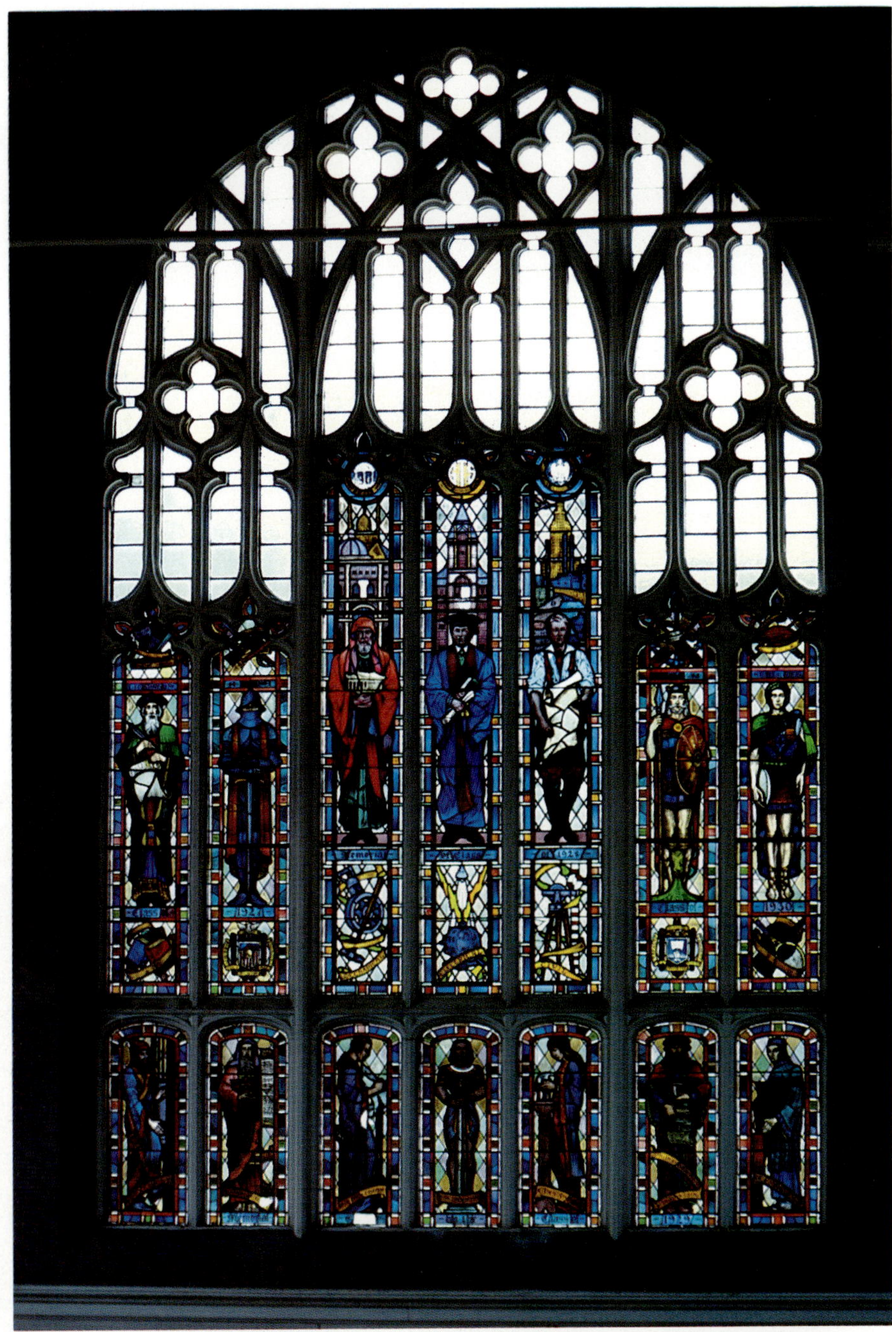

JOHN SAYLER COON BUILDING

The Technique
"The South's Livest College Weekly"
Georgia School of Technology
CUTS GRANTED

BRING
BACK
RAT
RULES
F.F.F.

LAVOISIER
CHEMISTRY

Mr. Pretty Legs

Sports
The Atlanta Journal   THE ATLANTA CONSTITUTION
TECH TEACHES THIS OL' DAWG A NEW TRICK
Roll over, UGA: Tech, 35-18!
So Curry flung his Jackets
into the Athens briar patch
Furman
Bisher

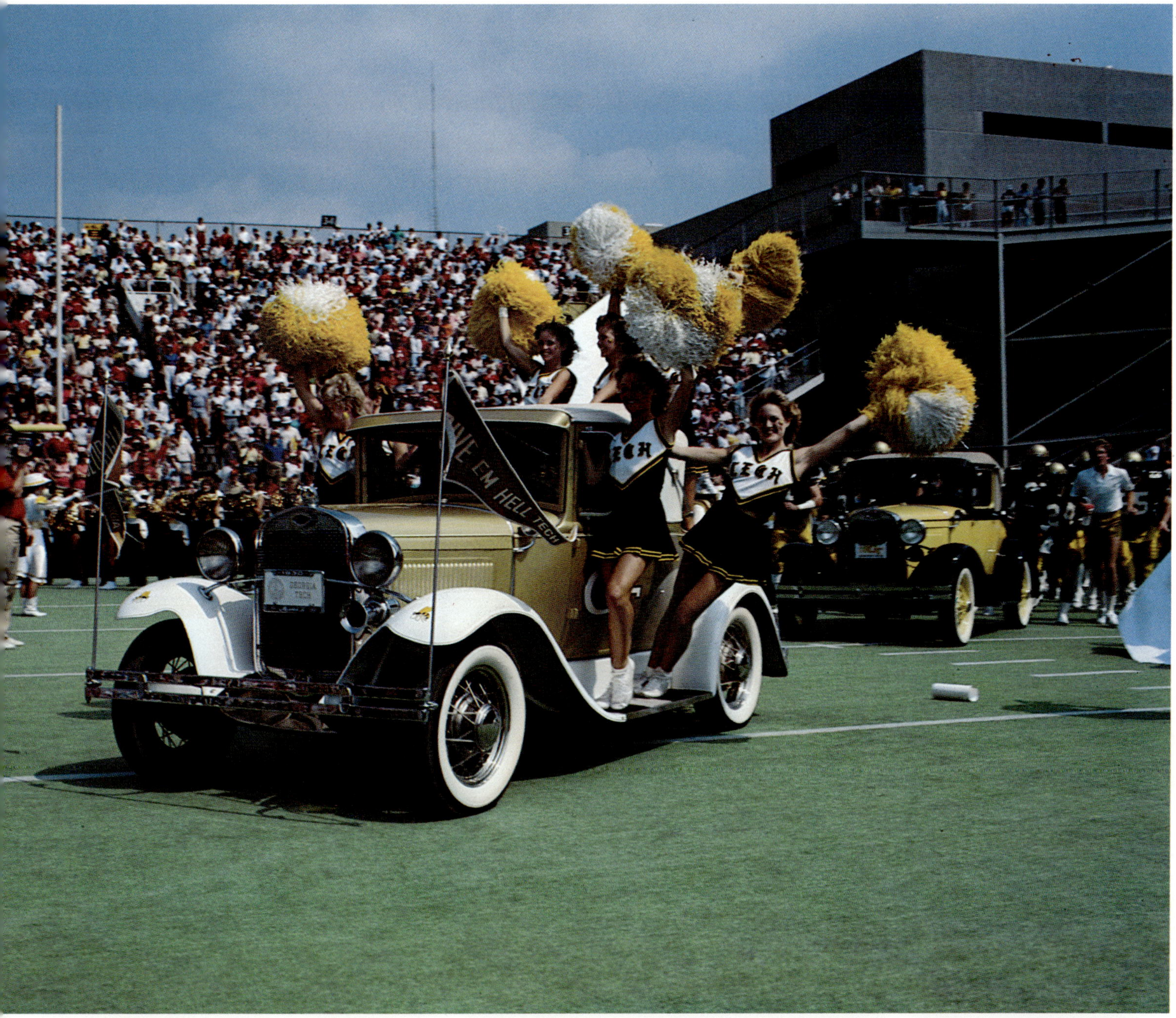
EM HELL TECH
TECH
TECH

TECH
24

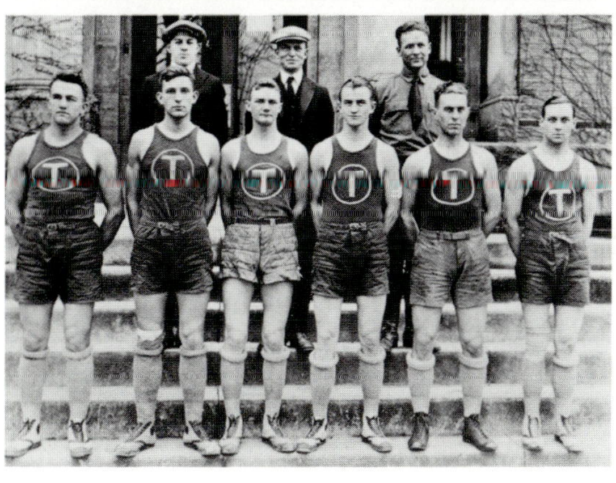

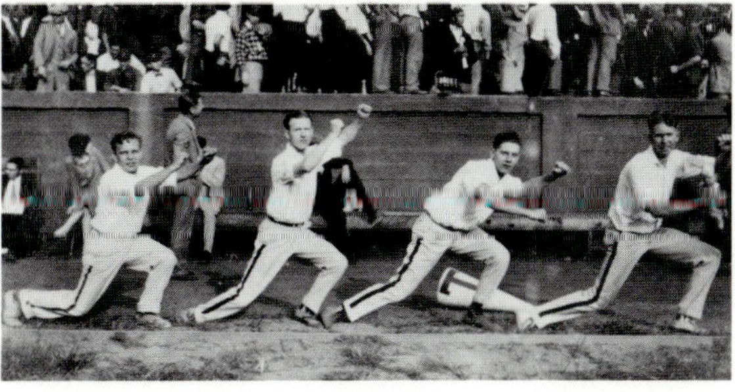

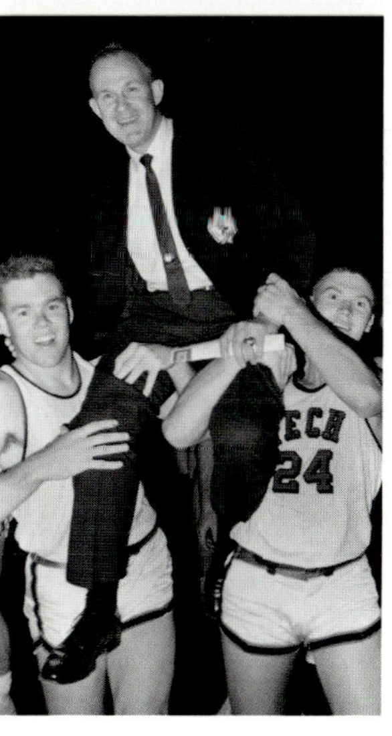

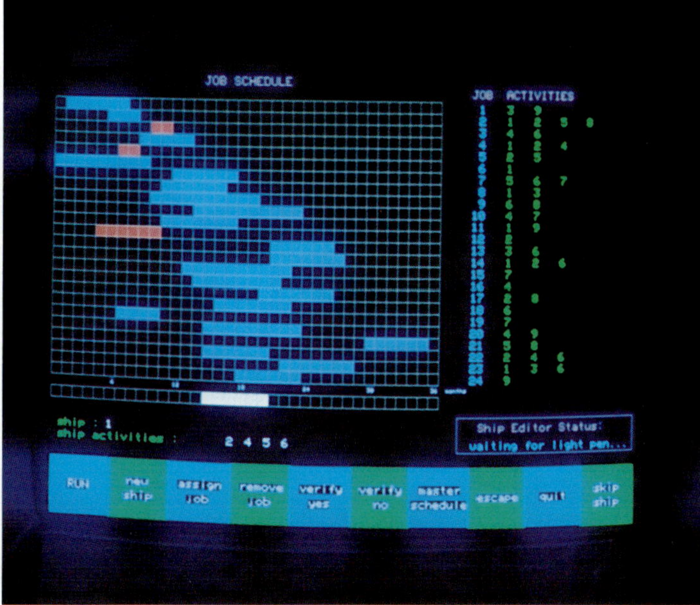
JOB SCHEDULE
JOB ACTIVITIES
ship : 1
ship activities :   2 4 5 6
Ship Editor Status:
waiting for light pen...
RUN   new ship   assign job   remove job   verify yes   verify no   master schedule   escape   quit   skip ship

GEORGE P. BURDELL
&DAUGHTERS
CONSULTING ENGINEERS

TO HELL
WITH
GEORGIA

CHINA

CHINA
7,000 YEARS OF DISCOVERY.

CHINA
TICKETS
ARE ALL
SOLD OUT
FOREVER
CHINA
TICKETS
ARE ALL
SOLD OUT
FOREVER

GEORGIA SCHOOL OF
TECHNOLOGY

GEORGIA TECH CENTENNIAL
TO KNOW. TO DO. TO BE.
DESIGNING TOMORROW TODAY
GEORGIA INSTITUTE OF TECHNOLOGY

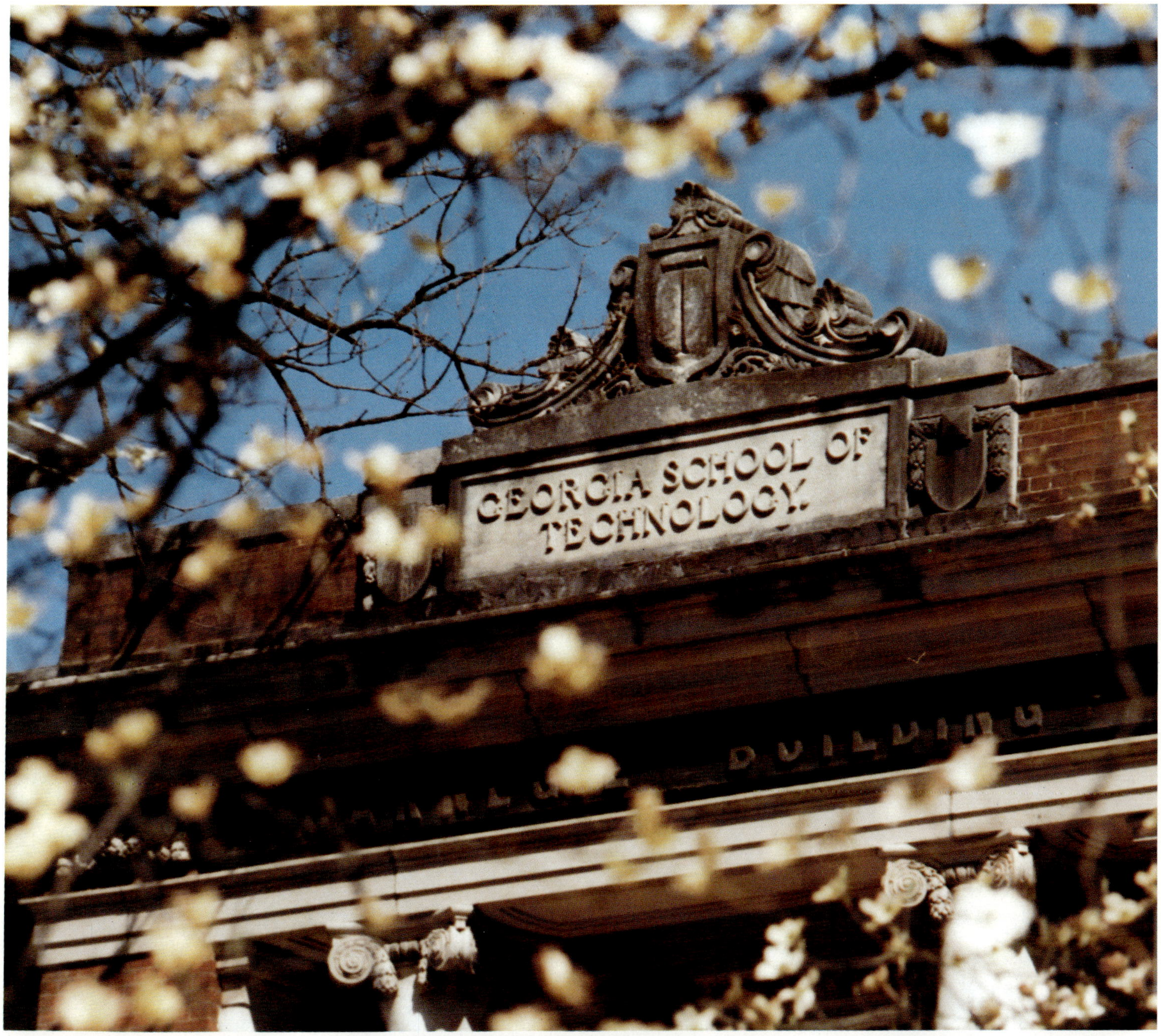

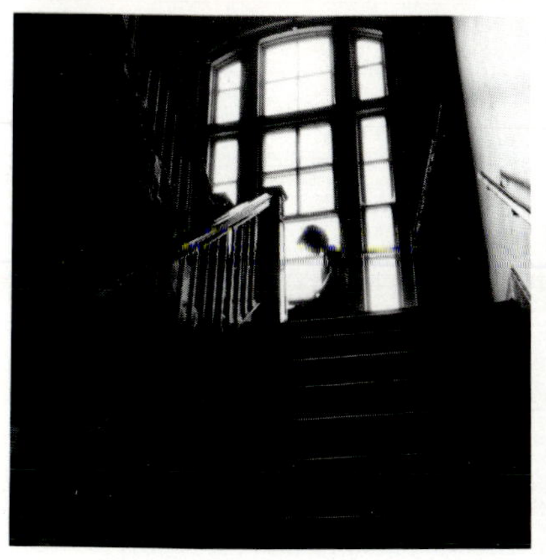

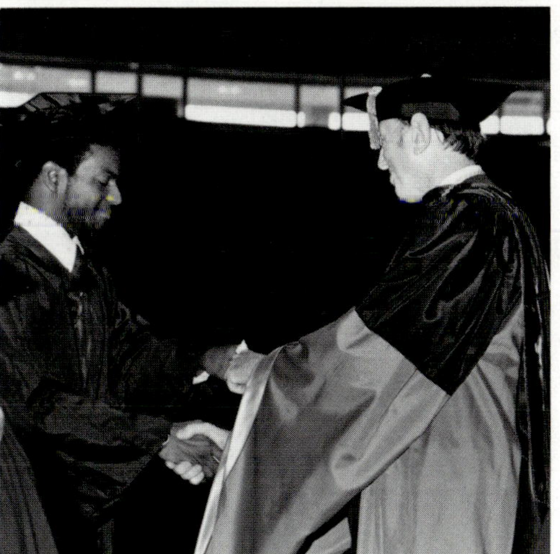

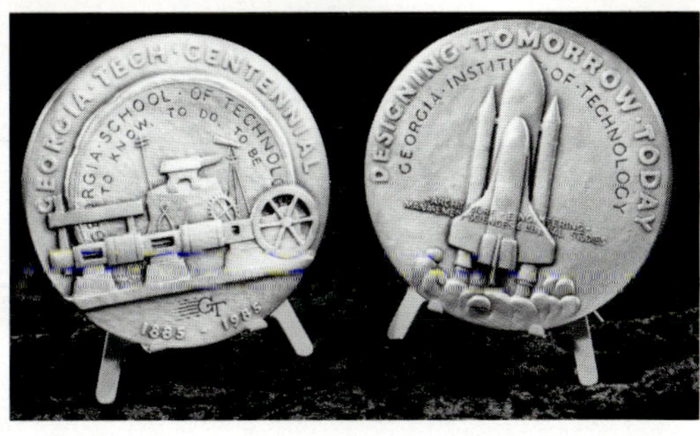

TECH